THE CHURCH IN ANGUISH

Has the Vatican Betrayed Vatican II?

Edited by
Hans Küng and Leonard Swidler

1817

Harper & Row, Publishers, San Francisco

Cambridge, Hagerstown, New York, Philadelphia, Washington
London, Mexico City, São Paulo, Singapore, Sydney

FIRST EDITION

Library of Congress Cataloging-in-Publication Data

The Church in anguish.

   Includes index.
   1. Catholic Church—Doctrines. 2. Catholic Church—
Controversial literature. 3. John Paul II, Pope,
1920–   . 4. Ratzinger, Joseph. I. Küng, Hans,
1928–   . II. Swidler, Leonard J.
BX1755.C53   1988   282'.09'048   87-45184
ISBN 0-06-254827-1

87 88 89 90 91 HC 10 9 8 7 6 5 4 3 2 1

Contents

CONTRIBUTORS

Wolfgang Bartholomäus, a priest of Germany, studied philosophy and theology in Frankfurt; education, communications, and religious education in Munich; and psychology in Vienna. In 1972 he received a doctorate in theology and is professor of religious education on the Catholic theology faculty of the University of Tübingen.

Leonardo Boff and *Clodovis Boff* are brothers, both of whom were born in and work in Brazil. Both are also priests. Clodovis is a member of the Order of the Servants of Mary and Leonardo is a Franciscan. They have written several works on liberation theology, individually as well as jointly.

Robert McAfee Brown is a Presbyterian theologian, former professor of ecumenical theology at Union Theological Seminary, and, at present, professor of theology and ethics at Pacific School of Religion in Berkeley. He was deeply involved in things Catholic at, after, and even before Vatican II.

Paul Collins, born in Australia and ordained a priest there, is a graduate of Harvard University; a research scholar at the Research School of Social Sciences, the Australian National University, Canberra; and author of *Mixed Blessings: John Paul II and the Church of the Eighties* (Australia: Penguin Books, 1986).

Charles E. Curran, a priest of Rochester, received a doctorate in theology from the Gregorian University and a doctorate in moral theology from the Academia Alfonsiana, both in Rome. Since 1965 he has been professor of moral theology at the Catholic University of America. He is a past president of the American Society of Christian Ethics and the Catholic Theological Society of America.

Andrew M. Greeley, a priest of Chicago, received at Ph.D. in sociology from the University of Chicago and is professor of sociology at the University of Arizona and senior study director of the

National Opinion Research Center, University of Chicago. He has published several novels and over a hundred books in sociology, theology, spirituality, and education.

Norbert Greinacher, a priest of Freiburg, Germany, studied philosophy and theology at Freiburg University and the Institut Catholique in Paris and received a doctorate in Catholic theology in 1955. He has been professor for practical theology since 1969 on the Catholic theology faculty of the University of Tübingen.

Bernard Häring is a priest and member of the Redemptorists and professor of moral theology at the Academia Alfonsiana/Lateran University in Rome. He was a major figure at Vatican II, has published over sixty books, and is known as the "father of modern Catholic moral theology."

Hermann Häring, a Catholic layman, studied philosophy at Pullach and theology at the University of Tübingen, where he received a Th.D. and Dr. Habil. from the Catholic theology faculty. Since 1980 he has been professor of dogmatic theology on the Catholic theology faculty of the University of Nijmegen, The Netherlands.

Jean-Pierre Jossua studied medicine in Paris, became a Dominican in 1953, was ordained a priest, and received a doctorate in theology from the University of Strasbourg. He was professor and later rector of the Dominican House of Studies at Saulchoir and is also the director of the "Centre de formation theologique."

Eugene C. Kennedy received a Ph.D. in psychology from the Catholic University of America in 1962 and has published scores of articles and books in the area of psychology and religion. In 1971 he directed the psychological study of American Catholic priests for the American bishops. He is professor of psychology at Loyola University, Chicago, and is currently at work on a book on "The Two Cultures of American Catholicism."

Madonna Kolbenschlag, a member of the Sisters of the Humility of Mary of Villa Maria, PA, received a doctorate in the philosophy of literature from the University of Notre Dame, served as a legislative assistant in the United States House of Representatives 1980–84, and is at present a senior fellow at the Woodstock Theological Center, Georgetown University.

Hans Küng, a priest of Switzerland, studied philosophy and theology at the Gregorian University in Rome and at the Sorbonne and Institut Catholique in Paris, from which he received his doctorate. He was professor of dogmatic theology on the Catholic theology faculty of the University of Tübingen 1960–80 and has been professor of ecumenical theology and director of the Institute of Ecumenical Research of the University of Tübingen since 1964.

Richard P. McBrien, a priest of Hartford, CT, received a doctorate in theology from the Gregorian University, Rome, is past president of the Catholic Theological Society of America, was professor of theology at Boston College, and is at present professor of theology and chair of the theology department at the University of Notre Dame.

Dietmar Mieth, a Catholic layman, studied philosophy and theology and received a Th.D. from the University of Würzburg and a Dr.Habil. in ethics from the Catholic theology faculty at the University of Tübingen. He was professor of moral theology at the University of Fribourg, Switzerland, 1974–81 and since then has been on the Catholic theology faculty at the University of Tübingen.

Ronald Modras, a priest of Detroit, studied theology and received a doctorate in theology from the Catholic theology faculty of the University of Tübingen. He was professor of theology at the archdiocesan seminary of Detroit and at present is professor of theology at St. Louis University.

Adam Nowotny is a pseudonym of an expert in Polish religious affairs. (In Hebrew *Adam* means "human being" and in Polish *nowotny* means "new.") The protective pseudonym reflects the need for this book.

Rosemary Radford Ruether, a Catholic laywoman, received a doctorate in classical studies from the Claremont Graduate School and has been on the theology faculties of Howard, Harvard, Princeton, and Yale universities. At present she is professor of theology at Garrett-Evangelical Theological Seminary.

Georg Schelbert has been on the theological faculty of the University of Fribourg, Switzerland, since 1972. He was professor of Old and New Testament at the Mission Seminary at Schöneck bei Beckenried, Switzerland, from 1953 to 1972.

Arlene Anderson Swidler, a Catholic laywoman, has graduate degrees in English literature from the University of Wisconsin and theology from Villanova University. She is currently on the religious studies faculty at Villanova.

Leonard Swidler, a Catholic layman, received a doctorate in history and philosophy from the University of Wisconsin and a licentiate in theology from the Catholic theology faculty of the University of Tübingen. He has been professor of Catholic thought and interreligious dialogue at Temple University since 1966. In 1964 he co-founded, with Arlene Anderson Swidler, the *Journal of Ecumenical Studies* and since then has been its editor.

David Tracy, a priest from New York, received a doctorate in theology from the Gregorian University, Rome, in 1967; taught for two years at the Catholic University of America; and, since 1969, has been professor of theology at the Divinity School of the University of Chicago. He is also a past president of the Catholic Theological Society of America.

Knut Walf, a priest of Germany, studied philosophy, theology, law, and canon law at the universities of Munich and Fribourg, Switzerland. He received a doctorate in 1965 and a Dr.Habil. in 1971 from the University of Munich. Since 1977 he has been professor of canon law on the Catholic theology faculty of the University of Nijmegen, The Netherlands.

Ad Willems is a priest of The Netherlands and a member of the Dominicans. He studied theology at Basel, Strasbourg, and Münster and received a Th.D. from the Catholic theology faculty at the University of Münster in 1957. He is professor of systematic theology on the Catholic theology faculty at the University of Nijmegen, The Netherlands.

Introduction

This book has grown out of the anguish engendered in the Catholic church during the past decade through what appears to many Catholics, and non-Catholics, as an attempt by the present leadership in the Vatican to reverse the momentous gains in maturity that were made at the Second Vatican Council (1961–65). An earlier version appeared in the summer of 1986 entitled *Whither the Catholic Church? Against the Betrayal of the Council.* * Twelve essays from that volume and fourteen new essays by American theologians make up this book for the English-speaking public.

With one exception, these essays are all written by Catholic theologians. With no exceptions, they are all written by Christians who care deeply about their church, experiencing with it its joy—and its anguish. Vatican II was clearly a peak experience. Today we seem to be going through "the valley of the shadow . . ." These reflections in anguish, nevertheless, are an expression of love for the church, faith in its God, and hope in its future.

Leonard Swidler

---

*Norbert Greinacher and Hans Küng, eds., *Katholische Kirche—Wohin? Wider den Verrat am Konzil* (Munich: Piper, 1986).

1. On the State of the Catholic Church

or Why a Book Like This Is Necessary

HANS KÜNG

No, the illustration on the jacket of our book is not a malicious caricature. It is an official Vatican postage stamp from the "holy year" of 1983–84, available for 400 lire: the Lord God walking the earth, Christ on the cross, the madonna with her protecting mantle—all these united in the single figure of the pope. Is this how the pope is seen in today's Vatican? The contrast to the image of church and pope during the Second Vatican Council, which ended in 1965, could scarcely be sharper. And the fact that this irony was not even noticed in the Vatican, that apparently no negative reactions from episcopate, clergy, or church people were anticipated, shows more than all the actions of this revived papal absolute monarchy just how far we in the Catholic church have regressed during the past two decades. Has the Second Vatican Council been forgotten, superceded, betrayed?

Yet our illustration is deceptive. It represents only the viewpoint of that Roman church bureaucracy which never did want and never did like the Second Vatican Council, which never ceased lamenting the loss of the medieval-counterreformation-antimodernist image of the pope which had prevailed in the preconciliar era, hoping to reinstate it as speedily as possible, although illuminated by modern techniques—rather like the newly lit frescoes in the Sistine Chapel. This ecclesiastical bureaucracy is fostering a restoration movement such as has taken hold of other churches, religions, and nations. The more tightly it tries to keep the gearshift of power in its own hands, the more urgently history calls for a reorientation not only of individuals but also of structures, including religious institutions. This conflict affects science, technology, the world economy, politics, and of course also religion: it is a question of humanity's survival.

The Catholic community, however, oriented to the New Testament, sees things quite differently than does the Roman ecclesiastical bureaucracy: not a pope *over* church and world in God's stead, but a pope *in* the church as a member (rather than head) of the People of God; a pope who is not an autocrat but a link in the college of bishops; not a ruler of the church but, in the Petrine succession, a "servant of the servants of God" (Gregory the Great). It needed a pope like John XXIII to reintroduce this original view of the church and the bishop of Rome. It took the Second Vatican Council to formulate the view in decrees. Even the "extraordinary" Roman synod of 1985, suddenly called by John Paul II to evaluate Vatican II on its twentieth anniversary, could do no more than confirm it.

Nevertheless, in many places the spiritual and organizational vitality of the Catholic church remains unbroken and, in fact, is reemerging. People at the base of their societies quiety labor in solidarity with the suffering: a "light of the world" and "salt of the earth." Latin American liberation theology, Catholic peace movements in the United States, the ashram movements in India, and base groups in many lands of the First and Third Worlds all demonstrate that the catholicity of the Catholic church is not merely a doctrine but a concretely lived human reality as well. The question "Where is the Catholic church headed?" will not be misunderstood as ecclesiocentric only if the broader problem of "Where is humanity headed?" is addressed simultaneously.

The affirmation of Vatican II by the 1985 Roman Synod of Bishops would have been much more striking

- if the bishops, in accordance with the rules for an "ordinary" synod (there was no occasion at all for an "extraordinary" one) had been able to choose their representatives themselves
- if the composition of the synod had mirrored the actual world church, and the curial bureaucracy—in line with a contemporary separation of powers—had been admitted only as an executive organ
- if the synod had been able to choose its own "editorial committee" and had been free from any pressure by the curia

This much at least can now be said: the vocal pre-synod criticism of Roman ecclesiastical politics since Vatican II and especially during the present pontificate certainly helped to generate serious, intensive discussion before and during the synod. The style of my own contribution (in the Toronto *Globe and Mail* of 4 October 1985, reprinted in this volume) was sharp, to be sure, but there are times when one must speak out clearly in order to be heard, even if cowardice and conformity again lead some people to discuss "the style" rather than the subject matter and even to malign one's Christianity and Catholicism.

The *Report on the Faith* from the German curial cardinal Joseph Ratzinger, head of the former Holy Office (now called the Congregation for the Doctrine of the Faith), was also helpful in an indirect way: now priests and bishops, laity and theologians, women and men could see how negatively many in the curia view the Council, how pessimistically they evaluate postconciliar developments, and how great is the danger of a rollback. The strong reaction from bishops, theologians, and church people meant that for practical purposes this *Report on the Faith* played no role at all (the synod, explained its president, Belgian Cardinal Daneels, at the very beginning, was not there to discuss a book). Despite all its concessions, the bishops' synod revealed an appraisal of the Council, postconciliar situation, and future very different from that of the Vatican powers that be and their support troops, constantly invoking the "mystery" of the church. Obviously the picture is not clear-cut. Nor is it in any way settled in just what direction that Catholic church will move.

What, then, did the 1985 synod add up to?

THE ACTIVE SIDE: VATICAN II—TRAILBLAZING FOR THE PRESENT AND FUTURE

1. *The warning voices were heard by the bishops.* No relapse or retreat into the past occurred. The synod in its overall spirit disavowed the "prophets of doom" of whom John XXIII had already warned. The final report of the bishops, with all its warnings and limitations, showed no pessimistic, illusionary nostalgia for the Middle Ages, no anti-Protestantism or antimodernism.

2. *The Roman traditionalists found themselves confronting a largely open episcopate.* Like the Council of twenty years before, the synod too displayed its own dynamics. Discussion was open. And while the German episcopate and the German curial cardinals were conspicuous for their pessimistic reactionary orientation and, together with the curia, made up the extreme right wing, quite different voices made themselves heard from Canada and the United States, from Latin America, Asia, and Africa, and from the Old World as well.

3. *Vatican II was not only affirmed, but it was proclaimed "the greatest grace of this century" and the "Magna Charta" for the Catholic church of the present and future.* In the final document we read: "At the conclusion of this gathering the synod, from the depths of our hearts, gives thanks to God the Father, through his Son, in the Holy Spirit for the greatest grace of this century, that is, the Second Vatican Council." The bishops "commit" themselves "to comprehend more deeply the Second Vatican Council and to implement it concretely in the church." "The message of the Second Vatican Council has already been welcomed with great accord by the whole church, and it remains the 'Magna Charta' for the future."

4. *The bishops discreetly affirmed the complicity of the hierarchy in the "estrangement from the church," especially among the youth.* "We are probably not immune from all responsibility for the fact that especially the young critically consider the church purely as an institution."

5. *The synod concretely affirmed its commitment to the inner renewal of the church and to social reform.* "Restoration" was not in the vocabulary of this synod, which instead centered on (1) the importance of the inner renewal of the liturgy (Latin was not mentioned; of 160 bishops, a total of 6 joined the Latin language group); (b) the necessity of pluralism within the unity of the church; (c) the bishops' collegial exercise of office with the pope, and their participation and co-responsibility on all levels of the church; (d) support for human rights, social justice, and peace, and opposition to any lack of freedom, disdain for the family, racial discrimination, excessive national deficits, and continual racing for better and more terrible

weapons. (From North America especially came protests against the state's neglect of its social tasks—understandable in the face of an immense national debt, new poverty, and simultaneous expenditures on armaments in the area of $300 billion a year in the United States—almost triple the entire budget of West Germany.)

6. *The synod, despite some opposition, affirmed ecumenical understanding among the Christian confessions and dialogue with world religions.* Not a word of the "come home" ideology represented in the Ratzinger report! The continuation of "ecumenism" was expressly recommended. That the curialists at the synod were not successful in integrating the Roman "Secretariat for Christian Unity" (the ecumenical secretariat under the presidency of Cardinal Willebrands) into Ratzinger's Congregation for the Doctrine of the Faith must be interpreted as a further sign of the failure of the reactionaries. Archbishop Samuel Carter of Jamaica commented candidly, "The proposed plan to downgrade the secretariat to a dependent office is another example of overconcentration of authority, which is a great threat to proper ecumenism and will hinder the secretariat from carrying out the function entrusted to it by the holy father."

7. *The synod advocated better collaboration with theologians.* Although, unlike in Vatican II, only a few of the court theologians designated by the curia ("Kaspar, Melchior, and Balthasar") were admitted by the pope, the final report of the bishops thanks theologians for their work in the postconciliar period. It calls for the elimination of a "confusion" of the faithful (although the hierarchy is partly to blame) and a greater and closer communication on both sides, as well as dialogue between bishops and theologians "for the building up of the faith and its deeper comprehension."

8. *The bishops were successful in publishing their final report despite the initial opposition of pope, curia, and conservatives.* In earlier synods the bishops had only been able to submit their recommendations privately to the pope. They went home without any concrete promise on the part of the curia, usually only to discover that the curia itself fabricated a document after the event (as, for example, "Familiaris Consortio" 1981 on the

family) in which any critical or dissident voices from the episcopate were hushed up and a consensus was simulated. This time the bishops shot the bolt on such proceedings, otherwise customary only in totalitarian systems, by their insistence on the publication of their own final report, though not, to be sure, without grave concessions: only a "second version" of the final report was permitted, in which many notoriously delicate points were deleted.

THE PASSIVE SIDE: RICH IN WORDS, POOR IN DEEDS

It would be easy to list eight points on this side as well. At bottom everything can be said in one sentence: The synod was rich in words, but poor in deeds. Words are important. They can *move*. They *can* move. But *will* they move? Will statements by the synod lead to actions by the pope?

Both the "Message to the People of God" and the final report are rich in words, seeking to please both sides and remain general on decisive points. All the "tedious old questions," such as birth control, the admission of remarried divorced people to communion, orphaned parishes, the marriage of priests, and so much else that is important for the faithful and had been brought up for discussion by the bishops, were completely missing in the final report. And this in the face of the recent statistics on the attitudes of Catholics which demonstrate to all the world the failure of papal preaching! While the synod was taking place the following statistics on United States Catholics were published by CBS News/*New York Times:*

- 68 percent approve birth control
- 52 percent approve the ordination of women
- 63 percent approve married priests
- 73 percent approve remarriage after divorce
- 15 percent oppose legalized abortion in all cases
- 55 percent approve abortion after rape or incest
- 26 percent approve the current abortion laws

According to other polls the situation is even "worse" among Catholics under thirty: scarcely 5 percent approve the official teaching on birth control and scarcely ten percent the official teaching on papal infallibility. These United States polls are to a large extent also representative for Canada and western Europe, and those who believe that these problems are any less relevant in the Second or Third Worlds are deceiving themselves. For example, the abortion rate in Poland ranks among the highest in the world, and the Polish pope's preachments to "increase and multiply" in those very African countries with the greatest poverty and the greatest increase in population (the population growth in Africa is fifteen million persons per year) has, not without reason, evoked indignation.

On the status of women in church and society—the litmus test of this misogynist pontificate—only a few lines occur in the final report of the synod, with not a single concrete word on those matters which are actually not only "women's concerns." The same is true of the questions of ecumenical understanding, which—this must be stated forthrightly—never got beyond the tediously familiar: nothing on the already existing unity documents, nothing on the recognition of Anglican orders and Protestant ordination, nothing on the recognition of the eucharistic liturgy of other churches and on a possible shared Eucharist. A shared prayer service—John XXIII had begun this a quarter-century before—serves in our day as a surrogate for a eucharistic community celebration of all those who believe in Christ and say "amen" to "the body of Christ."

For this reason both synod documents are full of the word "mystery," as if anyone among the theologians had anything against the transcendent inaccessible dimension in human life and the life of the church: deity itself as the great mystery. But now in this synod the word "mystery" actually helps the curial "mystifiers" to obscure the numerous contradictions between the institution and the Christian message, to ward off any criticism of the transparent Vatican mystery-mongering, and to keep the open "secrets" of the bishops from becoming generally known to the People of God by impeding or dressing up the final report. And this appeal to "mystery" ironically comes from that very apparatus that, under the aegis of the pope, is entangled in the greatest financial scandal of the century. Faced with a debt of over DM 1.4 billion, it finally declared itself prepared to pay out DM 250 million merely in order to beg more money off the faithful around the world in connection with the synod—all the time without disclosing its own balance, as is customary in every civil state and every respectable corporation. The poor Vatican . . . That "mystery" can be cleared up only by reliable financial management and complete openness. (On the appalling conditions in the Vatican—for example, the secret organization "Opus Dei," which the pope withdrew from episcopal control—see the recent book of the veteran Vatican journalist Giancarlo Zizola, *La restaurazione di Papa Wojtyla* [The Restoration of Pope Wojtyla], ed. Laterza [Rome, 1985].)

When it comes to catechism, of course, "mysterium" will not do. No, every Catholic in the entire world is supposed to eventually hear directly from the Congregation of the Faith what he or she has to believe about the immaculate conception of Mary and the virgin birth of Jesus, about the devil and original sin, birth control and divorce, papal primacy and infallibility. As if the fabrication of a new official confession of faith under Paul VI, with its attempt to define as much as possible, had interested or convinced anyone in the Catholic church to any extent worth mentioning! Even the bishops of the First Vatican Council, in 1870, oriented as they were to Rome in general, resisted such a regimentation of faith by Rome, so that the plan for a universal catechism was finally filed away. Should such a project be seriously taken up, it would again require, it seems to me, consultation with a council and not merely a handful of bishops in a Roman synod which is in no way fully representative. The days of *Roma locuta, causa finita*— "Rome has spoken, the case is finished"—are past, even if those behind the high walls of the Vatican insist on overlooking the fact.

Over and over the other Christian churches object that the pope, despite all the talk of collegiality, participation, and co-responsibility, has, now as ever, all the power in his hands in this one-man church-state. Although the order of the primitive church exhibits many democratic characteristics even in the liturgy, people in Rome—untroubled as always by any knowledge of New Testament research—continue to repeat the nineteenth-century adage that the church is "no demoncracy" without, of course, adding that, at least according to the New Testament, it should be still less a "monarchy" or even a "spiritual dictatorship."

So, people both inside and outside the Catholic church are asking, What will happen? Will the demands of this episcopal synod once again be shelved in the archives of the Vatican? This is what happened to the demands of earlier episcopal synods, of many national synods and ecumenical commissions. Why should it be any different today? It is not John XXIV who reigns, but Pius XIII, in the simultaneous roles of the "great communicator" and the "great conservator."

A STANDOFF

The outcome of the synod was mixed: neither a sense of breaking through nor one of breaking off, but an artificial apparent consensus on almost all points. It was certainly not a fiasco, but was it a real success? Hardly, in as much as the participants, like politicians, declared their agreement and acclaimed the event as event. The positive statements of Vatican II, thank God, will remain, and the betrayal of the Council—at least for the moment—was averted. But the Council is still by no means established in praxis as the Magna Charta of the Catholic church, nor is the betrayal of the Council deflected indefinitely.

What kind of attitude should we have? In the face of the positive assertions and the missing solutions, neither despair nor enthusiasm is appropriate. In between frustration and exaltation lies the true course of a watchful and incorruptible realism. Measured against the well-founded anxiety of many people before the synod, nothing absolutely horrible happened. But measuring it against our hopes, we as Catholic Christians can hardly be content with the well-intentioned words of those who ultimately lack the power to prevail. Herbert Haag is correct in his evaluation of the synod: "I can discover nothing creative in the results of the Synod. We find only declarations of intentions and banalities. I am astounded at the self-satisfaction of certain reporters who write it down as a great success that the Synod did not retreat behind the Council! As though the church could ever retreat back behind a council! Obviously the Synod had to proceed in the spirit of the

Council beyond the Council. Loyalty to the Council can thus be spoken of only with reservations."

To be sure, there were neither conquerors nor conquered. Still, the fact is that the bishops go home, but the Roman curia stays! It will once again devote its time to further announcements and decrees, to secret directives and actions, in order to strengthen the central power and weaken collegiality. The synod—to put it in a single word—resulted in a standoff. And the game goes on!

One thing has, in any case, become evident: Here two teams—perhaps equally strong—are playing. To put it still better, here "two competing views of the church and society," to use the words of the *New York Times*, are struggling. As "simple people" so often say, "They are living in another world" and, it could be added, "in another time as well." Taking both together, we can put it most precisely as "they live in another paradigm," in another "overall constellation of convictions, values, methods, etc." (Thomas S. Kuhn). Traditionalists are on the one side, reformers on the other. They collide not only on questions of procedure (from the selection of the members named by the pope to the publication of the final report), but also in almost all substantive questions: on the relationship between the Vatican on one side and the episcopal conferences and individual bishops on the other; on the relationship of "teaching office" and theologians; on the determination of the limits of dissent; on ethical problems such as birth control and divorce; on statements on the horizontal and vertical dimensions of the church, the relationship between "mystery" and "machinery" or "mystery" and "mysteriousness."

To put it another way: behind the tensions, parties, and confrontations are hidden not only various persons (the pope, the Germans Ratzinger and Höffner or the Brazilians Arns or Lorscheider), and not only various countries (in Brazil as well as in the United States there are newly named reactionary bishops and cardinals), and finally not only various theologies (curial neoscholasticism or liberation theology). Concealed behind all this are two differing world-time views, differing "overall constellations," two different paradigms of church and society. The battle therefore continues, as can be clearly seen in the Ratzinger report: either back to the Roman-medieval-counterreformation-antimodernist constellation or forward into a modern-postmodern paradigm!

CHURCH FROM BELOW AND CHURCH FROM ABOVE

In Catholic parishes and among the clergy there are certainly only a few who want to go back. In fact, in many places the pastor and the faithful quietly do whatever seems proper to them in matters like sexuality and marriage morality, mixed marriage and divorce, ecumenical collaboration and social commitment. They act in the spirit of the gospel and according to the impulses of Vatican II, unconcerned with the headwinds in the upper regions of the hierarchy. In many places, of course, people have again become anxious and have adapted. So much strength was consumed in the struggle for renewal, and the powers "above" again insist—in liturgy and dogma, morality and discipline—on the letter; to adapt is more comfortable. Many faithful ask themselves, Why have so many pastors who earlier welcomed reform learned to be silent again and to obey? Why have the critical voices among theology professors, for the most part more independent, become rarer? Why did so many progressive pastors, upon being named bishop, disappoint their people by their conformity to the curia? The pressure on the episcopate from the Roman central power has grown immensely in the past seven years, and this pressure is transmitted to clergy and congregations.

In this dispute the curia has on its side the medieval *Ius Canonicum*. Adapted to the present, it is a peerless instrument of power, especially for top personnel decisions: the naming of cardinals, which predetermines future papal elections; orders and honors of all sorts, linked with sonorous titles and imposing garments; but especially the naming of bishops, the criteria for which are not so much objective competence and acceptability to clergy and people as affability and strict loyalty to Rome. This is relentlessly tested, even before the nomination, by a detailed inquisition (What is your stance on birth control? the celibacy law? ordination of women? etc). Then it is sacrally safeguarded and reinforced in the episcopal consecration itself by an intensely personal oath of obedience to the pope, and it is constantly monitored by the nuncios. And if, at the periphery of the law on some disputed point, a bishop pleads for a humane Christian attitude, he is reprimanded by his brothers in office as well. Indeed, under this pontificate bishops have joined in executing the business of the curia against their fellow bishops: the archbishop of Washington, D.C., had to see to the carrying out of the rules in Seattle, as did the archbishop of Cologne in Sao Paolo, Brazil. While resignations for reason of age are accepted immediately from such progressive bishops as Lercaro of Bologna or Helder Camara of Recife, in the case of conservatives such as the archbishops of Cologne and Philadelphia, the age limit of seventy-five years formally determined by Vatican II is completely disregarded without scruple.

"Law" on one side—and "money" on the other. The two chief donors to the curia are the churches of the United States and West Germany. Of the two, the American episcopate is more dependent on the people and their voluntary contributions (not the least of the reasons for its greater openness to the concerns of the people).

The premoderns in the hierarchy unquestionably take great pains to acquire a postmodern varnish. On the one hand, as many useful external elements of the modern as possible are taken over, especially in communication arts and media politics, and incorporated into the medieval antimodernist paradigm. Thus there arise the paradoxical but effective folkloric images of baroquely clad and medievally hatted prelates riding in helicopters or participating before TV cameras in demonstrations and processions which could come from another century. On the other hand, the postmodern criticism of modern science, technology, industry, and democracy ("consumerism") is adopted whenever it costs nothing: "We too, we too! . . ." Positions favoring human rights and social justice and protesting all possible discrimination on the basis of religion and sex are courageously embraced, but women inside the structure are forcibly held in an inferior status. Ordination is forbidden to women and marriage to ordained men, and the church's own theologians are denied freedom of speech and a fair judicial process with inspection of files, counsel, and the right of appeal. So once again a paradoxical image arises: a Vatican which signs the Helsinki Accord in favor of disarmament, but neither will, nor in fact can, sign either the Declaration on Human

Rights of the United Nations or that of the European Council because first the medieval church law (which celebrated its joyful resurrection in the "new" codex) has to be brought up to the level of contemporary legal consciousness.

Nevertheless the critical voices "from below," from the Catholic episcopate and clergy, from theologians and laity, refuse to be suppressed. Theological research progresses; it has long since pointed out where, in the Roman Catholic tradition, the Catholic has been suppressed in favor of the Roman. The current pontificate has recently been subjected to sharp criticism in Italy itself from serious publicists like Pierfiorgio Mariotti (*Karol Wojtyla, profilo critico del papa polacco* [Rome, 1983]) and the already-mentioned Giancarlo Zizola. Against "law and money" the "spirit" can accomplish little, but in the long run, whenever it has truth on its side, it has proved itself stronger. Bottling up problems for a long time, as during the Renaissance or the era of the Pius popes, has ultimately and inevitably led to a revolutionary breakthrough like the Reformation or Vatican II, a lesson that the restorers of a new "balance of power" a la Metternich should not forget.

THE RESULTS OF THE SYNOD AS OPPORTUNITY

This critique—not of the Catholic church but of the medieval-counterreformation-antimodernistic Roman system—must be continued until the turning point of the Second Vatican Council is taken seriously within the Vatican itself. Many people, within and without the Catholic church, have given up hope that anything decisive will really change behind the Vatican walls. I do not share this pessimism after, despite everything, so much has in fact changed, much of it obviously irreversibly. The Roman episcopal synod made it clear that a significant portion of the episcopate supports a consistent renewal in the spirit of the Second Vatican Council. The pope and his curialists would be well-advised to take seriously the charges and claims of the episcopate whom they are to serve and translate them into concrete action this time. A mere ten words of the synod's report will be cited here. Each of them goes back to the Second Vatican Council and therefore has binding power on the Roman administration and on every subsequent synod, which are not supposed to "confirm" or "certify" this ecumenical council of the Catholic church but simply to translate it into action.

1. *Church as communio.* If the church is to be taken seriously not as "hierarchy" or rule by priests, but as *koinonia* or communion or community of the faithful with Christ and with one another, then the 1987 synod on the "Vocation and Mission of the Laity in the Church and in the World" must not be a synod of bishops *over* the laity, but a synod of bishops (and theologians) *with* the laity, men and women—and, let us hope, not only with those in conformist lay associations. Such a meeting would show clearly that the medieval superordination of the clergy over the laity, which contradicts the original constitution of the church, has given way to a reciprocal sub- and superordination in the biblical sense.

2. *"Pluralism" in unity.* If pluralism is to be not merely a word but a reality even in Rome itself, then we must expect that, not only in the Congregation for the Doctrine of the Faith (which still, contrary to Paul VI's mandate, has contributed but little to the positive illumination of the faith, but simply pursued its old inquisitorial activities in new ways), but in other Vatican offices as well, the dominance of the old medieval dogmacentric neoscholasticism will finally give way, and that all the current streams in Catholic theology—including Latin American liberation theology—will be represented.

3. *"Collegiality" of the bishops with the pope.* If limits to the authority of the pope really do exist and collegiality—the most important catchword of the most recent synod—is eventually to take effect fully in canon law, then the bishops' synod must change from what has until now been a largely ineffective advisory organ of the pope into a committee which truly collaborates in the legislative functions of the church. The bishops' conferences, the usefulness and benefits of which, strange to say, must be expressly confirmed in the face of the curia's claims to power, must in the future experience less obstruction and more help and support.

4. *"Participation"* and *"co-responsibility."* If this principle is to be valid on all levels of the church, then the decentralization process must continue; then bishops can no longer be

installed or even (as in Holland) imposed by Rome without the consent of people and clergy, if they toe the Roman line; then the bishops must be chosen by a representation of clergy and people, preferably through already existing priest and pastoral councils (perhaps with consultation with further representatives), and, when chosen, must be approved by Rome.

5. *"The vocation and the mission of women."* If the church wishes to provide that the women in the church "play a greater part in the various fields of the church's apostolate" and that pastors "gratefully accept and promote the collaboration of women in ecclesial activity," then in the future women cannot be relegated to service positions in the church. The equality women have attained socially must also take effect within the church. And church leadership will have to take care that the silent mass exodus of women from the church is countered by complete legal equality up through the ordination of women.

6. *The youth—"hope of the church."* If the synod expects "great things" from the "generous dedication" of youth, if it wishes to motivate youth to "embrace and dynamically continue the heritage of the council," then in the future the hierarchy must conduct itself more credibly vis-à-vis the youth. Contemporary faith expressions, spirituality, and praxis must not be suppressed by the official church. The students' own organizations must no longer be threatened and their own youth organizations no longer be disciplined (a concrete test case: the attitude of the hierarchy toward sexuality and partnership).

7. *"Base communities"* and *"the preferential option of the church for the poor."* When the synod describes basic communities as "a true expression of communion and a means for the construction of a more profound communion" and indeed calls them a "great hope for the life of the church," its words are credible only if the theology which has its *Sitz im Leben* in these base communities—namely, the liberation theologies of Latin America, Asia, and black Africa—is completely rehabilitated in the official church, and the disciplining of liberation theologians ceases.

8. *"Ecumenism."* If the bishops "ardently desire that the in-

complete communion already existing with the non-Catholic churches and communities might, with the grace of God, come to the point of full communion," their desires are credible only if the bishops do what is their responsibility alone: put into practice the positive results of the ecumenical commissions of the past twenty years in regard to reciprocal recognition of office and intercommunion. The bishops can underscore their ecumenical seriousness by integrating the Congregation for the Doctrine of the Faith into the Secretariat (Congregation) for Christian Unity, so that the former, with its wretched past, can fulfill the new task assigned to it—to clarify the content of Christian faith to contemporary people and to guard against real (not imaginary) misunderstandings and errors—in an ecumenical context.

9. *"Dialogue" with non-Christian religions.* When the synod advocates continuing dialogue with non-Christian religions and with nonbelievers, when it "exhort[s] Catholics to recognize, preserve and promote all the good spiritual and moral—as well as sociocultural—values that they find in their midst: all of this with prudence and charity, through dialogue and collaboration with the faithful of other religions, giving testimony to the Christian faith and life," such declarations of intent and challenges are credible only if concrete deeds follow from dialogue with Jews and Muslims, Hindus, and Buddhists.

10. *Aggiornamento.* When the synod advocates a correctly understood *aggiornamento* ("a missionary openness for the integral salvation of the world"), when it excludes "an immobile closing in upon itself of the community of the faithful," then its statements will be credible only if fear of the modern and postmodern has also ceased in Rome. Then realization of modern human rights will no longer be evaded in the church. Then liberation in the church will parallel liberation in society, and the "tedious old questions" remaining since the council will be settled. Yes, then a church which is open rather than closed in and concerned with itself will really become a "sign" to the peoples. Global problems like the East-West and the North-South conflicts,

the marginalization of millions of human beings (the number continues to grow explosively), the ecological crisis, the rising of new liberation and peace movements, new ethical questions in connection with gene manipulation, the growth of new sects and religions, the revolution in the communication sector—all of these developments will affect life in the third millennium more than church regulations and dogmatic statements will. No one who wants the church to remain, can want it to remain as it is.

THE CALL FOR A NEW COUNCIL

Ceterum censeo Romanam curiam esse reformandam!
This is why many people today are calling for a new council, from which, of course, the *curia romana* shrinks like the devil before holy water. The problems that became visible at the last bishops' synod (from the universal catechism shelved by an earlier council to the questions of birth control, celibacy, and infallibility) cannot be carried through to their solution by a new synod, but only by a new council. A Third Vatican Council or, better still, a Second Jerusalem Council (with the inclusion of other churches) must be the goal. The old "new course" and the old "new codes"—themselves the clearest signal of the restoration and the betrayal of the Council—must then be revised.

Translated by
Arlene Anderson Swidler

I. THE CHURCH UNIVERSAL
The Negative Impact of a Repressive Regime

2. Fortress Catholicism
Wojtyla's Polish Roots
ADAM NOWOTNY

On 23 October, 1978, the very day of his inauguration as pope, John Paul II wrote a letter to the people of Poland. After briefly recalling the difficult struggles the Polish nation and the Polish church had been through in recent centuries, he continued:

Behold! Extraordinary things are now happening beyond human explanation! In these last decades, the Church in Poland has taken on special significance both for the universal Church and for all of Christianity. The unique circumstances in which it finds itself—of incredible importance for the questions which modern society and various nations and peoples are raising with regard to social, economic and cultural problems–has made it an object of special interest. The Church in Poland has taken on a new image; it has become a Church of special witness on whom the eyes of the whole world are turned! It is through this Church that our people, this generation of Poles, live and speak forth![1]

Was the pope expressing here a mere pious platitude or was he serving notice that the model that would guide him in directing the destiny of the universal church was precisely that of the Polish church? Many are convinced that John Paul II's image of the church is deeply rooted in and influenced by his Polish background and experience. Peter Hebblethwaite commenting in this vein remarks that, "there could be no understanding of his papacy without an understanding of his Polishness . . . being Polish is the most important fact about him."[2] Giancarlo Zizola states even more explicitly: "As the first Polish Pope, Karol Wojtyla has been engaged precisely in this mission of moulding the Church's future in the shape of a Polish past."[3] If this be true, some insight into the characteristics of that Polish church ought to provide a valuable clue for understanding the actions and directions of our present pontiff.

One cannot understand the Polish church without an understanding of Polish history. The two are inextricably linked. The very first recorded act of Polish history occurred in 966 A.D. with the baptism of its first king, Mieszko I. This simple religious ceremony was not without political significance. It won for Poland the powerful protection of Rome and aligned this new nation culturally, politically, and religiously with the West. Poland thus became, as one pope entitled her, "the Gate of Christendom to the East."

Early in its history when King Boleslaw II began ruthlessly oppressing his own people—long before the Magna Charta was signed with King John—Bishop Stanislaus of Krakow stood up in defense of the common people. He repeatedly and publicly denounced the king's actions. On 8 May, 1079, the infuriated king had the bishop murdered at the altar and his body dismembered. This so enraged the people that they forced the king into exile and the murdered Stanislaus became a powerful symbol of the church's readiness to stand in defense of its people—so powerful a symbol, in fact, that when the newly elected John Paul II expressed a wish to return to his native country to take part in the nine-hundredth anniversary of Saint Stanislaus's death, the Polish government refused to accede to his wishes. The political implications were obvious to all!

In one of the turning points of Polish history, the combined Polish-Lithuanian army went into battle against the Teutonic Knights of the Cross, a medieval crusading order that made repeated incursions into Polish territories under the pretext of converting the heathens. Historians make special note that the Polish-Lithuanian soldiers marched into battle chanting the oldest known Polish Marian hymn, *Bogurodzica Dziewica*. Their decisive victory at Grunwald in 1410 put an end to the Teutonic threat and changed the course of Polish history. Popular sentiment attributed the victory to the special protection of the Holy Virgin.

Again, in 1655, when the Swedish armies had all but overrun the country, they were finally turned back and defeated attempting to besiege the monastery fortress where the miraculous painting of Our Lady of Czestochowa was kept. The astonishing victory was naturally attributed to the intercession of the Blessed Virgin. In gratitude, the then Polish king, Jan Kazimierz, proclaimed Mary "queen of Poland" and the shrine became a national symbol of Mary's unfailing protection of the Polish people.

In 1683 when King Sobieski defeated the Turks at Vienna and saved European Christianity, he gave expression to an underlying faith in divine Providence that has been a constant of the Polish tradition. He baptized Caesar's famous quote: *Veni, Vidi, Deus Vincit!*—"I came! I saw! but God conquered!" In announcing the victory to Charles II, the Holy Roman Emperor, he referred to Poland as "the bulwark of Christendom," renewing the conviction that by God's design Poland has a special role to play in the history of nations.

Unquestionably, the most significant role for faith and the church came during the darkest years of Polish history. From 1772 to 1918, during the long years of Poland's partition under Prussian, Austrian, and Russian domination, the church was the only institution where the native language, culture, and art could be publicly fostered. The impact this had on forging an identity between nationality and religion was considerable. Whereas most people, and Americans especially, would tend to separate religion and nationality, the Pole instinctively identifies the two. Czeslaw Milosz, the Polish poet laureate and Nobel prize winner, comments on the significance of this for the Polish church:

After Poland had disintegrated as a country and wounded nationalism made its appearance, the notions of "Pole" and "Catholic" became equated. . . . Thus religion was turned into an institution for preserving national identity; in this respect, the Poles were like the Jews in the Roman Empire. To make the analogy more complete, messianic currents were as popular with the Poles as they had been with Israel . . . when the line between national and religious behavior is erased, religion changes into a social power; it becomes conservative and conformist.[4]

The Nazi occupation from 1939 to 1945, which attacked the church with special viciousness and sent one-third of its clergy to death in the concentration camps, only served to further deepen this identity between religion and nationality and make of the priest-martyrs national heroes. Similarly, the church's role as the primary articulator, defender, and preserver of the deepest hopes and aspirations of the Polish people during the nation's continuing oppression by an imposed regime following World War II has only enhanced this conviction. It is small wonder, then, that today—despite over forty years of a relentless campaign to eliminate religion from Polish life—approximately 95 percent of its thirty-eight million population openly profess their allegiance to the Catholic church. It is out of such history that was born the proverb: *Polak, to Katolik*—"To be Polish is to be Catholic!"

MESSIANISM VS. HOPELESSNESS

As is evident from this brief summary of Polish history, the theme of suffering, oppression, and persecution dominates the Polish experience. Cardinal Wyszynski, in speaking of the Church of Silence (the Church behind the Iron Curtain), was wont to say that martyrdom has not ceased; it has only taken on a new and more violent form. Martyrdom in the early church was mercifully brief. Today, the persecution and suffering go on day after day, week after week, month after month, year after year. This modern form of martyrdom is far more difficult to bear. This sentiment is borne out in an inscription written across a widely distributed photo of the bombed-out ruins of the Warsaw cathedral:

It is easy to talk about Poland;
It is harder to work for Poland;
It is still harder to die for Poland;
But it is hardest of all to suffer for Poland!

How does one understand, interpret, make sense of such seemingly undeserved tragedy and misfortune? Poland's poets, dramatists, and artists—like the ancient prophets of Israel—have often portrayed Poland as a "suffering servant" nation destined one day to be the salvation of all peoples. Wojtyla's favorite poet Julius Slowacki (1809–1849) stressed the redemptive value of suffering for others as part of Poland's role in history and in one of his poems prophesied salvation through a Slavic pope:

Behold the Slavic Pope is coming,
A brother of the people.[5]

If poets, dramatists, and artists make this connection, should not those steeped in the writings of the prophets do likewise? Is it any wonder that John Paul II stresses the providential nature of his election to the See of Peter and its special significance for the

Polish church? His own personal history confirms the drama lived out by the nation as a whole. He was born in the small town of Wadowice about twenty miles south of Krakow and an almost equal distance from the concentration camp at Auschwitz. His mother, Emilia, died when Karol was nine years old. An older brother died while doing a medical internship, and an older sister died before he was born. His father was a retired Austrian army lieutenant who lived on a small pension. John Paul II's own reflections on this period of his life are telling:

At twenty I had already lost all the people I loved and even the ones that I might have loved, such as the big sister who had died, so I was told, six years before my birth. I was not old enough to make my first communion when I lost my mother, who did not have the happiness of seeing the day to which she looked forward as a great day. . . . My brother Edmond died from scarlet fever in a virulent epidemic at the hospital where he was serving as a doctor . . . I was twelve. . . . Thus quite soon, I became a motherless only child. My father was admirable and almost all the memories of my childhood and adolescence are connected with him. The violence of the blows which had struck him had opened immense spiritual depths in him; his grief found its outlet in prayer. The mere fact of seeing him on his knees had a decisive influence on my early years. He was so hard on himself that he had no need to be hard on his son; his example alone was sufficient to inculcate discipline and a sense of duty.[6]

Thus Karol's personal experience only served to confirm and deepen the conviction that suffering and tragedy—often undeserved and unmerited—are God's way of preparing for the future. If as individuals and as a nation we but remain faithful with discipline and sacrifice, God will help us overcome and become a source of salvation for others. The ancients used to say: "The blood of martyrs is the seed of Christians." John Paul II is convinced that the suffering and sacrifice that the Polish nation and church have been through have made it a strong, vigorous church that can serve as a model for others—especially for the western European and North American church. A pope deeply convinced that God is leading the way has no fear. Opposition, difficulty, and struggle will not discourage him. They are familiar territory and only serve to confirm and assure that he is doing the will of God. Such a deeply ingrained spirit of messianism, nourished daily in prayerful communion with his God, fills John Paul II with incredible courage and commitment for his task and is the source of the unbounded confidence and hopefulness he has for the future of the church.

CERTITUDE VS. CONFUSION

It is a noble thing to have a predisposition for understanding every person, analyzing every system and recognizing what is right; this does not at all mean losing certitude about one's own faith or weakening the principles of morality, the lack of which will soon make itself felt in the life of whole societies, with deplorable consequences besides.[7]

Polish Catholicism is remarkable for the consistency and certainty with which it proclaims official church teachings on faith and morals. It has experienced none of the theological tension, opposition, resistance, and dissent, especially in the area of morals, that has marked western European and American Catholicism in recent decades. In this regard, Polish theological development has been considerably less innovative and more reserved than trends found elsewhere in the world. The impact that Vatican II had on much of the rest of Catholicism has scarcely touched Poland.

Leszek Kolakowski, a well-known Polish philosopher, helps us understand the reason why:

Of course, Cardinal Wyszynski played an enormous role in the post-war history of Poland. . . . Without the enormous power that was Polish Catholicism one can easily say that Poland would have never survived; Poland would have been destroyed. The Church preserved our nation and our national culture. On the other hand, the Church was able to play this role only because it was characterized by a certain rigidity, an uncompromising attitude, a lack of flexibility which contributed to backwardness in our culture . . . at this moment it is hard to say whether it could have been different. . . .[8]

The church's struggle for survival against a regime thoroughly committed to its extinction is perhaps the best explanation for this need for absolute clarity and certitude. Our American experience has taught us how disturbing even insignificant changes can be; for the Polish church such divisiveness in their circumstances would have been fatal.

But John Paul II's emphasis on certainty in matters of faith and morals has a deeper source as well—his own life experience and educational formation. He acknowledges that personal experience and reflection have been his primary avenues for arriving at truth:

Circumstances have never left me much time for study. By temperament I prefer thought to erudition. I came to realize this during my short career as a teacher at Cracow and Lublin. My conception of the person, "unique" in his identity, and of man, as such, at the centre of the universe, was born much more of experience and of sharing with others than of reading. Books, study, reflection and discussion—which I do not avoid, as you know—help me to formulate what experience teaches me.[9]

John Paul II admits that it was his study of scholastic metaphysics that gave "solid confirmation" to what intuition and experience taught him about the world. This system of thought with its emphasis on unchangeable essences provided the philosophical underpinning for his absolutist convictions. It is a neatly ordered world in which God's eternal and unchanging plan is inscribed in the very nature and essence of things. His education in Rome at the Angelicum University under the direction of Garrigou-Lagrange—a strong advocate of rigid neoscholasticism—completed the framework through which John Paul II reflects on life experience.

Upon his return to Poland, the young Wojtyla became fascinated with the phenomenological approach of the popular German ethicist Max Scheler. He completed a second doctorate, studying the question of whether Max Scheler's ethics could serve as a basis for a Christian ethic. His dissertation reached two conclusions: first, Max Scheler's approach cannot be used as a basis for Christian ethics because it recognizes no absolutes; second, Max Scheler's use of language deserves to be imitated because it speaks to people. This double conclusion provides an important clue for understanding many of John Paul II's writings. On the one hand, it explains his heavy appeal to such concepts as experience, freedom, and human dignity, and to language that gives the impression of a very open, flexible, and dynamic understanding of the human person. On the other hand, it cautions us to beware that beneath that language lies a neo-Thomistic, essentialist understanding of human nature that inevitably leads to the inflexible conclusions he often reaches, particularly in personal ethics.

Knowing this, it should have come as no surprise that when addressing the American bishops during his last visit to America as well as during their *ad limina* visits to Rome, he would remind them of their responsibility to preach with absolute clarity and without compromise the church's position on such topics as abortion, artificial birth control, the indissolubility of Christian marriage, and the exclusion of women from the priesthood. It is only in this way that the right of the faithful to certitude about matters of faith and morals can be safeguarded and debilitating confusion eliminated.

SOLIDARITY VS. INDIVIDUALISM

Solidarity is a word which has taken on new life and new meaning in the light of events occurring in Poland in the early 1980s. Lech Walesa's efforts that brought about the swift and massive unionization of the majority of the industrial and agricultural laborers in Poland created a power that, temporarily at least, incapacitated the Polish government and military. It is small wonder that John Paul II in his encyclical "On Labor" called for a movement of solidarity among workers all over the world as the only effective means for bringing an end to the oppression and exploitation of workers and ensuring justice for all.

Solidarity in its union form was not the first experience of the power in community togetherness that the Poles had experienced. For centuries, religious pilgrimages to the various Marian shrines located throughout the country would attract pilgrims numbering into the hundreds of thousands. These clearly became occasions not only for manifesting their religious piety but also a show of strength for demonstrating their loyalty to the church and opposition to the government. Such manifestations have been an important part of Polish national and religious life and suggest something about the Polish religious experience.

Czeslaw Milosz, a contemporary of John Paul II, gives us an interesting insight into this trait of Polish Catholicism as he recounts his own early educational experience:

Hamster [his own religion teacher] was actually an extreme proponent of an old thesis in the Catholic Church: that man can approach God only through the intermediary of the senses; and that individual faith and virtue are a function of group behavior. By going to Mass and receiving the sacraments, we absorb, in spite of ourselves, a certain style, which, just as copper is a good conductor of electricity, serves to guide us to the supernatural. . . . I see this as a trait of Polish Catholicism, which, in putting the accent on responsibility to collective organisms (i.e., to Church and Fatherland, which are largely identified with each other), thereby lightens the responsibility to concrete, living people. . . . Religion is rarely an inner experience for him; most often it is a collection of taboos grounded in habit and tribal prejudices, so that he remains a slave to Plato's Social Beast.[10]

John Paul II acknowledges this trait but makes a much more sophisticated case for the kind of solidarity that is needed and rejects out of hand the crude conformism that Milosz suggests. In fact, he insists that genuine solidarity requires a healthy opposition and that both are essential for constructing a strong society. He waxes eloquent when he states "that the structure of community must not only allow the emergence of opposition, give it the opportunity to express itself, but also must make it possible for the opposition to function for the good of the community."[11] The attitudes that he regards as incompatible with solidarity are a mindless "conformism" utterly devoid of any personal conviction or an "avoidance" that is tantamount to evasion, escape, retreat. He recognizes that there may be reasons that justify the attitude of avoidance, but then these same reasons form an accusation of the community. These certainly are strong and courageous criticisms to make in a society which is tightly controlled and where rigid censorship and strict party supervision regulate every aspect of life.

His Polish experience thus gives John Paul II a high regard and deep appreciation for the importance of solidarity. But on the basis of ecclesial actions taken against Archbishop Hunthausen, Hans Küng, Charles Curran, and many others it is apparent that, in the mind of John Paul II, these observations about solidarity and opposition are restricted to civil society only. Solidarity and togetherness in the church are to be achieved in another way.

AUTHORITY VS. ANARCHY

Poles take great pride in their reputation as a freedom-loving and tolerant people. They like to point out that in the 1300s persecuted Jews from all over Europe fled to Poland as the one safe haven of refuge where they could be truly free. They boast about the fact that in the sixteenth century, during the time of the Reformation, many suffering persecution for their religious beliefs found in Poland a home where they could worship as they pleased. This respect for individual freedom and toleration of divergent views was carried to an extreme in the seventeenth and eighteenth centuries when the National Sejm passed the *Liberum Veto* permitting any member of the Sejm, by a single vote, to dissove a parliamentary session and annul its enactments. This absurdity resulted in the anarchy that eventually led to the downfall of the Polish republic.

Periods of tension, difficulty, and struggle make the toleration of freedom particularly precarious. It is generally acknowledged that Cardinal Wyszynski's strong and fearless exercise of authority played a crucial role in the church's survival and successful resistance to communist efforts to destroy it. On more than one occasion, this meant bypassing normal canonical procedures to remove from office duly elected leaders of religious congregations, summarily silencing or transferring outspoken clerical critics, unilateral rendering of decisions, and other markedly authoritarian actions. But in the final analysis, it is widely believed that it was this strong hand of authority that saved the Polish church.

Our present pope has not forgotten the lessons that history teaches: the painful lesson of anarchy and chaos that misused freedom can create; the power and strength that can result from vigorous exercise of authority. This is especially important when one remembers that he comes from a society which shares quite generally the Solzhenitsyn attitude that an exaggerated concept of freedom has left Western society weak, corrupt, and decadent. His own integration of these values of freedom and authority is best expressed in an article he wrote on his understanding of collegiality following his return from the bishops' synod in 1969, to which he had been a delegate. A proper understanding of collegiality, for John Paul II, can never result in conflict with papal authority because it is always exercised "with and under" (*cum et sub*) the guidance of the successor of Saint Peter. This is an expression that occurs again and again in his writings on this topic. For this reason, he sees no danger in extending collegiality beyond the bishops to priests and laity, provided, of course, they remain always "united with and under the guidance of the Successor of Saint Peter."[12] A review of the actions of his pontificate indicate that he has not hesitated to exercise strong, authoritarian leadership to ensure the kind of certitude, solidarity, and freedom he believes necessary for the church's well-being. His actions with the Dutch church, the Jesuit superior general, Sister Agnes Mansour, as well as his unilateral correction of the New Code of Canon Law and personal decision to draft all final reports of the bishops' synods have ample precedent in Polish experience. John Paul II readily acknowledges the debt he owes to his long-term mentor Cardinal Wyszynski on how to lead a church through difficult times.

SOCIALISM VS. CAPITALISM

Officially, the Catholic church is very clear in maintaining a neutral stance toward the form of government and economy by which a people choose to rule themselves. Though the church does not become involved in the politics of economic systems, it has much to say regarding the moral and human values such systems may foster. Poland has never experienced capitalism in full bloom. The privileged status of the nobility and landed gentry that oppressed the landless peasants and other minorities throughout much of its history right into the twentieth century prepared the way for the socialist experiment that was imposed by the regime after World War II. Thirty-five years of failure of this experiment resulted in the Solidarity explosion of 1980. What is interesting to note is that the leaders of Solidarity were not clamoring for capitalism; they explicitly rejected such an option. In their terms, all they were asking for was "to put a human face on their socialism." They had come to appreciate socialism's ability to reduce some of the extreme inequalities that existed in prewar Poland. Had the Solidarity experiment succeeded, the world might have witnessed the gradual coming into being of a political–economic system incorporating the best elements of the capitalist and socialist experiences. Unfortunately, that did not happen! But this is not to say that the experience of Polish society has not had its impact on the political and social thought of John Paul II. His most mature thought on this topic, recorded in his encyclical "On Labor," attempts to incorporate this experience. Although he clearly rejects the Marxist analysis, he is no less vigorous in condemning the inequalities that result from extreme capitalism. His frequent appeals, as he travels around the world, for a more equitable sharing of the world's resources will probably mark his most important and valuable contribution to the church. No previous pope has focused world attention on the problems of poverty, oppression, and injustice as insistently as has John Paul II. It is a hard message for American ears to hear, but we can continue to expect to be reminded of our heavy responsibility to abandon our consumerist attitudes and ways and to share our resources more generously with the poor of the world.

CHURCH VS. STATE

Throughout this essay it has been indicated how historical circumstances have led Poles to forge an identity between nationality and religion. Some question whether their professed adherence to the church is a genuine profession of faith or merely the only available expression of their opposition to the ruling government. For nearly two centuries Poles have experienced governing authorities hostile to their language, culture, religion, and most deeply cherished human values. Various forms of government have come and gone but the church has remained the one source of support and strength for everything that has constituted them as a nation. Such an extended historical experience has made John Paul II acutely aware that the state in a political sense is a transitory reality of no great fundamental importance. It is the church that is the real guardian of the nation's culture and values.

This background helps one understand his deep reluctance to allow priests and religious to become involved in politics. Their commitment calls them to the more serious task of safeguarding the morals and values of the nation. Whenever the church intervenes in public affairs, such as during the Solidarity movement, its role is not to meddle in political pragmatics but rather to give moral guidance and direction regarding basic human values. Westerners generally find it difficult to make so neat and subtle a distinction between moral values and pragmatic politics when so often it is the very political structures that prevent the realization of the moral and human values. Perhaps in a country where the government is clearly hostile to religion, such distinctions are easier to apply.

QUEEN OF POLAND—MOTHER OF THE CHURCH

Marian devotion runs deep in Polish spirituality. It draws much of its strength and force from its rootedness in Polish history. The major victories and successes of the Polish nation have been attributed to her intercession and providence. The title bestowed upon her by King Jan Kazimierz as queen of Poland is much more than a pious invocation. It is a deep religious conviction that has been nurtured through the centuries in prayers, novenas, devotions, pilgrimages, and shrines dedicated to the Virgin Mother of God. The strong belief in Mary's intercessory role led the Polish bishops at Vatican II to lead the intervention that resulted in the Council's declaring Mary mother of the church. Renewed impetus was given to this devotion by Cardinal Wyszynski when in 1966 he initiated throughout the nation a nine-year Novena of thanksgiving to Our Lady of Czestochowa to commemorate the millennium of Christianity in Poland.

John Paul II shares in this deep devotion to the Mother of God. His consciousness is so attuned to this relationship that he finds special significance in the fact that John Paul I was elected on the Feast of Our Lady of Czestochowa and that the assassination attempts on his own life took place on the Feast of Our Lady of Fatima. The conviction that Mary's intercession spared his life resulted in a pilgrimage of gratitude to the shrine at Fatima on one of his first trips after his recovery. With such confidence in the power of Mary's intercession, we should not be surprised at the pope's frequent invocation of her help in his public speeches and addresses, his strong encouragement of devotion to her, and, most recently, his proclamation of a worldwide year of devotion to Mary, beginning Pentecost Sunday, 7 June, 1987.

WOMEN—PRIESTS?

One of the strong criticisms of John Paul II in some American circles is over his failure to advance more forcefully the issue of equal rights for women in the church and particularly his absolutely adamant position against the ordination of women. Are there reasons in his Polish background that might explain this? His own alleged explanation is that it is the will of Christ even though the Vatican biblical commission has concluded that there are no clear obstacles in the Scriptures to such a development. His strong conviction is rooted rather in his own personal experience and reflection with strong support from his Polish environment.

The church in Poland has not yet made any significant steps to involve the laity, men or women, in a more active role. It remains a largely male, hierarchical, clerical institution. Even women religious are not admitted, for the most part, to positions of catechizing or education. This responsibility is entrusted to the parish vicar who often spends forty to fifty hours per week catechizing the youth of the parish. Women, lay or religious, are restricted to caring for the elderly, the blind, the sick, providing some secretarial help, and servicing the kitchens, sacristies, and other maintenance tasks of church institutions. At a theological congress called by the then Cardinal Wojtyla in Krakow in 1978, among the more than eight hundred delegates present, there was not a single woman. Certainly John Paul II's background would not suggest a wider role for women in the church.

There is one experience in particular that may have had a negative effect on his thinking regarding this question. In 1893, a certain Felicia Kozlowska began a movement to deepen the prayer life and spirituality of the Polish clergy. Her efforts were received initially with great enthusiasm and attracted a great number of priests to her center. Because of her extraordinary visions and revelations, the Vatican investigated and in 1906 condemned her. Many of the priests who had been spiritually renewed under her direction refused to heed the Vatican ban and remained with her. Eventually, the movement set up its own parishes and dioceses, encouraged mystical marriages between priests and nuns, and even ordained and consecrated women priests and women bishops. The movement created a disturbing wound in the Polish church that has continued until the present. It is difficult to judge what impact this experience had on John Paul II, but it is surely one he cannot easily dismiss from his mind.

In light of his manner of arriving at truth through personal experience and reflection and his insistence on clarity and solidarity for the Christian community, there appears little likelihood of any change on this issue. His charge to the American bishops on this matter is more likely to be the continuing policy: "The Bishop must give proof of his pastoral ability and leadership by withdrawing all support from individuals or groups who in the name of progress, justice or compassion, or for any other alleged reason, promote the ordination of women to the priesthood."[13]

ECUMENISM VS. ISOLATIONISM

One of the important changes in Polish society since World War II is the marked homogeneity of its people. In prewar Poland, Catholics constituted approximately 65 percent of the population. The remaining 35 percent consisted of sizable minorities of Jews, Ukrainians, Bielo-Russians, and Ruthenians. Of the more than 3.5 million Jews before the war, there remain at present less than five thousand. The vast majority of the Ukrainians, Ruthenians, and Bielo-Russians have been placed under Russian rule due to boundary changes. As a result, Polish society today is 95 percent Roman Catholic.

In one sense this homogeneity of religious environment constitutes a real handicap. The lack of close, personal encounters with persons of other faiths does not permit the development of the kind of trust and openness that paves the way for meaningful ecumenical dialogue. The high level of ecumenical activity that has taken place in the United States since Vatican II certainly has been facilitated by the daily interaction in all forums of life of Catholics with people of other faiths. This experience is credited with enabling the grass-roots ecumenical encounters to far outstrip any progress that has been made on the theological or official levels. John Paul II has certainly declared his ready commitment to foster the unity of the church, but his lack of personal experience and familiarity with other believers may well explain some of the hesitation and fear that appears to have brought a halt to the hoped for ecumenical progress.

CHURCH STATESMAN—MASTERFUL POLITICIAN

The whole world recognizes John Paul II's superstar status as the "great communicator." Less widely known and appreciated are his abilities as a superb administrator. In fact, there has even been some criticism heard that his frequent trips abroad have left him little time for effective administration of the Petrine office.

A review of his accomplishments, however, will clearly indicate a masterful administrator who knows how to influence and control the structures of the church on which the effective realization of his vision of the church ultimately depend. His close scrutiny of the appointment of bishops has assured him of a loyal cadre of faithful supporters who will implement his views and carry out his policies on the local level. Assuming responsibility for the final statement of all bishops' synods enables him to make sure that there will be no discrepancy at the official level between his views and those of his brother bishops. His innovative resolution for the crisis in the Dutch church served notice that he is capable of handling opposition even at the regional level of the church. His personal review and correction of the New Code of Canon Law has assured that the legal structures of the church will support and foster this vision. His intervention in the Jesuit affair sent a message to all religious orders of the action that can be taken if they stray too far from the appointed path. His removal of official Catholic theologian status from dissenting creative thinkers such as Hans Küng and Charles Curran has sent a freezing chill down through the whole theological community. His investigation of American seminaries is meant to ensure that future generations of priests will be properly formed in a spirit of fidelity and obedience to this vision. His study of American religious and the careful scrutiny of their renewed constitutions is designed to put an end to some dangerous tendencies and return this largest group of dedicated church servants to their rightful place in the ministry of the church. A soon to be published document in Catholic higher education aims to secure our Catholic colleges and universities for more faithful and loyal service to the mission of the church. No pope in the entire history of the church has in so short a time so effectively and masterfully restructured the church to serve the vision shared so forcefully by its supreme pastor.

EPILOGUE

John Paul II by any standards is an exceptional and extraordinary human being. There is no question that his views of the church have been deeply influenced and conditioned by his Polish background and experience. Will they be adequate for the church he is preparing to enter the twenty-first century?

His Polish messianism can prove to be an incredible source of strength, courage, and hope, provided it does not degenerate into a fanaticism that fails to distinguish between the divine will and one's own stubborn convictions. His desire to dispel the doubt and confusion regarding church doctrine disturbing so many of the faithful is well-intentioned, but if it insists on clarity and certitude where neither faith nor reason can guarantee such, his efforts will only provide a false security that prefers even the certitude of error to the ambiguity of reality. His strong sense of the importance of both solidarity and opposition to create a society where communal and individual needs are integrated will serve the church only if these attitudes are regarded as equally valid not only for civil society but for the church as well. Otherwise, the way of "avoidance" that many in the church have already chosen will increase and prove to be in John Paul's own words a well-deserved judgment upon the institution. His hope to avoid anarchy by a forceful use of authority needs to be carefully tempered lest it degenerate into a destructive authoritarianism that stifles freedom and inhibits growth. The church-state relationship he has experienced in Poland suggests a separation of sacred and secular, priest and politics that is far more radical than even the American tradition warrants and runs counter to the Christian tradition calling for the integration and restoration of all things in Christ. His reservations regarding socialism and capitalism and insistent calls for justice will be heard more clearly only when the church itself, through its institutions, becomes a model of justice and compassionate care for the poor and oppressed. The Polish devotion to Mary likewise could find greater acceptance in the West if Mary's intercessory power brought about, not only the liberation of Poland or the church, but of women as well—both in church and society. Ecumenically, unless the pope can transcend the limiting homogeneity of his Polish experience, he will never be able to lead the universal church to the kind of unity that this generation had hoped for. Only time will tell, however, whether history will remember John Paul II as an eminent church statesman whose legacy will live on because his vision was right or simply as a masterful politician who for a short period turned the wheels of power.

NOTES

1. John Paul II, *Kultura*, n. 12/375 (December 1978): 3–4.
2. John Whale, ed., *The Man Who Leads the Church: An Assessment of Pope John Paul II* (New York: Harper & Row, 1980), 25.
3. Giancarlo Zizola, "The Counter Reformation of John Paul II," *Magill* 7 (1985): 10.
4. Czeslaw Milosz, *Native Realm*, trans. Catherine Leach (Garden City, N.Y.: Doubleday, 1968), 82.
5. Paul Collins, *Mixed Blessings: John Paul II and the Church of the Eighties* (Australia: Penguin Books, 1986), 159.
6. Andre Frossard and John Paul II, *Be Not Afraid*, trans. J. R. Foster (New York: St. Martin's Press, 1984), 15.
7. John Paul II, *Redemptor hominis* (Washington, D.C.: USCC, 1979), 18, par. 6.
8. Leszek Kolakowski, translated from "Wywiad z Leszkiem Kolakowskim (fragmenty)," in *Zeszyty Literackie*, 2 (Wiosna, 1983), 53–54.
9. Frossard, *Be Not Afraid*, 17–18.
10. Milosz, *Native Realm*, 84–85.
11. Alfred Bloch, ed., *The Real Poland: An Anthology of National Self-Perception* (New York: Continuum, 1982), 199–201.
12. John Paul II, *Redemptor hominis*, 12, par. 5.
13. John Paul II, *Origins*, vol. 13, no. 14 (15 September 1983): 239.

3. A Man of Contradictions?
The Early Writings of Karol Wojtyla
RONALD MODRAS

What in another science would be called a contradiction, in theology often goes by the name of paradox. Whether viewed as contradictions or paradoxes, the apparent incongruities in the theology of Karol Wojtyla abound almost as much as the ironies in the man's career. Given his genius for languages (virtually every one spoken in Europe), it is ironic that he should open himself to the accusation of being provincial. It is ironic that the most traveled man ever elected pope should be the one to demonstrate how culturally limited and particularist any and every human perspective is, including that of the papacy. It is ironic, too, that a former academic should be perceived as lacking sympathy for academic freedom.

But is it a paradox or a contradiction that a pope who speaks out so much on social justice should be critical of a concept like social sin? Is it a paradox or a contradiction that the most politically involved pope of this century should forbid priests and religious any similar involvement? Is it a paradox or a contradiction that someone who argues philosophically like a modern phenomenologist or personalist comes up with conclusions as ancient as any Stoic's?

Karol Wojtyla is not inconsistent. The theology he propounds today as bishop of Rome he propounded as bishop of Krakow and earlier still as a priest. Shortly before issuing his inaugural encyclical, "Redemptor hominis," the pope announced that there would be found in it thoughts which "had been maturing in me during the years of my priestly and then episcopal service." He expressed the conviction that Providence had brought him to the chair of Saint Peter to disseminate his ideas to the church and the world at large.[1] Clearly he does not believe that God called him to the papacy to change his mind.

Many if not all of the apparent contradictions in the pope's pronouncements can be found in and explained by his early writings. An examination of those writings throws light on some of his central concerns today. His scholarly achievements, however, must be seen within the context of his origins. One cannot understand Pope John Paul II without understanding Poland and Polish Catholicism.

Poland was a land with a vigorous Reformation but an even more vigorous Counter-Reformation. The partitions by its despotic neighbors at the end of the eighteenth century put an end to a brilliant, but all too brief, encounter with the Enlightenment. Then, for 120 years, when Poland had been wiped off the maps of Europe, a militant Roman Catholicism helped to keep Polish identity and culture alive, vis-à-vis Russian Orthodoxy and German Lutheranism, with a fateful equation of nationality and culture with religion. Like it or not, the Catholic church in Poland has had to learn the art of politics. In the last century it learned to struggle with agents of Christian kaisers and czars. For the last 40 years it has had to reckon with a regime that is avowedly atheist. Today it functions virtually as an opposition party.

The Catholic church in Poland, with reason enough, has come to assume a stance similar to a fortress under siege. Its survival and success in the face of official governmental atheism can be ascribed in great measure to its militance and martial discipline. No bishop, let alone a priest, dares express an idea or policy at odds with that of the cardinal primate. Pluralism is a luxury the church in Poland deems neither useful nor affordable for its purposes.

The history of Poland and the character of Polish Catholicism have left their marks on Karol Wojtyla and are reflected in his writings. From 1949 right up to 1978 when he became pope, Wojtyla enjoyed a remarkable publishing career, generating a bibliography of more than 250 entries: books, popular and scholarly articles, pastoral letters, poems, and even a play; on topics ranging from the anniversaries of Polish saints and Vatican II to Mary, marriage, and Immanuel Kant. Despite the wide range of subjects, however, certain topics and themes recur regularly, such as anthropology, ethics, ecclesiology, and sex. Even a cursory review of these more prominent interests reveals a unity behind the apparent incongruities.

THOMISTIC PERSONALISM

The earliest of Wojtyla's scholarly publications were based upon his studies first of theology in Rome and then of philosophy in Poland. At Rome's Angelicum University he wrote a doctoral dissertation on faith in the writings of the Spanish mystic Saint John of the Cross.[2] Once he returned to Poland, his interests quickly shifted from mystical theology to ethics, so that there is no need to dwell at length on this work, except to point out that it was written under the tutelage of Reginald Garrigou-Lagrange, the leading exponent of neo-scholasticism in his day. The result of the future pope's research was that Saint John of the Cross had substantially the same concept of faith as Saint Thomas Aquinas, a conclusion that would gratify his mentor and surprise no one, since neo-scholasticism claimed to find the answers to virtually all questions in the thought of Saint Thomas.

Neo-scholasticism represented a twentieth-century rejection of modern philosophy in favor of the well-ordered medieval worldview and thinking of Saint Thomas, with its roots in Plato, Aristotle, and the primitive science of ancient Greece. Whether neo-scholasticism understood Saint Thomas correctly is debatable but need not detain us here. What is worth noting is its intellectualist notion of faith as an "assent to revealed truths." In almost Platonic fashion, Wojtyla speaks time and again of faith as uniting the "intellect" with God. He simply assumes as self-evident the neo-scholastic understanding of revelation as "conceptual propositions" (p. 246) which impart a "type of information" (p. 263).

Though few Catholic theologians would deny the cognitive value and implications of revelation, few today would simply equate revelation with doctrinal propositions that communicate factual data. Such a concept of revelation does not take sufficient cognizance of the historically and culturally conditioned nature of all language in general and the symbolic nature of religious language in particular. The neo-scholastic identification of revelation with the church's doctrinal propositions is closer in some ways to the theories of fundamentalist, evangelical Protestants than it is to the theology of the church fathers or Saint Thomas Aquinas.[3]

That Wojtyla in his early years would adopt neo-scholastic thinking is understandable enough. The more important question is, has he continued to hold it? At first glance, it appears he has not. For the Middle Ages, the fundamental category for theology was nature, whether the consideration was God, Christ, grace, or ethics. Wojtyla appears to have made the "anthropocentric turn" from nature to the human subject that modern philosophy did with Descartes and Kant, that contemporary Catholic theology did with Karl Rahner. It appears that Wojtyla broke with his early training and came to adopt the human person and not nature as the starting point and fundamental category of his thinking. But appearances, as the saying goes, can be deceiving. He did not break with the medieval mentality at all, as his subsequent writings show clearly.

Wojtyla's second major study was a philosophical dissertation on the possibility of constructing a Christian ethics based on the system of phenomenologist Max Scheler.[4] In it he admits that he was attracted to Scheler's system in the first place because of its personalism and objectivity. He analyzes and then evaluates Scheler with "the revealed sources of Christian ethics" as a criterion, not any one particular system of Christian ethics but "the ethical truths revealed by God and taught by the church as the basis for moral behavior" (pp. 25–28). It was his neo-scholastic propositional concept of revelation that led Wojtyla to a substantially negative conclusion. Scheler's method of investigating consciousness does not allow one to determine whether acts are good or evil in themselves. Wojtyla sees this kind of moral evaluation of acts as indispensable for any objective ethics, and certainly for a Christian ethics. A Catholic, he maintains, may not be a phenomenologist (p. 125). Scheler's system can only be "accidentally helpful" by allowing us to penetrate and analyze Christian ethical experience.

Karol Wojtyla is a neo-scholastic Thomist. He has described Thomism as a work of "monumental proportions not only for its own era, but capable to this day of arousing the admiration of anyone who only takes the effort to understand and evaluate it."[5]

But Wojtyla is an energetic evangelist as well and knows that a message needs to be translated into the language of those you wish to convert. For the sake of discussion with contemporary philosophy and, as he apparently believes, for the sake of wider popular acceptance, Wojtyla has resorted to the methods of phenomenology and the language of personalism to translate neo-scholasticism into what he describes as "Thomistic personalism."

In a 1961 article under that title,[6] Wojtyla assembled and analyzed what he regarded as the personalist elements in Saint Thomas's writings. He described personhood as the "highest perfection" in the created order, but derived his concept of the person not from modern philosophy or psychology but from Boethius's classic definition: a person is an individual substance of a rational nature. Rational thought lies at the basis of the foremost characteristic of the human person, namely, morality, whereby through free decisions not only the will but the whole human person becomes good or evil.

One cannot help but be struck, when reading Wojtyla, by how often he emphasizes the will and the concept of domination. "It is through the will that man is lord of his actions, and self-consciousness reflects that domination in a particular way" (p. 669). He describes love as truly human only when sensual energy and appetites are subordinated by the will. Similarly, the individual must be subordinated to the common good of society. "Totalism," as he calls it, subordinates the individual to society "for the supposed common good" and invariably violates rights like the freedom of conscience. Individualism, and with it liberalism and capitalism, puts the individual's welfare above the common good. The individual, Wojtyla insists, must be "subordinated" in all that is indispensable for the common good, even if it means "heavy sacrifices."

For all its references to persons, Wojtyla's philosophy is not personalist. It bespeaks an attempt to translate a medieval theory of the human person and society into modern categories, based on the conviction that such a thirteenth-century anthropology and social theory is still fully adequate. It goes without saying that his anthropology has implications for such apparently disparate but in actuality intimately related issues as sexual ethics and authority in the church.

SEXUAL ETHICS

The most extended expression of Wojtyla's anthropology is his 1969 book *The Acting Person*,[7] an obscure work that leaves even some sophisticated readers puzzled. In it he attempts to demonstrate human transcendence and spirituality. *Transcendence* he defines as self-determination or self-governance. Once again we are struck by the category of domination as pivotal to his thinking. *Spirituality* is the source of our self-domination and allows us to experience ourselves as a unity amid complexity. The soul is the principle of integrity whereby we possess and govern our bodies by employing them like a "compliant tool."

Wojtyla's is a hierarchic or stratified conception of the human person. With his Stoic and neo-scholastic forebears, he speaks of "lower" and "higher" spheres as he situates the psychic or emotional sphere midway between the physical and spiritual. Authentic spiritual power consists in the intellect and will subordinating the physical and emotive sphere, if need be in an "absolute" manner (p. 315, n. 72). Such self-control, he writes, is "probably the most fundamental manifestation of the *worth* of the person" (p. 264).

This anthropology lies at the basis of Wojtyla's *Love and Responsibility*,[8] the fullest exposition of his thinking on sexual ethics. Trying to solve problems of overpopulation with artificial birth control and the changes in traditional forms of family life have led to what he calls a "state of crisis." Married women working outside the home appear to be the "main symptom of the crisis." His response to the crisis is a presentation of neo-scholastic teaching and argumentation in personalistic form.

Although he uses words like "person" and "love" freely, Wojtyla's understanding of those terms is hardly that of his readers. Like his arguments, his definitions refer constantly to nature. The sexual urge is a specific force of nature whose proper or natural end is procreation. True love, the kind commanded by the gospel, is not an emotion but the virtue of goodwill (*benevolentia*) whereby the rational will affirms the value of a person. Such affirmation requires "subordination" to the laws of nature. He draws a direct connection between subordination to natural law and love. "In the order of love a man can remain true to the person only in so far as he is true to nature. If he does violence to 'nature,' he also 'violates' the person by making it an object of enjoyment rather than an object of love" (p. 229).

Wojtyla's argument for his thesis appeals to the Kantian moral imperative: a person must not be *merely* the means to an end for another person. Artificial contraception, he contends, is a matter of two people using one another for "mutual, or rather, bilateral 'enjoyment.' " This, he insists, is utilitarianism, not love. It is worth noting that, although he states the Kantian imperative correctly the first time he cites it, thereafter he regularly omits the crucial word "merely." In fact, we cannot help but make use of other persons as means, whether dealing with each other as teachers, hairdressers, or grocery clerks. Kant's principle forbids using persons "merely" as means without recognizing their value "at the same time as an end." Wojtyla simply asserts without any argumentation that "anyone who treats a person as the means to an end does violence to the very essence of the other" (p. 27).

Before the Second Vatican Council, Catholic tradition described procreation as the primary end of marriage, mutual help as the secondary end. The Council deliberately omitted any reference to a hierarchy of ends. Writing a decade before the Council, Wojtyla upholds the hierarchy but rejects the widespread equation of mutual help with love. The aims of marriage are one complex aim. Procreation is not distinct from love. Rather, "the correct attitude toward procreation is a condition for the realization of love" (p. 226). With no attempt at anything like an empirical proof, he simply claims that contraceptive measures "have a damaging effect on love" (p. 53).

In his treatment of the erotic and emotional aspects of sexuality, Wojtyla says at first that genuine love or goodwill can "keep company" with the love that is desire, so long as desire "does not overwhelm all else" (p. 84). Later, however, he writes that the will "combats" the sexual urge and "atones for the desire to have the other person" (p. 137). Genuine love is the antithesis of emotional desire. Couples "must free themselves from those erotic sensations which have no legitimation in true love" (p. 146). To a stoic distrust of the emotions he adds a Kantian appeal to duty when he writes that sexual desire or concupiscence "means a constant tendency merely to 'enjoy,' whereas man's duty is to 'love' " (p. 160).

Assisting us in performing this duty is the virtue of chastity, which he says "implies liberation from everything that 'makes dirty.' Love must be so to speak pellucid." Wojtyla does not explicitly describe sexual feeling as dirty, but does state that "sensations and actions springing from sexual reactions and the emotions connected with them tend to deprive love of its crystal clarity" (p. 146). Wojtyla does not regard sexual emotions or enjoyment as evil in themselves but only if dissociated from procreation. With a homespun analogy he compares God's attitude toward contraception to that of a father when his child, having been given bread with jam, throws away the bread and eats only the jam (p. 309, n. 66). Self-control and continence are the only acceptable methods for regulating births. Overpopulation and all that it implies, like poverty and hunger, are relegated by Wojtyla to the sphere of economics. Needless to say, personhood, which for Wojtyla means nature, may not be subordinated to "economics" (p. 65).

Wojtyla continued to write regularly in this vein. In a 1965 article on "The Problem of Catholic Sexual Ethics,"[9] he reiterated his claims that Thomism has lost none of its value, that its natural law ethics of sexuality is implicitly personalist, that birth control "degrades" the person. What he adds, however, is that the norms of medieval sexual ethics are not simply authentic Catholic teaching but "revealed." The hierarchy of ends, which views procreation as the primary end of marriage, Wojtyla sees as implicitly contained in the biblical command of love. The Thomistic doctrine about the laws of nature and ends of marriage are "confirmed by revelation." It would seem to follow from this that, for Karol Wojtyla, an exercise of papal infallibility, a solemn *ex cathedra* definition of those norms as revealed, constitutes a distinct possibility.

As priest and as pope, Wojtyla has demonstrated an unrelenting interest in sexuality. He virtually identifies human dignity with discipline. In 1971 he wrote about concupiscence or sexual desire as impoverishing the world and destroying human dignity. Even concepts like salvation and "Savior of the world" are more fully intelligible in the context of "overcoming concupiscence."[10] Clearly, birth control is not a peripheral issue of secondary importance for him. In 1978 he described marital ethics as possessing "such powerful anthropological implications" that it has become the field for a "struggle concerning the dignity and meaning of humanity itself."[11]

Karol Wojtyla appears to view himself as a warrior anointed to wage a struggle for human dignity on the battlefield of sexuality. But he need not battle alone. As bishop of Rome he has at his disposal the formidable forces of the Catholic church. How he views the church is also clarified by his early writings. Here too, as elsewhere, Wojtyla's anthropology colors his thinking.

CHURCH STRUCTURES

December of 1965, the end of the Second Vatican Council, marked the introduction of sweeping changes throughout the Catholic church. In Poland, however, less than a month later, the end of the Council was overtaken by another event. On New Year's Day, 1966, the Polish Catholic church began its celebration of one thousand years of Christianity in Poland. Preparations for Vatican II and the Council itself had occurred during the nine-year Novena of preparation for the Polish millennium, and then the implementation of the Council commenced with the observance itself. With triumphal solemnity the Polish church celebrated its medieval origins and undaunted loyalty to tradition. So imposing an exercise in recollection served effectively to hold the forces of change in check. While elsewhere in the church the word on everyone's lips was Pope John's *aggiornamento,* in Poland the watchword was *remember.*

When Wojtyla came to discuss the council in his book *Sources of Renewal,*[12] it is no surprise that he concerned himself not with what Vatican II changed but with what it had reaffirmed. He downplayed "divisions and differences between so-called integralists and progressives" (p. 4). Both groups, he insisted, "must be unswervingly guided" by what he called "the principle of integration." Here is the key to how Wojtyla interprets the documents and achievements of the Council: "On the one hand we can rediscover and, as it were, re-read the magisterium of the last Council in the whole previous magisterium of the Church, while on the other we can rediscover and re-read the whole preceding magisterium in that of the last Council" (p. 40). The significance of this hermeneutical principle for Wojtyla is obvious from his pontificate. For the former cardinal archbishop of Krakow, the way to interpret Vatican II is not with its vision of the future but its ties to the past.

Poland's tragic history has experienced little of what we know as modern Western democracy. The only forms of societal organization which could possibly serve as models for Polish Catholicism have been medieval, monarchial, and now, more recently, totalitarian. The medieval view of church structures is very much in evidence in Wojtyla's book on the Council. The concept of hierarchy predominates over all other categories. For most other commentators on the Council, the central teaching of Vatican II was its focus on the church as the People of God; but not for Wojtyla. For him, the key passage is the conciliar statement that the priesthood of the faithful and the hierarchic priesthood are interrelated yet differ from one another in essence and not only in degree (*Constitution on the Church*, no. 10). This doctrine, writes Wojtyla, "contains in a certain manner all that the Council wished to say about the Church, mankind, and the world" (p. 225).

The church's hierarchic structure is a "divine constitution," which guarantees its apostolicity. Although Vatican II speaks of a "true equality" among all members of the church, this is in the invisible order of grace. A lay member may well be more effective in the order of grace than a member of the hierarchy, but there is no way of measuring. When it comes to the "order of authority," however, there is no such equality. Wojtyla highlights the division between clergy and laity. "The sacerdotal ministry in a sense separates bishops and ordained priests from the members of the People of God who only share in the general priesthood," Wojtyla writes (p. 228). As in his anthropology and sexual ethics, the overriding operative principle is "subordination."

Bishops are the pastors and preachers of the church who, in communion with the bishop of Rome, constitute the communion of churches. To them is owed "the obedience of each and every disciple of Christ" (p. 253). *Priests* are the bishops' "helpers," related to their bishop as to a father. The bond which unites priests around a bishop is a "kind of reflection" of the collegial bond uniting bishops around the pope (p. 380). Though Wojtyla does not draw the conclusion himself, it would seem to follow that the relationship between the college of bishops and the pope is analogous to that of a bishop and his priests, one of filial assistance. The *laity* have as their specific task the "sanctification of the world." In Polish, the very word for laity "implies a connection with the world, and the vocation of lay people is thus different from that of priests and religious, on whom Christ and the Church have enjoined a certain detachment from the world" (p. 341). Wojtyla's idea of the laity clearly precludes anything like lay leadership in the church. His conception of the priesthood and religious life hardly leaves room for social and civic involvement let alone political activity.

CONCLUSION

These then are some, obviously not all, of the central ideas in Karol Wojtyla's early, prepapal writings. There are other key concepts in his thinking, but these are among the most operative. Instead of an anthropology that would see all the physical, emotional, social, and spiritual dimensions of human existence as mutually interrelated and interpenetrating, he has adopted and internalized a medieval philosophy of nature with a hierarchy of lower and higher orders. With repeated references to personhood and love, it is this hierarchic anthropology he attempts to translate and thereby restore to respectability the sexual ethics of natural law it gives rise to, with its hierarchic ordering of primary and secondary purposes for sexuality and marriage. Hierarchy governs his concept of the church as well, as he banishes equality to the realm of the invisible and reduces collegiality to filial assisting and giving advice.

Karol Wojtyla is not a man of contradictions. There is an inner logic to his thinking: a medieval model of the human person, sexuality, marriage, and the church in which hierarchy and subordination serve as the dominant principles. The logic of his ideas is sometimes lost on audiences and readers who do not understand his mindset and idiosyncratic use of personalist terminology. No attempt can or need be made to evaluate those ideas here, but only to point out their inner coherence and the consistency with which he has proclaimed them both before and after his election as pope.

"If God has called me with such thoughts," he said on the eve of his first encyclical, "it is so that they could find resonance in my new and universal ministry."[13] Wojtyla experiences himself as one who has been called. More than a pope who would have come up the curial or diplomatic ranks, he sees Providence more than political forces as furthering his career. Not only his own personal spirituality but his Polish origins contribute to a sense of mission. Early in his pontificate he referred to the election of his predecessor, John Paul I, as being on the Feast of Our Lady of Czestochowa, and to his own election on the Feast of Saint Hedwig, another Polish patron. Mere coincidence? On his first visit to Poland, he alluded to himself as the "Slavic Pope," for the Poles a clear reference to a nineteenth-century poem, some take to be prophetic, by Julius Slowacki, an exponent of Polish messianism. The Polish church has long prided itself as the "bastion of Christianity," with a mission to defend Catholic tradition from all onslaught from the east. The military commander of an army of priests, Poland's foremost son sees himself called to a similar mission, to defend the truth. He has no doubt but that his ideas are the truth. A sense of destiny explains the self-confidence that constitutes what is most likely Pope John Paul II's greatest strength. It also contributes to what may well be his greatest weakness, the dark side of self-assurance, a lack of self-criticism.

Visiting nations the way he once visited parishes, he relates to other bishops the way a bishop relates to parish priests. Confident of his truth and his power, he governs the universal church as if it were one immense diocese. The technology that created the "global village" has made it possible for him to actualize what medieval popes could only claim. There is no doubt in his own mind, and he would have none in anyone else's: He is pastor of the world.

NOTES

1. John Paul II, *Origins* (1979): 627.
2. Karol Wojtyla, *Faith According to Saint John of the Cross* (San Francisco: Ignatius Press, 1981).

3. A. Dulles, S.J., *Models of Revelation* (New York: Doubleday, 1983).
4. Karol Wojtyla, *Ocena Możliwości Zbudowania Chrześcijańkiej przy Założeniach Systemu Maksa Schelera* (Lublin: KUL, 1959).
5. Karol Wojtyla, "Etyka a Teologia Moralna," *Znak* 19 (1967): 1079.
6. Karol Wojtyla, "Personalizm Tomistyczny," *Znak* 13 (1961): 664–76.
7. John Paul II, *The Acting Person* (Dordrecht, Holland; Boston: D. Reidel, 1979).
8. John Paul II, *Love and Responsibility* (New York: Farrar, Straus, Giroux, 1981).
9. Karol Wojtyla, "Zagadnienie Katolickiej Etyki Seksualnej: Refleksje i Postulaty," *Roczniki Filozoficzne* 13 (1965): 5–25.
10. Karol Wojtyla, "Notatki na Marginesie Konstytucji 'Gaudium et Spes,'" *Atheneum Kaplanskie* 74 (1970): 3–6.
11. Karol Wojtyla, "Antropolgia Encykliki 'Humanae Vitae,'" *Analecta Cracoviensia* 10 (1978): 13.
12. John Paul II, *Sources of Renewal, The Implementation of Vatican II* (San Francisco: Harper & Row, 1980).
13. John Paul II, *Origins* (1979): 627.

4. The Peripatetic Pope
A New Centralizing of Power
PAUL COLLINS

An entirely new phenomenon has emerged in the Church—the omnipresent papacy. This has been created by the speed of travel and by the media, especially television. Pope John Paul II has exploited these new possibilities to the full. Previous popes have claimed a universal jurisdiction and pastorate; John Paul II has made it a reality. This can be expressed in simple geographic terms: by the end of 1986 he had made thirty-two pastoral trips—that is one trip every three months since his election in 1978. The thirty-second trip was to Bangladesh, Singapore, Fiji, New Zealand, Australia, and the Seychelles, the longest trip yet made. Several trips will be undertaken in 1987: the first to Uruguay, Chile, and Argentina and then to Poland, Germany, and the United States.

Having intimately experienced the tour of Australia in November 1986—I covered it for the Australian Broadcasting Corporation and saw every move on TV and heard every word spoken—I will try to place it within the context of other papal journeys.

What is the purpose of these pastoral visits? The pope has said they are to strengthen the faith of the local church and to be a visible symbol of the unity of the universal church. There certainly were good effects for the local church in Australia. In a country which sees itself as "secular," the pope placed spiritual and Catholic values squarely on the national agenda. Issues concerning religion, church, and faith were widely debated in the media. The large public liturgies attracted enormous crowds and gave many people a sense of belonging to the church again, a pride in being a Catholic. And, as he has consistently done in Western countries, the pope made a stand for minority groups. He gave strong support to aboriginal Australians, stressing the worth of their culture and supporting their claim for land rights. He also emphasized that the gospel must be fully integrated into the local culture and called for "a second evangelization." The pope's speeches were prepared in Australia and the changes made by the Vatican were insignificant. There was a sense that the local church really participated.

The Australian experience can be duplicated in other countries. In India in February 1986 there was a strong emphasis on the values enshrined in Indian society and culture, and during his twelve-day tour to Africa in August 1985 he told the young people of Cameroon that the Christian faith "must be able to be fully assimilated into the language of other people. . . . A rupture between gospel and culture would be a tragedy." In theory, at least, there is no doubt about the pope's commitment to enculturation.

Two extraordinary scenes from the trip to Australia linger in the imagination. The first was during a visit to an ordinary parish in a working class suburb in Melbourne. The pope visited the parish grade school, and he sat down in grade four with the children gathered around him on the floor and answered their questions. Peter Hebblethwaite has emphasized that John Paul is very much the catechist. He is, but he is also an instinctive master of media imagery. The spontaneity of the children, the warmth of the pope, the charming contrast between Australian and Polish accented English, even the difference in colors between the red uniforms of the children and the white of the pope created a marvelous television image. The second scene that lingers is that of the pope at a youth rally in Sydney. John Paul joined hands with the youngsters, sang, and kissed them. The pope's words were lost in the visual images. It was so good, the overseas networks picked it up.

Pope John Paul has great ability to fit into a scene and dominate it. A close examination of the Australian trip shows that image—especially TV image—was more important than word. The visual settings and the groups with whom the pope identified (handicapped, youth, aborigines, workers, politicians) were more important than what he said. Certainly, this visual approach is part of the Catholic tradition, for it conjures up the sacramental nature of the church—persons, actions, and experiences that symbolically make present the power and reality of God. Some critics have argued that John Paul gets in the way, that his personality obtrudes, and that God is hidden. But many who attended the liturgies denied this. For them it was a real religious experience—although any well-celebrated liturgy, especially with a large faithfilled community and effective music, can give participants a real sense of God's presence. Something similar was experienced during the recent visit to France (October 1986). Here John Paul was enthusiastically received by large crowds who participated fully in the liturgies.

Yet despite all of this, the peripatetic pope leaves me with a deep sense of uneasiness. This is not because I think the papal tours will change the local church. As Father Bartolomeo Sorge says, such trips "are like summer rain—refreshing without lasting effects." Certainly the Australian church will muddle along in much the same way as it always has, and one suspects that France, India, and Cameroon will not change much either.

But the tours effect a shift at a deeper level of perception, for they change the image of the papacy by making the pope seem *present.* People see him, especially on television, as an accessible and humane figure who stands for justice and for a return to traditional values. He is no longer remote, like the "quasi-divine" Pius XII, but a man of the people. Television focuses on John Paul alone; we only see *him.* Local leadership, bishops, and communities fade into insignificance. The pope has given a new lease of life to the papal monarchy. Henri Fesquet has commented perceptively in *The Tablet* (29 November 1986) on the three visits to France:

When John Paul II visits France . . . and the cheers resound without reserve, one reason for his popularity is that, deep down, the French have remained monarchists, and the pomp of the grandiose receptions meets their need for security and social stability, together with the consummate art of the actor—an orator . . . who speaks with supreme authority as leader of a huge confessional body.

It is not the French alone who long for a "monarch," it is a need deeply embedded in many people as they search for certainty in a world of shifting values. In all of this, collegiality has been pushed into the background. It is the captain, not the team, that is highlighted. Lip service may be paid to the authority of local bishops, but as archbishops Emmanuel Milingo and Raymond Hunthau sen discovered, there are limits to Rome's tolerance of local churches.

Many participants in papal ceremonies or viewers of papal TV feel an intimacy with John Paul. But the questions is, are they intimate? Can you reach out and touch him? I doubt it. The problem is that the media creates a false sense of intimacy—and this is especially true of television. TV can create a situation wherein images are more important that reality. A critical regression occurs wherein complex realities are reduced to simplistic slogans and ideologies. The TV evangelists are clear examples of this. An unreality creeps in wherein viewers believe that the image conveys the whole truth. There is a real danger of this with Pope John Paul. People begin to believe the simple equation that the pope equals the church. This equation—the origins of which lie in the nineteenth century—cannot be sustained since Vatican II. Anyone who understands the tradition of the church and its present reality knows that it lives as a careful counter-balancing of forces—pope, bishops, and theologians. The problem is that a high-profile pope destroys the balance that makes up the reality of the Catholic church.

Obviously, papal trips differ according to the area visited. In places where Rome has a clear agenda because of specific issues or because of the importance of the religion or country visited—such as Latin America or the United States—there is no doubt that the Vatican keeps tight control of what is said. There may be some local input, but the speeches are clearly designed to express the papal agenda. But in most countries Rome is content to go along with the local preparation. Media—especially TV—assume much more importance in developed countries. In Third World countries the emphasis is on mass gatherings of people. But the core agenda is always the same—the pope must be at center stage.

A focus on Roman leadership inevitably weakens the position of local leadership. His visits could be more helpful if they were much more low-key—and less expensive—and if he came, listened, and learned and, after dialogue, re-enforced the efforts of Catholics to confront local realities. But the way in which the tours are organized prevents any chance for input during the actual visit. Local participation has to be vetted well in advance.

The sheer length and speed of such trips prevent any time for discussion, let alone a chance to stop and experience the local church or local environment. The pope covered the whole of Australia (a country the same size as the United States) in six and a half days. In another example, in 1985, he visited Togo, Ivory Coast, Cameroon, Central African Republican, Zaire, Kenya, and Morocco in twelve days. One can admire his stamina, but the purpose of such speed must be questioned. Is it to avoid having to hear the local people, to prevent the expression of agendas different from that of the Vatican? Local bishops' conferences—which should speak for the local church—are marginalized; John Paul spent less than two hours with the Australian bishops as a group. There is no doubt that the pope is a humane and kind man. But he is also a strong man with a clear agenda for the church. The human image belies a tough determination to bring the church under control. During the very week he was demanding justice for aborigines, workers, and the unborn in Australia, the Congregation for the Doctrine of the Faith was beginning an investigation of one of the country's best theologians—a man from the center of the Catholic tradition—on the say-so of unknown and unnamed accusers. It is this conflict between image and reality that troubles many loyal Catholics.

I am not suggesting that Pope John Paul is merely a cynical power broker. At heart he is probably a populist evangelist. At Mass in Sydney, in a powerful (if overlong) sermon, he cried out to those who had strayed from Catholicism, "Do not be afraid! Come home!" He has constantly called for enculturation demanding that the church must become an integral part of the local scene. But it is always *he* who is the evangelist. The ministries of others pale into insignificance beside his. As a populist, his lifeblood seems to be enormous crowds. But there is a danger built into this style. It can so easily become a personality cult, a form of manipulative demagoguery. It seems to be precisely for this reason that Jesus was so careful of avoiding it. While Jesus was surrounded by crowds, he was constantly on his guard against the cult of personality. He refused to allow the crowd to project onto him any political or ecclesiastical role. He avoided using the term "messiah" precisely because of its overtones. He always pointed beyond himself to the God who sent him. He had no institutional power and no established church to support him. His influence flowed from the power of the Spirit within him, from the strength of his personal conviction, from the gentleness of his humanity, and from his intimacy with God. And Jesus—as the New Testament and the Catholic tradition constantly maintain—is the sole norm and final judge of all that is Christian and Catholic.

Thus I must admit that I think Pople John Paul's "pastoral visits" to the local churches are, at best, mixed blessings. They certainly give many Catholics a sense of identity, belonging, and certainty in a world involved in one of the great mutations of history. But the problem is, does this certainty come through a retreat to the past, through identification with the central figure in a powerful institution? Does it imply an abandonment of the commitment in faith and hope to live a Christian life and build up the body of Christ in everyday reality? In other words, is it a failure to confront the very reality that the pope mentions so often—enculturation? Is it a failure to incarnate the Catholic Christian tradition in this time and this milieu? In my view, it is.

5. Cardinal Ratzinger, Pope Wojtyla, and Fear at the Vatican

An Open Word after a Long Silence

HANS KÜNG

Conformism means death for any community; a loyal opposition is a necessity in any community.

—KAROL WOJTYLA, 1969

For a long time I have withheld judgment on the present course of the Vatican. Old wounds still smarted and new tasks challenged. Naturally, as a theologian and a Christian, I have never stopped considering the Catholic church to be my spiritual home. Nor, as an ecumenical theologian, have I ceased to work for people in all Christian churches.

But because I am constantly made to feel how many men and women—especially fellow priests—suffer under the Vatican's present course, I can no longer keep silent. What is happening to our church in the eighties makes me both sad and angry, particularly after the conciliar awakening made the sixties such hopeful years.

I do not wish to engage in cheap polemics against individuals. Instead, I want to give public expression well beyond the Catholic church to the deep-seated anger and sadness felt by so many people. Very few people can do this—unfortunately—so I feel a greater obligation and responsibility to air the grievances of the

Editor's Note: This essay was published by Professor Küng in several languages simultaneously in various newspapers (in North America only in the Toronto *Globe and Mail*) on October 4, 1985, shortly before the 1985 synod.

many. Without fear before the thrones of prelates, I want to speak clearly and with Christian freedom.

THE GLOOMY VISIONS OF THE CARDINAL

This must be done in the light of a recent publication, the *Rapporto sulla fede (Report on the Faith)* by the number two man in the Vatican, Cardinal Joseph Ratzinger. In it we find the curia's analyses and aims for the upcoming episcopal synod (fall 1985). Cardinal Ratzinger is afraid. And just like Dostoyevsky's grand inquisitor, he fears nothing more than freedom. The sounds from Rome are both old and new: for Cardinal Ratzinger, the curia's claim to power is still a divine privilege. Criticism, not to mention resistance, has no place. "Persistent doubt" about a truth of the faith is a "crime against religion and the unity of the church," something that, according to Canon 751 of the "new" Vatican canon law (1983), is punishable with excommunication.

The current effective head of the ex–Sanctum Officium is a man who previously passed sentence on French catechesis at Notre Dame in Paris; who dismissed the ecumenical proposals in Karl Rahner and Heinrich Fries' *Unity of the Churches—An Actual Possibility* as theological acrobatics; who shelved the memorandum of agreement of the official Anglican–Roman Catholic International Commission (ARCIC) as premature; and who personally corrected and indoctrinated the Latin American bishops in Bogota.

This man has now finally laid his cards on the table. The tone of the document is hard, even if moderated. There is very little talk about faith, but a great deal about the institutional church, about dogmas and doctrines, and above all about "un-Catholic" deviants in the episcopacy and among theologians. Cardinal Ratzinger's skillful arguments lash out on all sides, aiming at every discipline and at every continent. Are we at the threshold of another antimodernist campaign?

In the first chaper of the document, the "prefect of the faith" defends the necessity of excommunication, clearly threatening critical Catholic theologians with a censure that has never been pronounced against notorious "Catholic" criminals like Adolf Hitler or Latin American dictators. The old Inquisition is dead;

long live the new one! The cardinal who "daily receives top-secret information from every continent," evidently does his best daily to take top-secret action on the basis of all this information. It doesn't take much. By chance, he hears a church broadcast from Austria that displeases him, and already the speaker's bishop is entangled in a lengthy official correspondence demanding measures against the miscreant.

It's common knowledge: bishops, superiors, nuncios are always to be at the disposal of the highest guardian of the faith and his holy office. The public becomes aware only of the better known victims. And woe to the weak! No one is burned at the stake any more, but careers and psyches are destroyed as required. (The former dean of Le Saulchoir Faculty of Theology in Paris, dismissed and suspended from ecclesiastical functions, now earns his living working in an office.) In very important cases, such as the recalcitrant Latin American episcopate, Cardinal Ratzinger journeys with a whole posse to the relevant country to make unequivocally clear what the "Catholic truth" is. Alternatively (as in the cases of Holland and Switzerland), a whole episcopate is invited to Rome for a "closed session" ("special synods" as the new instrument of curial domination). In light of this global activity by a German curial cardinal who projects his fears on the world around him, is it any wonder that some people in Germany accuse him of having betrayed the reforming tradition of German Cardinal Frings? Twenty years ago this cardinal, to whom Cardinal Ratzinger was theological adviser, was the first, to the thundering applause of the Council, to denounce the inquisitorial practices of the Congregation for the Doctrine of the Faith—at that time still called simply the Sanctum Officium (Romanae et Universalis Inquisitionis).

The prefect of the Congregation for the Doctrine of the Faith will of course never admit that the postconciliar crisis of the Catholic church is substantially "home brewed." In fact, the errors of the Roman teaching office during the last centuries are altogether passed over in silence: from the case of Galileo and the Chinese ritual dispute to the indexation of the most important thinkers of Europe (Descartes, Kant, Sartre, etc.); from the condemnation of human rights to the case of Teilhard de Chardin, the French worker priests, and the relentless purging of theologians under Pius X and Pius XII. Just recently, the pope solemnly told an international convention of historians in Stuttgart that the Vatican would open its secret archives right up to the 1920s. But the most secret archive of all, that of the inquisitorial authority, remains totally closed as before. We know why.

Instead of finding the source of all evil in the church itself, Cardinal Ratzinger, the former reform theologian, has suddenly found it in a "modern world" that has invaded the church. The self-righteousness, ahistoricism, and blindness to reality that this displays is something one wouldn't have held possible in the light of the remarkable theological works this man produced in the sixties. Of course, as a theologian, Cardinal Ratzinger has always leaned more toward the pessimistic Augustine than toward the realistic Thomas Aquinas. Now he has entirely become the "prophet of doom." At the opening of Vatican II, Pope John XXIII even warned of this type.

The methods are the usual ones: the opponent is caricatured as a troublemaker who presumes to disturb the holy order; one's own past and present are painted in rosy colors; the defamatory language of the conservative is cloaked in modern liberal garb; not infrequently, false oppositions are constructed and false fronts opened—actions that culminate in witch-hunting. Reflected here is the arrogance of power. From this elevated position, the former professor now denies the (uncomfortable) conference of bishops all theological authority. Open-minded theologians from around the world, from exegetes to dogmaticians and ethicists right up to the pastoral and liturgical theologians, all are condemned by someone who is himself a former theologian and bishop.

Yet now, this same man, because of his recently achieved Roman office, believes he can act like the incarnate norm of Catholic orthodoxy: *la vérité catholique—c'est moi!* "I have the feeling that Satan's smoke has entered through a crack into the temple of God." These words by Paul VI are quoted positively in the *Report on the Faith*. In his book, *Introduction to Christianity* (written while on the Catholic theological faculty of the University of Tübingen, 1968), Cardinal Ratzinger politely passed over the devil. Now he sees in him "a secret and, on the whole, objective reality." Those theologians who prefer to see the "devil" as the "power or powers of evil" (thus Vatican II, according to the Bible passages it quotes) and not as a "fallen angel," are disqualified by Cardinal Ratzinger as rationalistic "philosophers or sociologists" who are simply accommodating themselves to the modern world.

He sees the devil at work in the modern world, though not at the head of the church. More than five hundred years after Pope Innocent VIII's infamous 1484 anti-witch bull (as many as *nine million* became the victims of witch trials, products of belief in the devil and pathological sexual behavior), we hear such opinions from the representative of an institution which even today is involved in one of the greatest financial scandals ever, complete with Mafia intrigues. But hitherto, no structural or personal consequences have been drawn from these events. In all conscience, what a contrast between pretence and reality!

RETURN TO ROMAN CATHOLICISM

Nevertheless, the engagingly presented doctrine in the report of our "prefect of faith" is consistent with the covering up of all these past and present errors and scandals:

1. The Protestant Reformation (the beginning of "modern decadence") is written off in theological superficiality. We are warned against "protestantization" (the beginning of pernicious "modernization") and against a Catholic "masochism" that is all too exuberant in confessing guilt. Luther should still be condemned as an un-Catholic heretic because he denied the infallibility of the councils, despised tradition, and put the authority of the individual above Scripture and tradition. (I wonder whether Protestants will now take up the protest themselves again, instead of leaving it to critical Catholics.)

2. In spite of all the work by ecumenical commissions over almost two decades and all the resultant official consensus documents, ecumenical agreements, not only with the Protestants, but also with the Orthodox and the Anglicans, is put off until the cows come home. After all, the Protestants just don't have validly ordained ministers or a valid Eucharist (there is therefore no common Communion with them).

Moreover, the Orthodox deny the prerogatives of the bishop of Rome (primacy of jurisdiction and infallibility) and the Anglicans have recently endorsed such un-Catholic ideas as the re-admission of remarried divorcees to the sacraments, the ordination of women, and other prolematic moral-theological reforms. Accordingly, pointing to the "Catholically" appropriated Bible, Cardinal Ratzinger bluntly calls the Protestants to return to the Roman Catholic Church: "But the Bible is Catholic! . . . to accept it as it is, . . . therefore, means to join the Catholic Church."

3. The Middle Ages (and Bavarian Catholicism) are variously presented as exemplary: "the great tradition of the Church Fathers and the masters of the Middle Ages were for me more convincing" (than the Reformation and modernity). Medieval usages and conceptions are again recommended by Cardinal Ratzinger as essentially Catholic. These include not only indulgences, Rosary, Corpus Christi processions, and celibacy, but also the exaltation of Mary ("never enough about Mary!"), visions of Mary (the obscure "secret" of Fatima), and the inferior position of women.

4. Every modern interpretation of problematic church doctrines is rejected. From personal devils and guardian angels to original sin to certain theories about Christ and the church, everything is judged without taking into account the history of dogma or historical criticism in biblical exegesis, both of which are supposedly always ideological. Instead we get a groundless appeal to the "unity of the Bible and the church" and to a supposedly uniform church tradition, with the result that Scripture is dismissed as a critical norm for the church and the postbiblical tradition.

5. According to Cardinal Ratzinger, Vatican II hardly produced anything good. Rather, the "misleading" and "disastrous" elements that it introduced led to a "progressive decay" against which he wishes to bring to bear "full and integral Catholicism" and a "recentrage," that is, a "recentering" on Rome (and a shift in focus from episcopal conferences to the more easily manipulatable individual bishop). That the number of nuns has declined just as drasti-

cally as the number of priests is not attributed to something like the misogynic policies of the Vatican (in Quebec, a region that used to have the highest number of nuns per capita, the number of sisters declined by 44 percent between 1961 and 1981, the number of novices by 98.5 percent). Cardinal Ratzinger traces it to feminism in the cloisters, to psychoanalysis, sociology, and political theology. And what is the cure for the modern emancipation of women and feminist theology according to Cardinal Ratzinger? "Mary, the Virgin, enemy of all heresies."

RESTORATION AS THE PROGRAM

The editor-in-chief of the not exactly progressive Catholic *Herder-Korrespondenz*, David Seeber, has analyzed the central issue in Joseph Ratzinger's *Report on the Faith* quite correctly: "His strict rejection of everything that is even remotely connected with the 'rationalistic' spirit of the Enlightenment, meanwhile, reveals what Restoration as Program really means for him: purging the Council and the life of the faith of all the impurities that are rooted in the Reformation and find expression in a form that definitively distorts Christianity. . . ."

To what does this *Report on the Faith* boil down? In terms of practical politics, its preconciliar demand for an "integral Catholicism" and "re-centralization" on Rome comes down to one thing: the threatened power of "Rome" (read: the church, Christ, God) over the souls of believers in dogma, morals, and church discipline must, according to Cardinal Ratzinger, be secured and reconsolidated by all means possible (papalism and Marianism rolled up into one). Once this curial power and its centrally directed Roman system are secured, the church will be saved. For this, we don't need democratic societies with their largely pernicious modern freedoms. No, for Cardinal Ratzinger, the church today really only functions properly in the totalitarian states of the East, where, after all, pornography, drugs, and the like are simply not permitted.

If these regimes would allow the bureaucratic church a little more freedom for its proclamation, its schools, its associations and other establishments, and if they wouldn't so imprudently make atheism the state ideology, it seems that they would be fundamentally more acceptable for the church than those Western democracies that the pope constantly—and indeed not without justice—berates for their permissiveness and consumerism. In this connection, one is reminded of how the Vatican has often enough manifested sympathy for totalitarian Catholic regimes. One is also reminded of the concordat with Hitler in 1933. Today this agreement still serves financially and legally to guarantee the German hierarchy its unassailable position of power in German society as a "state within a state."

In response, Cardinal Ratzinger ignores the latest historical research which has copiously documented the baneful silence and conformism of the German episcopate in the face of Nazism. Instead, he transforms the Catholic church into an institution of resistance, whereas Protestantism could of course only produce individual resisters.

What, then, are we to think of the *Report on the Faith?* Are these really only the private visions of an official of the Roman curia who projects his own fears of the world on the church as a whole? No, this book wouldn't be worth the mention if it weren't precisely a church policy signal of the first order and if it weren't for the fact that one can also hear the master's voice in the book. Consequently, it is a double signal. It is the signal from a pontificate that, for the past seven years, has progressively been maneuvering itself farther into a dead end. It is also a signal to the upcoming episcopal synod that this fall will once and for all be made to ply the Roman course.

THE POPE'S SEVEN LEAN YEARS

The good intentions of Pope John Paul II and his untiring efforts concerning the identity and clarity of the Catholic faith have to be recognized. But one mustn't be fooled by media spectaculars. Compared with the Catholic church's seven years of plenty during the time of John XXIII and Vatican II, the years of the Wojtyla pontificate, which marks its seventh anniversary this month, look rather lean. Notwithstanding many speeches and costly pilgrimages that have put some local churches deeply into debt, there has hardly been any meaningful progress in the Catholic church and ecumenicity.

Even though he is not Italian, John Paul II does come from a country that experienced neither Reformation nor Enlightenment; he seemed to be just what the curia wanted. The former archbishop of Krakow did not in any way distinguish himself at the Council. Even as a member of the critical papal commission on birth control (which by a large majority recommended to Paul VI that freedom of conscience be allowed in this matter), he was conspicuous by his consistent and politically well calculated absence. As pope, this archbishop adopted the style of the populist Pius popes, although he used entirely different technical means. With his charismatic radiance and his acting ability, he finally gave the Vatican what the White House was soon to have and what the Kremlin, at least until recently, lacked. He was the media-wise "great communicator," the man who with charm and flair, with athleticism and symbolic gestures, could present the most conservative doctrine or practice as acceptable. The accompanying change in climate would first be felt by priests asking for laicization, then by the theologians, and soon by the bishops.

In spite of all the verbal assurances, what have from the beginning been the real intentions of this pope are becoming increasingly clear, even to his admirers: the conciliar movement must be halted; church reform should be stopped; ecumenical understanding with the Eastern churches, Protestants, and Anglicans must be blocked; and dialogue with the modern world must again play second fiddle to unilateral teaching. What are the signs of this change of weather? John XXIII, who is held responsible for the postconciliar decline in the power of the curia, is hardly mentioned any more. Instead, efforts are under way for the beatification of the infallibility pope, Pius IX, a controversial figure in every way.

To be sure, Vatican II is emphatically confirmed by both John Paul II and Cardinal Ratzinger, the number two man at the Vatican. However, what they have in mind is not the progressive spirit of the Council but rather the "true Council," the one that simply stands in continuity with the past and did not signal a new beginning. There are certainly conservative passages in the historical documents of Vatican II, passages that were demanded by the curial faction, and in the case of the *nota praevia* about papal privilege, formally imposed on the Council by Paul VI.

It is these passages that are now definitively interpreted backwards while all the progressive and epoch-making departures are passed over at critical points. For example, instead of the programmatic words of the Council, we are again presented with the language of an authoritarian teaching office. Instead of an *aggiornamento* in the spirit of the gospel, a revival of so-called traditional Catholic teaching. Instead of "collegiality" of the pope with the bishops, a revival of strict Roman centralism. Instead of *apertura* to the modern world, renewed and increasing indictment, lamentation, and accusation of presumed "accommodation." Instead of "ecumenism," renewed emphasis on everything narrowly Roman Catholic. There is no more talk of a distinction between the Church of Christ and the Roman Catholic Church, between the substance of the faith and its linguistic and historical garb; no more talk of a "hierarchy of truths."

In all this the Vatican is not simply riding the waves of a worldwide conservative current like some cork. No, it is actively engaging in politics, and, with respect to Central and Latin America, it is in direct accord with the White House, a fact that President Ronald Reagan has emphatically and publicly confirmed. Moreover, this is all done without regard for the frustration and disappointment at the grassroots. Even the most modest internal or ecumenical desiderata are dismissed out of hand. For example, the German, Austrian, and Swiss synods worked for years, devoting a great deal of idealism, paper, and money to frame proposals that a high-handed curia refused without so much as an explanation.

One puts up with it. Who cares any more? The levels of church attendance, baptisms, and church weddings are constantly declining anyway. Cosmetically rejuvenated and dressed in modern clothes, the Roman clericalism, triumphalism, and legalism that the bishops of the Council so roundly criticized is being happily revived all the same. Chief among these is the "new" canon law (1983 *Code of Canon Law*). Contrary to the intentions of the Council, this law sets virtually no limit to the power of the pope, the curia, and the nuncios. Indeed, it narrows the relevance of the

ecumenical councils, it concedes to bishops' conferences only an
advisory role, it continues to keep the laity in complete dependence on the hierarchy, and it thoroughly neglects the ecumenical dimension.

Even during the frequent absences of the pope, his curia trans-
lates this canon law into entirely practical policies using a plethora
of new documents, ordinances, admonitions, and directives.
These range from decrees about heaven and hell to blatantly
ideological refusal of the ordination of women; from the prohibition of lay preaching (now even lay theologians) to the prohibition of altar girls; from direct curial intervention in the affairs of
the larger orders (selection of the Jesuit general, regulation of the
Carmelites, inquisitorial inspection of the United States female
orders) to the notorious proceedings to ban certain theologians
from teaching.

During the Council years, one would have hardly thought it
possible. Now and again the Inquisition changes its name: right
now it is called the Congregation for the Doctrine of the Faith. It
has changed its method a bit: now the tone is softer, it has "information meetings," and acts behind the scenes. The principles,
however, have hardly changed at all: secret proceedings, refusal
of access to files, denial of defense counsel or appeal, the same authority as both prosecuter and judge. The Inquisition is once
again in full swing. It has been especially active against North
American moral theologians, Central European dogmaticists,
and Latin American or African liberation theologians. By contrast, every means is used to encourage Opus Dei. This reactionary Spanish secret organization has its politico-theological hands
in banks, universities, and governments. It also displays the marks
of the medieval counterreformation and has been removed from
episcopal jurisdiction by the present pope, a man who was already
closely associated with it in Krakow.

The list of contradictions has no end. We hear a lot of talk
about human rights but no justice is given theologians and nuns.
We hear vehement protests against discrimination in society, but
within the church discrimination is practiced, particularly against
women. We get a long encyclical about compassion, but no compassion is shown the divorced or the married priests (there are

about seventy thousand). The list could go on. Even in this respect, they have been "lean years."

MORE DISCORD THAN CONCORD

The media have discussed at length the benefit of the papal
tours. Certainly the positive results for individuals and certain nations should in no way be denied. Some spiritual impulses will undoubtedly have been produced by the countless speeches,
appeals, and divine services. But what about the church as a
whole? Have not these papal visits raised great hopes for real results in so many countries, hopes that were then bitterly disappointed? Have there been any significant improvements in any of
these countries? As regards his own Polish homeland, the pope
obviously overestimated his chances for real political change.
Now he must watch helplessly as enthusiasm in that country gives
way to widespread resignation. In Western Europe and the United States, the polarization and antagonism between conciliar progressives and traditionalists in the church have been increased
and hardened rather than overcome.

Far from healing the wounds of the church, this pope rubs salt
in them, so often unintentionally promoting more strife than harmony. It is true that perfect Vatican pre-censorship does its utmost to prevent the pope from being confronted with the
questions of clerics and people during his tours. He does, after all,
come not to hear but to teach. However, when he is confronted
with uncensored questions, as happened in Switzerland and—for
all the world to see—in Holland, it becomes apparent how little
the teaching office really has to say on the most urgent needs of
the people and their pastors. This is especially evident with the
problems that are of particular relevance for women. The pope is
leading an almost unbelievable battle against those modern wom-
en who are seeking a life-style that corresponds to the times. The
battle ranges from the prohibitions against birth control and female acolytes to similar positions against the ordination of women
and the modernization of the female orders. But let us not be de-
ceived: the women's question will increasingly become the test
case of this pontificate.

In Latin America, the pope has forfeited that obvious sympathy he used to have. This loss in popularity is a result of the Vatican campaign against liberation theology as Marxism, the "penitential silence" imposed on professor Leonardo Boff of Brazil, and Rome's degrading treatment of Latin American cardinals and bishops. The ambivalence of many of his social appeals is becoming increasingly clear there as well.

Even in Africa, where initially the mass enthusiasm was especially great, a more sober atmosphere is spreading, much like during the trips to Switzerland and Holland where there was for the first time a significant decrease in the number of the curious. While paying lip service to the "Africanization" of the church, the pope polemicized relentlessly against "African theology." He did not show the least understanding for deeply rooted, if problematical, tribal traditions. These find expression, for example, in "sequential marriage" (first the child, then the marriage), in the primitive polygamous order (which, as we know, can also be found among the patriarchs of Israel), and in the practical toleration of married priests.

The programmatic proclamation of "be fruitful and multiply" right across Africa, combined with the condemnation, contradictory in itself, of abortion and birth control, allows media commentators to make the pope jointly co-responsible for the population explosion, for hunger, and for the pitiable and endless misery of millions of children. The canonization of a murdered nun as a "martyr of chastity" and the dedication of a prestigious $12 million cathedral, the largest in Africa, in the middle of the poverty of Abidjan, neglect African reality just as much as the calls for sexual abstention (or the rhythm method) and celibacy.

Many people are asking themselves what good all the social speeches on humanity, justice, and peace are if the church is failing above all in those problem areas where it could itself make a definitive contribution. This is certainly the case in the whole area of ecumenism. It is a tragedy that real ecumenical progress has not been made in any respect under this pontificate. On the contrary, non-Catholics are talking about Roman Catholic propaganda campaigns by the pope because their representatives are practically being treated like extras rather than equal partners. This has all led to a disquieting chill in the ecumenical climate, as well as to disappointment and frustration among the ecumenically minded in all churches. It has regrettably also led to a revival of the old anti-Catholic paranoia and defensiveness that disappeared during the "seven years of plenty."

Cardinal Ratzinger's *Report on the Faith* will make it abundantly clear what the Sunday sermons from Rome imply for ecumenism. What we have is the coming together of inner-Catholic and ecumenical stagflation: the stagnation of real change and the inflation of non-commital statements.

BISHOPS UNDER A DOUBLE PRESSURE

Fortunately, although the conciliar and ecumenical movement is constantly being obstructed and frustrated from above, it continues at the grassroots, in individual congregations. The result is increasing alienation of the "church from below" from the "church from above" to the point of indifference. More than ever, the extent to which a congregation is pastorally alive, liturgically active, ecumenically involved, and socially committed depends on the individual pastor or on individual lay leaders. However, between Rome and the congregations stand the bishops. These, therefore, attain a decisive significance in the current crisis.

The bishops are therefore currently under a double pressure: that of grassroots expectation and that of Roman directives. Yet the pope occasionally works on bishops personally so that they will publicly take a negative position on the ordination of women or birth control. Indeed, the pope can fly into a rage when confronted with the fact of thousands of married priests whose representatives have just finished holding their own synod before the gates of Rome and have asked for re-admission to their priestly functions. This has to be seen in the context of the steadily worsening shortage of priests and a decline in the care of souls. (Much as in the German-speaking parts of Switzerland, in five to ten years only half the parishes in other countries will be served by a parish priest.)

With a view to long-term changes, personnel policy is of decisive importance for the Vatican, as it is for every other political system. And in the light of Rome's current change in direction, the main instrument of this policy is undoubtedly the privilege of nominating bishops (a privilege that has accrued to the curia by historical accident)—not to mention the appointment of cardinals and the promotion of conformist theologians, powers that have always been vested in Rome. Only a few dioceses have maintained any vestiges of the former right of clergy and parishioners to nominate their bishops. (These rights have, as we know, also been a central bone of contention between the Vatican and China, which is pushing for the self-administration of its churches.)

More than ever it is the long–term strategy of Rome (even Cardinal Ratzinger talks about it) successively to replace the open episcopate of Vatican II with bishops that toe the doctrinal line. (This is especially regrettable in Holland; in Paris, Detroit, and the Vatican candidates of Polish or Slavic origin were preferred.) No less thoroughly than high functionaries in the Kremlin, new bishops are to be tested for complete orthodoxy and sworn anew to it. However, it is not just in the large orders such as the Jesuits, the Dominicans, and the Franciscans that one faces this authoritarian pope with reserve. Even in the Roman curia one can hear complaints and jokes about the "Slavophilism" of the pope and the "Polonization" of the church.

AN APPEAL

For the Vatican, the upcoming episcopal synod in November (1985) is a suitable tactical means for a long-term strategy that aims at a comprehensive restoration as well as a definitive subjugation of the still much too independent episcopate. This synod is intended for the review of the results of Vatican II and the formulation of interpretative measures, general directions, and demarcations (Catholic/un-Catholic). It should be pointed out that in the absence of any urgency, Rome has called an "extraordinary" episcopal synod, rather than an "ordinary" one, for which the bishops could have selected their own representatives. As such, only the more conservative presidents of episcopal conferences and, in any case, only those approved by Rome, have a seat in the synod. Naturally, even these do not have a vote. Only the pope has a vote. The collegiality that the Council solemnly decreed has remained a mere word for the Vatican. Indeed, Rome almost succeeded in reducing the episcopal synod to a mere tool for legitimation. Thus the curial apparatus is again controlling everything in this synod as well. Already simply in terms of numbers, the curia is overrepresented with its curial cardinals and members appointed by the pope.

Also, in the Ratzinger spirit, it has gone beyond the preparation of the documents to put the agenda and the chairmanship in its hands. The separation of powers is still foreign to Catholic canon law. And critical theologians are kept at arm's length. (For the curia, Vatican II was a regrettable "theologians" council.)

In the enlightened opinion of Rome, everything could and should therefore transpire quite quickly. The estimate is that all problems should be resolved in two weeks. Truly, in the light of this whole apparatus, a bishop who wanted to criticize the current course would have to possess the apostolic daring of a Paul, who according to his own witness, opposed Peter because he "did not act according to the truth of the gospel."

First steps have been taken: a French bishop has criticized Cardinal Ratzinger's *Report on the Faith* as "vacation proposals" because it was impossible to tell whether the author of the report spoke as a private citizen, a professional theologian, or a functionary. The decisive question is, therefore, Are things going to work out for the curia this time as well? Are the bishops going to tell the truth? Are they going to address the taboo needs and hopes of their congregations and their clergy whether it is opportune or inopportune? Are they, where necessary, going to break the curial spell the way cardinals Josef Frings and Achilles Lienart broke it at Vatican II? These men protested against the whole authoritarian procedure and set in motion a process of reflection. To be sure, just like their predecessors at the Council, the bishops are faced with a dilemma.

1. They could look for the future in the past and fall completely into line with the restoration course of the Roman curia. In this case, as became only too obvious in Holland, they would have to submit to a dangerous test of cohesion among the episcopate, the clergy, and the people.
2. They could plan the future in the present and, with Christian freedom, risk a conflict with the curia, just as at Vatican II. On this option, they would be declaring themselves firmly

for the consistent continuation of the conciliar renewal with respect to the controversial points, and would thus maintain the broad support of their people and their priests.

The public reply that a group of priests from Munich gave to the *Report on the Faith* by their former bishop, Cardinal Ratzinger, should give the bishops food for thought: "Our pastoral practice has let us see a good many of the unhappy side effects of the conciliar renewal. But we also know that a church that wants to turn back from Vatican II divorces itself from modern society and will be reduced to marginal significance. And those who, like Ratzinger, exalt themselves in such a triumphalistic manner above everything that is not or does not seem Roman Catholic, exclude themselves as dialogue partners." Indeed, those who want to restore the *ancien regime* after a revolution like Vatican II deceive themselves—as did the late Metternich and other restorers of the "new balance."

Therefore, in solidarity with these fellow clerics and with countless Catholics, I make my appeal as someone who helped to mold that Council twenty years ago as council theologian: Let the bishops in the synod and in the dioceses act as they did at the Council. Bound by their consciences in the spirit of the gospel, may they take part of the congregations and pastors entrusted to them. Above all, let them act on behalf of the youth that is so largely alienated from the church and on behalf of the women who, faced with an authoritarian and celibate male hierarchy, are increasingly taking their leave in silence. Let them take the part of those theologians and nuns in the church who have been browbeaten or unjustly reprimanded. Let them work for the final understanding among Christian churches, for an unprejudiced dialogue with Jews, Muslims, and other religions. And not least, in the light of the self–produced Inquisition, let them work for freedom of thought, of conscience, and of teaching in our Catholic church. Can one episcopal synod accomplish all this? Hardly. For that we will probably need a Third Vatican Council.

6. Joseph Ratzinger's "Nightmare Theology"

HERMANN HÄRING

In Tübingen, he was my teacher. As students in 1966, we welcomed him there enthusiastically. His university lectures left a lasting impression on us. We listened to him attentively, even when not uncritically, as a well-known theologian at Vatican II and as a critical participant and commentator on its achievements. I evoke these recollections with grateful appreciation and state that I am not his biographer, much less his censor or interpreter of his theology. Still I do hope that one can openly and fairly discuss his theology and its methods, since more than ever it has become part of the public domain which affects all of us.

THE TURNING POINT

In 1981 in the theological review *Concilium*, Michael Fahey published a notable article concerning Ratzinger's theological development.[1] In Fahey's judgment Ratzinger changed from a critic of ecclesiastical narrowness to an opponent of reforms. It is true that after a number of calls to boldness and renewal, warnings began to appear after 1966. Still, even in 1968, he provided a constructive critique of the *Dutch Catechism* and hailed it as an important book.[2] At the same time, however, Ratzinger spoke of an "emergency situation" affecting theology which had not yet accomplished its task of translating yesterday into today. His first call to alarm appeared in 1970 with the essay "Democratization in the Church." Here he states only opposition to other positions but no recognition or nuanced discussion of them. In Ratzinger's view, democracy, whether in student circles or even in the writings of Karl Rahner, had become "a buzzword for the doctrine of salvation." Freedom was being "identified with total lack of restriction of the ego which admits no social constraints. According to this view, institution implies manipulation."[3] No proofs are given for this assertion, but what we have are the first global attacks on critics and intellectuals, in short, on "those circles which talk especially loud about democratization of the Church" but who "manifest the least respect for the faith shared by the community."[4] He cites only an (unverified) memorandum concerning a course on ordination in which its authors were prepared to offer "only the barest minimum of service" and an unwillingness to contribute anything of themselves.[5] Isn't this a clear case of overstatement on the part of Ratzinger?

From that point on, Ratzinger's approach and methods became more and more entrenched and sharpened. When he is reporting in 1978 about some villages in Latin America (presumably on the basis of episcopal accounts) which became Protestant because what the inhabitants wanted over and above social aid was "a religion too,"[6] one finds the same spectrum of sweeping judgments, even the same use of generic, unverifiable denunciation, best understood as a reflex reaction of a most profound uncertainty and mistrust of painstaking argumentation. Such mistrust and polemic as a means of diagnosing crises at every level reached a high point in 1985 with the publication of his interview, *The Ratzinger Report*.[7] This book, with its tone of catastrophe and its claim of comprehensiveness, hardly permits any response beyond the remark of Fergus Kerr, who in typical, classic English understatement simply notes that Ratzinger has lost his bearings. The church Ratzinger describes is certainly not the church that Kerr experiences in England. Ratzinger's transition from being a critic of criticism and of reform efforts has led finally to his becoming a solitary judge.

One must further note that this perplexing document is, to be exact, not a work of Ratzinger himself but of a journalist. This helps make perfectly clear that what are presented are not longer precise theological arguments but the thumping conclusions of the prefect of the Congregation for the Doctrine of the Faith. And here we note an important difference. To be sure, Ratzinger had in his writings already argued at sufficient, even excessive, length. He had developed his understanding of belief and church in some detail,[8] and he did this on the basis of his own approach, long before the much invoked "praxis," by noting perhaps surprising developments within the church. On the basis of this perspective he stressed correctly the observation that he himself had remained loyal. It was not Ratzinger but others (such as his colleagues on the board of *Concilium*) who had changed. Of course his arguments were never without special pleading, and what he saw as the best interests of the church (as they were represented by the hierarchy) were always brought into his arguments. How could it have been otherwise? He could not and did not want to eliminate this context, so that even his theology changed according to its context (which is nothing to be ashamed about!).[9]

We do not wish to go into questions such as whether and to what extent Ratzinger, even at an early phase of his shift, hid his new interests (namely, opposition to change). Nor do we treat the question of to what extent his own personal, difficult experiences during the days of student protests and with the rebellious young generation of theology students in Swabia played any role in this shift. In a time when a still unstructured reaction was taking shape after four hundred years of truce, when progressive and restrictive forces were only gradually emerging, it would be surprising if Ratzinger had not first of all discovered and explicated for himself where this journey was leading. The chicken takes shape first in the yolk of intuition.

I proceed therefore from the conviction that we can properly judge his writings from 1965 to 1970 only in connection with later developments. This conclusion is especially clear in the "ideal case" of a theologian who put his theories into praxis as a prince of the church. Interests emerge that at first lay hidden in theory. What is interesting is that Ratzinger's thought served as an impulse and legitimation for events about which this present book is reporting. As a test case I have chosen to make use of his book *Introduction to Christianity*,[10] which at the time of its publication in 1968 received widespread international acclaim and was perceived as an inspiring work for belief and church. Many were later amazed to discover in him a different, suddenly argumentative, conservative colleague and bishop. Appearances are deceiving to be sure, because already at that time all the elements were present that later, in light of new developments, assumed central importance and increasingly dominated Ratzinger's thought. This is a work whose goal it was to discover and to bring to an end, through reflection upon the past, a supposed sellout.

The book opens with a note of warning and with ambitious claims. The "fog of uncertainty" is surrounding us "as hardly ever before in history" (p. 9). We are introduced to the story of "Lucky Hans." In the book's preface we are told how a character named Hans exchanged in turn a precious piece of gold for a horse, then for a cow, a goose, and eventually for a millstone that he then threw into the water. The myth of "watered down" theology had found its metaphor. Hans is happy at being free from the weight, but he is without any provisions for his journey because he has been outfoxed by offers of a smart world all too ready to swap. It is clear that, over the long haul, such images affect Ratzinger's thought more than reservations about generalizing. Since Ratzinger rejects from the very beginning any close analysis of critical voices and trends, there is nothing to stop his passage from diagnosis to projection. The question of where he stood amid the battlefield he had sketched for himself in his role as director of the restoration then becomes all the more important.

REJECTION OF THE MODERN AGE

Ratzinger perceived not only a sellout in modern times but also a deep displaced hopelessness. He asserts this also by emphatic and emotionally charged images and stories. People do not accept the gospel from a theologian who is wearing a clown's custume (p. 16). Worse yet, not even a change of costume is of any further help because, in the meantime, the threat of uncertainty lies bare in each believer, just as even the unbeliever can be uncertain of his position (p. 20). This double stalemate calls for conversion to belief, which must be newly achieved daily. "Belief is change in one's being; only one who has changed receives belief " (p. 20).

Ratzinger's use of language in his introductory chapter about belief provides some useful insights. To be sure, it contains the story about the clown who calls for help in vain and the story about the disarming response of the Hasidic Jew ("perhaps it is true after all"). Ratzinger mentions Theresa of Lisieux ("placed inside the body of a sinner") and he interprets the opening scene of Paul Claudel's play *The Satin Slipper* ("fastened to the cross— with the cross fastened to nothing"). In these accounts I find personal experiences, questions, points of conflict between belief and doubt. But as much as these pictures and stories have taken on the character of fundamental experiences, all the less clearly do they seem to be incorporated into the text. What is present is an unclear and ambiguous appeal to verbal gestures. There are issues of "existence" and "frustration," of "daring" and "shift," of "existential locus" and "depth," of "being," of "the impenetrable," and of the "fundamental shape of human destiny." The theological linguistic culture of the fifties, with its concentration on individual decision making, with undifferentiated complaints from Kierkegaard and late reformulations from Heidegger, as well as the influence of Guardini and the liturgical movement are all mirrored in these passages.

Accordingly, many academically trained men and women readers allowed themselves to be drawn into this familiar world of existential challenge and response. They allowed themselves to be influenced by the breath of the otherworldly and the ceremonial ("only the bottomless depth of nothingness can be seen, wherever one looks"), which really is not so festively glorious, because his book is already characterized by an interwoven arrangement of serious concerns and (here the problem begins to emerge) of devastating sideswipes. These remarks cause one to sit up and take notice, especially since nobody knows very clearly who is being attacked. Where exactly is this "plain and unadorned theology in modern dress appearing in many places today" (pp. 16–17)? Who exactly is involved in the banal "spiritual costume switching"? Not only the disciples of Bultmann are involved, but even those overly enthusiastic disciples of Vatican II, which led to unacceptable results: "That neither the profound intellectualism of demythologization nor the pragmatism of *aggiornamento* can supply a convincing solution certainly makes it clear that this distortion of the basic scandal of Christian belief is itself a very far-reaching affair . . ." (p. 27).

Once again we have a verdict based on a generic analysis. But the abstractly positive affirmations still assume a very interesting shape, even if the persons addressed by them had scarcely reflected on it. What emerges is a clearly negative assessment of recent attempts in Protestant and Catholic settings. The fact that even the people he has in mind in no way deny these dangers and seek to eliminate them by carefully identifying the problems, the fact that they regard Ratzinger's own starting point as at least a serious alternative and not as a decidedly contrasting plan, means that those who agree with him come largely from among those whom he regards with high suspicion. His intention is not to distinguish between common goal and conceivably different means (at least he shows no trace of any such effort).

Two reasons for this were already clear in 1967. Ratzinger rejects using historical-critical and sociocritical methods because he sees in both of them an unwarranted submission to unacceptable erroneous developments of the modern age. He describes the first erroneous development as the "tyranny of the *factum*" which he takes to mean "man's complete devotion to his or her own work as the only certainty" (p. 33). Because human beings stand in the midst of this historicism they discover only their own finitude and so "the heaven from which they seemed to come has been torn down" (p. 34). This first faulty development is intimately connected with the second, namely, scientific and technical thought patterns—"devotion to reality in so far as it is capable of being shaped" (p. 36). Thus Ratzinger has pointed to two central problems and holds on to his predictions that today what is at stake is "cybernetics, the 'planability' of the newly-to-be-created man" so that "theologically, too, the manipulation of man by his own planning is beginning to represent a more important problem than the question of man's past . . ." (p. 37). Quite right. But what are the consequences?

In Ratzinger's view theology encounters this reduction of truth to "fact" by allowing "belief to be essentially centered on history" (p. 37). Theology has fallen into a trap; theology has provided its own reduction for itself. The same goes for the reaction to the second error. People feel tempted to put something "on the plane of fact on to that of the *faciendum* and to expound it by means of a 'political theology' as a medium for changing the world." Humankind's response is "to transpose belief itself to this place" (p. 38). We shall come back later to this question of historical reconstruction. Ratzinger squeezes together into the same box such unfriendly siblings as technical rationality and Marxism. Finally his argument begins to break down: what seems perhaps diagnostically enlightening emerges analytically as completely insufficient clichés when he speaks about *the* modern age, *the* flaw of historicism (as though there were no historical thinking), *the* technological thought (as though there is no obligation to be in touch with the world), and *the* theological enterprise (as though there has ever been only one theology). Whoever makes use of this "friend or enemy" paradigm will of course critically evaluate as unacceptable the new attempts subsequently cited. The names which he cites in the following footnote (p. 38, n. 14), namely, H. Cox, J. Moltmann, and J. B. Metz are part of this rejection. The fact that later he adds liberation theology to this list and attacks it the most vehemently because of its enormous impact is a logical step.[11]

Why then were we so surprised about Ratzinger's development? Probably because he subsequently relativized his own rejection, even if he did so rather late, and because he recognized that "Christian belief has a decisive connection with the motivational forces of the modern age" (p. 38). His objections remain unconvincing. They apply only then "when the two named attempts become exclusive." From the perspective of the present period, these reservations seem to be a smoke screen, since later there is nowhere visible any sort of an exhaustive argumentation with these theological proposals. Those who were criticized perceived these remarks in fraternal naiveté as a contribution to dialogue, but now in retrospect they must be seen as an overly hasty cutting off of discussion. This is what was meant, then, by the innocent thesis that "the act of believing does not belong to the relationship 'know-make' which is typical of the intellectual context of 'makability' thinking" (p. 39). In point of fact, Ratzinger was retreating from dialogue as he formulated these remarks. From subsequent events we can judge that he was retreating from the modern era before he had entered into it with any intensity.

RETURN TO THE FATHERS

Ratzinger's reservations vis-à-vis new approaches in theology can of course be questioned even by his own approach. Most appropriately, he expressed his opposition to every form of biblicism, whether sophisticated or naive. The question, however, is, Toward whom was this objection articulated? He was quite justified to begin his inquiry into Christian belief by means of the

Apostles' Creed. What remains to be determined is the extent to which he allows other ways of doing so. Ratzinger points to the challenge of our contemporary paradigm shift as parallel to that crucial development whereby Christianity took on a Hellenistic-Greek form. For him the two situations are not comparable. Inasmuch as today there is a narrow concentration of the terms *knowledge* and *praxis*, in those days the issues were *truth* and *understanding*. What can one say? Are we dealing here with a certain nostalgia of a humanistically educated person who so loves his church fathers and the Christian Western tradition and so ends his discussion with Heidegger's critique of technology? This concentration on European culture can hardly be pardoned nowadays.

Still once again one would have to hesitate placing narrow boundaries to Ratzinger's theology. His contributions to Christology ("this is how it is with humanity" [p. 223]), to the Resurrection ("love is strong as death" [p. 230]), and to Christian living ("one becomes truly human by being a Christian" [p. 204]) breathe a broad and open framework even when the more restrictive vocabulary keeps returning. Once again he uses polemic as a musical accompaniment. He never shows any excitement for Bultmann or Pannenberg, for the continuous efforts of historical-critical exegesis, or for the emerging hermeneutical movement. In the framework of his own systematic theology these opponents are simply caricatured.

The dilemma of modern theology—"Jesus or Christ"—is caused, he argues, by the "barrier of historical science" (p. 144). Pannenberg tries to "prove"; Harnack, that scapegoat who is constantly dragged in, "reduces"; Hegel and Bultmann try to "escape" from the historical. Everywhere people are trying to escape from the dilemma: from Jesus to Christ and from Christ to Jesus. He concludes by explaining why people are fleeing back "from the pale ghost of the historical Jesus to the most human of all human beings, whose humanity seems to them in a secularized world like the last shimmer of the divine left after the 'death of God' " (p. 147). No atrocious cliché is left unchallenged. From looking at the humanity of Jesus to the death of God, only two lines are needed. The decadence and absurdity of such a theology (if it exists) is quite obvious. The question is, Who has ever argued for such a stupid theology?

At this point Ratzinger offers, to use his own expresssion, a "modern cliché." A prophetic teacher appears on the scene in the overheated atmosphere and is executed for obscure reasons; there follows a gradual growing perception of his survival (p. 157). Extremely nuanced and complex discussions are here reduced to the level of banality. I find this passage today quite scandalous, because in it Ratzinger abusively denounces not only theological efforts and faith-inspired efforts but (as the years that follow confirm) actually hinders necessary discussions and clarifications.[12] This conglomeration of hypotheses is mixed up by Ratzinger, but is not fed by the mainstream of working theologians of that time. And if he asserts, in apparent innocence, that he would "more readily and easily" believe that God became human, then he has achieved only a Pyrrhic victory since he provides by this remark nothing illuminating about the incarnation of God. He should have been able to say once and for all, in an understandable way, what earlier affirmations meant.

There is no point, then, in responding in moralistic indignation. Still, this use of historical and sociocritical counter-questions helps us to understand what Ratzinger meant in fact by expressions such as "logos-bearing" or "reasonable-reasoning speech about God" (what a beautiful expression!). This was the unmistakable conclusion of his conviction that "at the bottom it was no accident that the Christian gospel in the period when it was taking shape, first entered the Greek world and there merged with the inquiry into understanding, into truth" (p. 46). Ratzinger meant exactly what he wrote. Only then did gospel become truth, did belief become understanding, did Scripture in the traditionally Catholic formulation (even though it had been reformulated by Vatican II's Constitution on Revelation) become tradition. Not only is our understanding of Scripture and of Jesus' preaching dependent on Greek thought patterns, but so is contemporary preaching.

New dimensions in theology and new breakthroughs in the church are thereby equivalently put to rest just as a direct, scientifiically responsible familiarity with the witnesses of Scripture. For if at the end of the chapter he writes of "understanding's responsibility without which belief would be undignified and bound in the end to destroy itself" (p. 47), then one can see very well that anyone who dares to step outside the house of our Greek heritage is personally involved in this ruinous enterprise. Throughout this entire publication Ratzinger's thought is not only Platonizing, as W. Kasper correctly observed in a thought-provoking review,[13] he is quietly raising Hellenism to the level of an exclusive norm for a church which is attempting both to become a worldwide church and, ultimately, to promote dialogue between cultures. By doing so, out of the enriching achievement of a brilliant era, he has fashioned an oppressive cage to hinder discussion of new questions, a cage reducible in times of necessity to a collection of magisterial texts and exhortations from hierarchical authority.

Am I overinterpreting the author? At least it is no coincidence that nowhere in his book does one find texts attempting to deal with more recent hermeneutical questions. It is no coincidence that he consistently argues from the viewpoint of specific church fathers or early ecclesiastical texts or precritical philosophical positions and that he forces discussions always on unhistorical, fundamental alternatives (belief vs. unbelief, Christian vs. secularized, rational vs. worthless) that threaten the possibility of discussion, so that ultimately only an authoritative intervention can ensue. This refusal to dialogue is intimately bound up with Ratzinger's view of the church.

THE WAY TO ETERNAL LIFE

From the beginning of his theological career Ratzinger concentrated on ecclesiology and thus connected to it questions relating to church structures, sacraments, and ecumenical issues. At the Council he contributed much to renewal. Also in his *Introduction to Christianity* he still described the church as "pneumatical and charismatic" and related the church to liturgy and sacraments. He was not inclined to describe the church from its ecclesiastical ministries or its organizational structure (p. 257 ff.). The primacy of Rome was not something that pertained to the primary elements of the concept of the church. Even episcopal structure "is not there for its own sake, but belongs to the category of means" (p. 268). The central spiritual reality of the church is representation and not power. Thus he displayed understanding for the complaint against a church that in antiquity and in modern times had betrayed the witness of unity and that even today has not yet brought together the rich and the poor so "that the excess of rich might become the nourishment of the poor" (p. 268). He quoted William of Auvergne: "Bride is she no more, but a monster of frightful ugliness and ferocity" (p. 262).

But here too these texts should be read exactly and his astute dialectic perceived. Since organization belongs to the means, it belongs "essentially to the marks" of the church in the world (p. 268). Criticism understood as a critical "reckoning of the past" is to be disqualified, for it contradicts the church's call to be "life for our torn world" (p. 268). Being Christian implies an endurance that leads to support (p. 262). This paradoxical view of the church, this ever present "nevertheless" of God's love, was for Ratzinger the ceaseless consolation of unholy holiness (p. 265). Thus even then he already had no sympathy for criticism. Even the self-critical language of Vatican II he ascribed to a "Lutheran theology of sin" (p. 262). What remains is a totally devasting arsenal aimed against criticism: hidden pride, rancorous bitterness, and thoughtless jargon. What follows is isolation of the self, spiritual teaching, reduction of the church to a political goal to "organize, reform, and govern." Now suddenly all that becomes secondary, which before had pointed to the monster.

And once again there appears that destructive club that allows no distincition between personal position and enmity toward the church. Read the following passage attentively: "Those who really [sic] believe do not attribute too much importance to the reorganization of church structures. They live on what the church is." Then he adds the key sentence of the entire book (and of Ratzinger's thought) which overly stresses the following distinction between edifying and destructive criticism: "Only the one who has experienced how, regardless of changes in her ministers and forms, the Church raises persons up, gives them a home and a hope, a home that is hope—the path to eternal life—only such a one who has experienced this knows what the Church is, both in days gone by and now" (p. 266).

In this sentence we see the whole context of Ratzinger's *Introduction into Christianity*. He is attempting to provide an introduction into the doctrine and praxis of the Catholic church.[14] He takes as his point of departure that his own experience shows the way to heaven. Seen from this vantage point, all his clear, often abstract, and allusive statements and his many highly emotional signals take on clearer significance. Already in 1967 Ratzinger understood the church's role as threatened and saw a decisive reason for that in the church's critics and reformers. In them he could discover only unbelieving criticism, but he does not name these critics, following an ancient taboo. So he is not prepared on his own part to comprehend all-embracing theological discussions and long-maturing processes as moments in the church. So he comes into conflict with them, he thrusts them outside, he analyzes them in completely vague terms as symptoms of unbelief, *Zeitgeist*, Enlightenment, and decline. All the elements of his conservative worldview are here present. The fact that he regards belief in God and in Jesus Christ as part of being church explains why a priori he opposes constructive discussion.

Let us go one step farther and ask what church Ratzinger is talking about. It is noteworthy how intensely Ratzinger was involved, before and after publication of his *Introduction to Christianity*, with the church fathers, as well as ecumenical councils of earlier times, and the churches of the East.[15] Questions of modern times (except those about the papacy and infallibility) play no role in his framework. The reckoning with the churches of the Reformation is not undertaken, in my judgment, beyond a few global remarks.[16] Nontheological ways of constructing theories, whatever shape they might have, are not fundamentally taken into consideration.[17] This is not a question of lack of ability but really a fundamental option not to do so. Such a view is clearly articulated in Ratzinger's essay "The Significance of the Fathers in the Elaboration of Belief," which he also wrote in 1968 and which he had reprinted in 1982 for his book *Theologische Prinzipienlehre*.[18] The church fathers possess for him a level of preeminence because, on the one hand, they are teachers from the still undivided church and because, on the other hand, Scripture and the fathers go together as closely as word and response. Whoever wants to discover truth should read Scripture as interpreted by the fathers of the church.

We can see therefore that even then Ratzinger had already restricted himself to a very narrow criterion for legitimate theology. The criterion is, in addition to episcopal structure, the creedal doctrine of the early church.[19] And it is precisely here on this point that Ratzinger seemed for a while to be progressive. Even he expressed his dissatisfaction with the theology of the Roman school and with Roman centralism.[20] Then came a time of serious disintegration and of challenging church leaders. They are criticized by some for "having become dogs without a bark who out of cowardice in face of the liberal public stood by fecklessly as faith was bit by bit traded off for the mess of potage, of the recognition of modernity."[21] There was no longer appeal to the "acquired reality of Catholicism."[22] In light of this crisis situation, Ratzinger apparently became quite ready to call upon Roman centralism and neo-scholastic theology as defensive measures.[23] The inexorability with which he attacked variant theological conceptions because of their criticism of the church increased with his anxiety that what might be lost would be the ancient view of the church (episcopal structure, linked with liturgy and sacrament, according to the norms of the first four ecumenical councils).

REPRESENTATIVE OF AN ANXIETY-BOUND THEOLOGY

Ratzinger lives from the thrust of a theology that, before the rediscovery of Scripture, called for a rehabilitation of the fathers, whose writings were seen as enrichment. A tragic aspect of his development is that he has not been inspired by the breadth of vision of an Yves Congar but rather by the antimodern predisposition of a Hans Urs von Balthasar.[24] Precisely because Ratzinger wants in an authoritarian way to obviate opening new questions and new challenges; because he does not admit for our present age the epochal transformation which he hailed in the Hellenization process, because he is no longer a Jew for the Jews, or a person free from the law to persons free from the law, or one who is weak to the weak (1 Cor. 9:20); but has instead become a Romanized Greek; his own call upon Catholic identity can no longer be qualified as catholic. He has restricted this prestigious title to one historical era and thereby has contributed to the withdrawal from the church by all those men and women of our century who want to remain and who want to make Jesus' message a foundation stone for a better world.

Still I do not wish to end on a polemic note. What is being debated here are not questions of personal integrity, not even questions about what theology is better or worse per se. I only wish to state, in agreement with many persons, that Ratzinger's theological schema would harm the church if it were to be translated into church policies. I readily admit that many in the Catholic tradition argue in a "more differentiated fashion" (as they would describe it) and claim Ratzinger is, after all, a great theologian and in many matters quite right. However, one cannot treat human beings as the pope and his prefect for the Congregation for the Doctrine of the Faith do. Those who argue that way are misguided right from the start. I prefer to agree with Jesus, who meant his remark to be understood as an ideology critique: "by their fruits you shall know them" (Mt. 7:16).

I know also the warning about not ignoring the plank in one's own eye while looking at the speck in another's eye (Mt. 7:3). In our present situation, my proposal can only be directed to those of us who are responsible for managing the theological enterprise: be much less silent then we have been up to now or at least abandon our barrage of safe words. Our fear of giving offense has paralyzed most of us; we have made this fear into an ideology called ecclesial spirit. Instead of calling a spade a spade, we ramble on in generalities, talking of historicity, of proper meaning, of content and form—and so that one should not be contrasted with the other—we claim that the problems are essentially much deeper and that, in particular, hermeneutical or dialectical mediation is much more complicated. Such jargon usually hides, I think, our fear or inability to articular a clear "yea" or "nay." In regard to the present Roman use of theology and ideology, such speaking out is overdue. We should simply ignore the reproach of being "lucky Hans," for Ratzinger has quite misunderstood the point of the story and, as elsewhere, has thought too late about the freedom of the children of God. The point of the story also has something to do with how Christians relate to those who hold offices in the church, to creedal formulas, and to new contexts. What seems to me most important is not what Origen, Augustine, Athanasius, or Tyconius once said, but what they would say today. Were they to come back today, they would have to either repeat themselves or be condemned by a Roman verdict. What a Spirit-less alternative!

Translated by
Michael A. Fahey, S.J.

NOTES

1. Michael Fahey, "Joseph Ratzinger as Ecclesiologist and Pastor," *Concilium* 141 (January 1981): 76–83. This article is part of a special issue devoted to "Neo-Conservatism: Social and Religious Phenomenon," edited by Gregory Baum.
2. Joseph Ratzinger, "Theologie und Verkündigung im Holländischen Katechismus," in *Dogma und Verkündigung* (Munich, 1973), 65–83, esp. 82. English translation of this article in *Furrow* 22 (1971): 739–54.
3. Joseph Ratzinger, "Demokratisierung der Kirche?" in *Demokratie in der Kirche: Möglichkeiten, Grenzen, Gefahren*, ed. J. Ratzinger and H. Meyer (Limburg, 1970), 12.
4. Ibid., 45. The attempt to protect the faith of the "simple faithful" from that of the intellectual has since then become a constantly recurring theme.
5. Ibid., 25, n. 15. For lack of space we cannot discuss here Ratzinger's rhetorical device of morally disqualifying the thoughts of other people.
6. Joseph Ratzinger, "Wandelbares und Unwandelbares in der Kirche," in *Theologische Prinzipienlehre: Bausteine zur Fundamentaltheologie* (Munich, 1982), 139.
7. Joseph Ratzinger with V. Messori, *The Ratzinger Report: An Exclusive Interview on the State of the Church* (San Francisco, 1985). On this book see the special number of *New Blackfriars* 66 (June 1985), especially the article by F. Kerr, "The Cardinal and Post-Conciliar Britain," 299–308.
8. Joseph Ratzinger, *Volk und Haus Gottes in Augustins Lehre von der Kirche* (Munich, 1954). Also important studies on the history of theology in *Das Veue Volk Gottes: Entwürfe zur Ekklesiologie* (Düsseldorf, 1969) and his *Theologische Prinzipienlehre* (see n. 6 above). On Ratzinger publications, see Fahey, "Joseph Ratzinger."
9. R. J. Schreiter, *Constructing Local Theologies* (New York, 1985).
10. Joseph Ratzinger, *Einführung in das Christentum* (Munich, 1968); idem, *Introduction to Christianity* (New York, 1969). These Tübingen university lectures were given in the summer semester of 1967. Page references cited in the text are to the English translation.
11. In later writings of Ratzinger we find numerous indications of his growing aversion for liberation theology. The Vatican declarations on liberation theology are influenced by his own views. Hans Urs von Balthasar made the astounding remark in the *Frankfurter Allgemeine* (25 October 1985) that the silence imposed on Leonardo Boff did not proceed from Ratzinger, "although he had no choice but to sign the directive." Well, if he signed it, then who directed it? A clarification of these facts would certainly be in the interest of all concerned.
12. In 1976 there appeared a volume of collected essays criticizing Hans Küng's *On Being a Christian* entitled *Diskussion über Hans Küng's "Christ Sein"* (Mainz, 1976)—to which, as usual, the one attacked was not allowed to respond—containing Ratzinger's clearly stated position: "Whoever poses a discussion thus has a faith that is corrupt at its very foundations" (p. 17).
13. Joseph Ratzinger, "Das Wesen des Christlichen," *Theologische Revue* 65 (1969): 182–88.
14. Ratzinger's view of the church is marked by liturgical experiences considered normative. Note the similarity of his thought with that of Balthasar and with the phenomenological thought of Pope John Paul II. Other important influences have been R. Guardini and M. Scheler.
15. Ratzinger, "Das Credo von Nikaia und Konstantinopel," in *Theologische Prinzi-*

pienlehre, 116–27. Athanasius and the Fathers of Nicaea are presented as models for the less brave who today in a "weakened Church" (p. 121) and amid theological factions (p. 121) should imitate the former who chose truth not "through compromise and adaptation" but through the "depth of their faith" (p. 127).

16. It is significant tht he often cites the work of P. Hacker, *Das Ich im Glauben bei Martin Luther* (Graz, 1966), a work preferred to others (see O. Pesch, *Hinführung zu Luther* [Munich, 1982], 66ff.). This work is compatible with Ratzinger's unecumenical assessment of Luther. I find quite disappointing his 1978 publication "Anmerkungen zur Frage einer 'Anerkennung' der Confessio Augustana durch die katholische Kirche," in *Theologische Prinzipienlehre*, 230–40, in which the question (with objections from Ratzinger) about the recognition of the Augsburg Confession is christened as an ecumenically "hasty procedure" into a "dialogue about the theological and ecclesial structure of the Evangelical-Lutheran creedal statements and their compatibility with the teaching of the Catholic Church" (p. 240). Surely such dialogues do not have to be repeated indefinitely.

17. Of course I do not know what Ratzinger is familiar with, what he has read and reflected on. One has to ask, however, why some theologians toil over historical, linguistic, social-theoretical, psychological, and other problems, and others know so quickly the why and wherefore that their conclusions are not legitimate. There is a gaping chasm, at any rate, between Ratzinger's criticism of contemporary life and his theological reflection on the present age.

18. Ratzinger, *Theologische Prinzipienlehre*, 139–59.

19. Karl Rahner and Joseph Ratzinger, *The Episcopate and the Primacy* (New York, 1962), was significant for the Council; see further Ratzinger's essay "Primat und Episkopat," in *Das neue Volk Gottes*, 121–46.

20. Joseph Ratzinger, "Free Expression and Obedience in the Church," in *The Church: Readings in Theology* (New York, 1963), 194–217.

21. This citation occurs precisely in his discussion about the relationship between church and scientific theology. See *Theologische Prinzipienlehre*, 341.

22. Joseph Ratzinger, "Widersprüche im Buch von Hans Küng," in *Zum Problem Unfehlbarkeit*, ed. K. Rahner (Freiburg, 1971), 104ff.

23. The way in which Ratzinger reacted to the Windsor report of the International Anglican/Roman Catholic Commission in *Communio* [German edition] 12 (1983): 244–59, and his reaction to the volume by H. Fries and K. Rahner, *Einigung der Kirchen—reale Möglichkeit* (Freiburg, 1983), because of its proposals, imitates earlier practices which Ratzinger once criticized.

24. One can scarcely overestimate the influence of H. U. von Balthasar upon Ratzinger. From Balthasar's *Cordula oder der Ernstfall* (Einsiedeln, 1966) to his most recent publications, one can see an increasing aggressiveness. The correct criterion is almost equated with Scripture as explained by the fathers within an episcopally structured church. Likewise, every expansion of problems that might go beyond the perspective of patristic horizons is equated with heresy.

7. The New Canon Law—The Same Old System
Preconciliar Spirit in Postconciliar Formulation
KNUT WALF

In his Apostolic Constitution, *Sacrae Disciplinae Leges,* in January 1983, John Paul II promulgated the new lawbook of the Catholic church, more precisely, of the Latin church. In it he recalled that his predecessor Pope John XXIII announced a reform of the old code in 1959 at the time he announced his intention of calling a council. The present pope then stresses even more frequently in his constitution how strong the bonds are between the last Council and this book of law. One finds similar expressions in the lengthy preface to the new code as well as in countless commentaries that wish to conjure up the spirit of the Council in this lawbook. Again and again one meets contemporaries who have more or less carefully examined the new code and have arrived at the conclusion that one can encounter the spirit of the Council in this code. As a jurist, when one hears or reads a bit too often about this kind of "spirit conjuration" one becomes suspicious. Usually this simply means that one cannot concretely ascertain in the code that which the Council really clearly wished or intended. Our suspicion should at least induce us to look for traces of the conciliar spirit in this code. This means, therefore, that we should dig beneath the surface or look behind the facade erected in this case by the text of the lawbook.

THE NEW CODE: RESULT OF THE SECOND VATICAN COUNCIL?

In the following it will be shown by means of examples, both from language and content, the extent to which the much adjured spirit of the Council is present in the new code. But it will also become clear from examples of what is *not* present in this lawbook whether the Council indeed influenced the shaping of the new code. We shall begin with several linguistic or terminological examples.

THE LANGUAGE OF THE COUNCIL—FORMULATION OF THE CODE

The last Council was supposed to have been or wanted to be, according to its own aim, a "pastoral" council. That's why the Council's language was tuned to the care of souls and received a preaching character rather than strove for static dogmatic or juridically univocal formulations. Many Council fathers, profiting by their manifold experience with juridical red tape, preferred, moreover, a pronounced antijuridical quality. At least that's what some participants or observers of the Council reported. To this can be added that not a few of precisely the important utterances of the Council have the character of compromise formulations. These are formulations, therefore, which were deliberately so shaped that they are susceptible to different, possibly even self-contradictory, interpretations. These formulations were supposed to facilitate agreement to conciliar decrees for as many participants and voting members as possible.[1]

That all of this taken together does not form a very favorable point of departure for the formulation of an ecclesiastical lawbook is obvious. To transpose conciliar utterances to such a book of law, to bring pastoral assistance through ecclesiastical norms, and to translate dogmatic, especially ecclesiological, formulations into lucid juridical language and a good legal system all seem nearly impossible. At the very least it requires an immense effort. And if they had to work almost sixteen years on the new code it was largely on account of these problems. The code of 1917 was finished in thirteen years, despite World War I.

From the beginning yet another problem played a decisive role in the work on the new code. The representatives appointed to the Commission for the Revision of Code of Canon Law were, almost without exception, of a conservative bent. A number of commission members had taken part in the Council and knew by personal observation the substantive problems which lay behind a goodly number of conciliar utterances. The language of the Council and many of its central concepts were not suitable for a book of law, in the view of commission members. The Council spoke quite readily about the church as community (*communio*). Regarding this beautiful idea, canon lawyers wrote half a library in the postconciliar years; in the code of 1983 it surfaced only marginally. In its stead, the Catholic church is defined according to the obsolete doctrine of the church as "perfect society" (*societas perfecta*) in the fundamental Canon 204 as *societas*, not as *communio*.[2]

In another example, the Council spoke with predeliction of the service (*munus*) of the ordained to and for the members of the church. It thereby took a decided distance from the notion *potestas* (meaning power, but also force), which played a central role in traditional canon law. The new code, on the contrary, returns to the old *potestas* notion when it speaks of the authority of the "sacred pastors." The notion *munus* appears in the new code only in the titles of Books III and IV and in the rather generally oriented formulations, as in Canons 204 § 1 and 375 § 2. But when the new code speaks of actual competencies it again employs the conventional concept *potestas*, but not the Council's *munus* (service).

A further example is found in marriage law. The Council saw marriage as a covenant (*foedus*) for life, not—as in the traditional marriage law of the church—as contract. The new code could hardly help but repeat the teaching of the Council in its Canon 1055 § 1, but the old conception of marriage contract, according to juristic criteria probably "safer," comes pushing in behind in paragraph 2.

Language is certainly indispensable for doctrinal systems and ideologies. Its preeminent task is to convey contents and to clarify. When we turn to the expressions of the Council and the code we immediately recognize clear discrepancies.

THE POPE AND THE BISHOPS—THE PRINCIPLE OF COLLEGIALITY

Just as in the exposition of the notion *communio*, so also with that of collegiality can one speak of downright enthusiastic expressions of this central conception of the Council in commentaries and interpretations of the conciliar texts. While the First Vatican Council had put forth and defined the primacy of the pope so strongly, the Second Vatican Council completed these assertions with its decisions on collegiality that form the foundation of the relationships between pope and bishops. In their enthusiasm, many ignored the fact that the "Prefatory Note of Explanation" to the "Dogmatic Constitution on the Church" of the Second Vatican Council really wished to see the word *collegium*, as contained in the concept of collegiality, unequivocally interpreted in a sense preserving papal primacy. Others, who thoroughly understood the implications of this explanation, intentionally appeased, perhaps desiring the expected enhancement of the meaning of the principle of collegiality between pope and bishops.

But then most things turned out other than had been expected by the majority of bishops and also many theologians. The new code presents us with the results today.

Even in the texts of the First Vatican Council one has to search far for expressions on papal primacy which compare with those of the new code. While the code of 1917—a canonical recapitulation of the First Vatican Council, at least as far as the constitutional structure of the church is concerned—perhaps assigned to the pope "the highest and complete jurisdictional authority over the entire church" (Canon 218 § 1, 1917 Code), the new code now supports the view that the pope "enjoys supreme, full, immediate and universal ordinary power in the Church" (Canon 331). If one points to this broadening of the epithets in the description of papal supremacy, it might perchance be answered that this is certainly nothing new. The earlier code and also the texts of the Second Vatican Council both know and recount all these and more properties of papal primacy. That might indeed be so. But in this connection what must be pointed out is the concentration of all these epithets in the one canon. But that's not all there is. In the new code, expressions about the pope are utilized which the earlier lawbook did not know, even though they appeared elsewhere. New in the code is this, that the pope is designated as the "Vicar of Christ" (*Vicarius Christi*, Canon 331). It is also new that the book of law now speaks of a "primacy" (*principatus*, Canon

331 § 1) of the pope not only over the entire church, but also over all of the particular churches and their associations. It is already worthy of note when the (official) German translation of the code dilutes *principatus* into the sleek work *Vorrang* (precedence). The French translation reads "primauté du pouvoir"—also not suitable—while the English translation "pre-eminent ordinary power" elucidates the meaning the best.

But one finds this kind of strong underscoring of the pope's power not only where the new code explicitly treats his position in the church. Again and again one encounters similar expressions elsewhere, for example, in the book concerning the ecclesiastical teaching office (Canon 749 § 1) and also in the matter of the rules governing formation in seminaries. Thus, Canon 245 § 2 prescribes that the students be formed in such a way "that, imbued with the love for the Church of Christ, they are devoted with a humble and filial love to the Roman Pontiff, the successor of Peter." The earlier code knows no comparable regulation!

The new code has naturally taken from the earlier book of law regulations that use this approach. But even then Catholics who knew the church of the Council and had consciously shared in shaping and carrying out its postconciliar development often have the greatest difficulty grasping regulations of this kind. Thus Canon 113 § 1 specifies that the Catholic church and the Apostolic See have, by divine law, the character of juridic persons. How can anyone make such an ahistorical divinizing of ecclesiastical law plausible to contemporary members of the church? Moreover, the results of more recent theological research give as little support to such expressions as to those of the code concerning the institution of all (seven) sacraments by Jesus Christ (Canon 840).

The collegial collaboration of pope and bishops finds, according to the utterances of the Second Vatican Council, its special expression in the ecumenical council ("Lumen Gentium," 22,2). Since indeed in the schema for the new code of 1980 the council receives not a word of mention and in the schema for a "Fundamental Law of the Church" of the year 1976 is treated only after other institutions in which the pope and bishops collaborate, many observers of the new ecclesiastical legislation were anxious to see how the new code would classify the ecumenical council.

Because the further development of the fundamental law was set aside, the pertinent passages had to be worked into the code. Statements about the ecumenical council can indeed be found in the new code (Canons 337–41). Yet two things in that regard are striking. In the first place, the new code does not devote to the council its own chapter as the code of 1917 knew it. The new book of law speaks about the council in the second article ("the college of bishops") in the first chapter of the part that speaks of "Supreme Church Authority." The subordination of the council to the primacy of the pope is therefore legislatively much more strongly elucidated than in the earlier code.

A further point is worthy of note. The 1917 code, in its Canon 228, spoke of the ecumenical council as exercising "supreme jurisdiction" over the entire church. While the epithets describing the pope's position of power have now been multiplied, the opposite is the case for the council. The new code in Canon 337 § 1 speaks only of the "power" of the council in reference to the whole church, omitting any embellishing adjectives. Furthermore, in this connection the defenders of the new code and its virtues counter the criticism by arguing that people misunderstand the matter because in Canon 336 "supreme and full power" over the universal church is conferred upon the college of bishops. And in fact this cannot be overlooked. But one must here immediately point out that in hardly any other definition of ecclesiastical law is immediate emphasis made of the close bond of the college of bishops to its head, the pope—without which it is incapable of action.

Furthermore, we should note that a separate chapter is devoted to the new collegial institution, "the synod of bishops." It stands just about in that place where the code of 1917 spoke of the ecumenical council, namely, after the chapter on the pope and before that which treats the law on cardinals.

THE CONFERENCE OF BISHOPS: DECENTRALIZATION OF THE CHURCH?

The positively disposed commentaries on the new code point precisely to the fact that through the new book of law the competence of the conferences of bishops is significantly broadened or at least defined completely in accord with the Second Vatican Council. It is, in fact, notable that the new code talks about the competence or at least the collaborative rights of the conference of bishops in about ninety places. When these ordinances are examined more closely, two things are discovered. In the first place it is noticed that the competencies of conferences of bishops are frequently given an explicitly secondary importance. In questions having broader implications, conferences require the approval of the Holy See for their decrees and resolutions. The predominance of the pope, therefore, is in no way infringed upon by this kind of decentralization. Rather, it is made even clearer. In addition, the new code does not give a complete picture of the supervision which the conferences of bishops are under from the side of the Holy See. It may be remembered that according to the *motu proprio* of 1969 entitled "Sollicitudo omnium Ecclesiarum," issued by Paul VI concerning the office of papal delegates, a measure which remains in force, the influence of papal delegates on conferences of bishops is very much greater than one could conjecture from these rather veiled, indeterminate formulations of the new code. Canon 364 lists among the chief tasks of a papal legate "to foster close relations with the conference of bishops by offering it assistance in every way" (§ 3). To be sure, the papal legate is not a member of the conference of bishops, but the Holy See can demand that he be invited to their deliberations (furthermore he must be invited to the opening meeting of every session).[3] If one considers that the conference of bishops has to forward its agenda to the papal legate promptly before each meeting and later forward the minutes of the meeting, one grasps just how complete is the supervision by the Holy See over this much-praised intermediate body that stands between the local bishop and the pope.

THE POPE AND THE LOCAL CHURCH

Contrary to the intention of the Second Vatican Council, the new code has strengthened rather than lessened the influence of the pope upon the particular or local church. This can be shown by countless other examples heretofore not cited. We shall single out only two which are especially striking.

First of all there is the new canonical institute of the personal prelature. This concerns what is, in fact, a personal bishopric that is, moreover, directly subordinate to the pope.[4] The new regulations (the earlier code knew absolutely nothing of personal prelatures!) are like a Roman made-to-measure suit cut from the present pope's favorite personal prelature, the Opus Dei. The canonical positioning of these regulations between those concerning the clergy and those concerning ecclesiastical societies (Canons 294–97) should be noticed. Because personal prelatures are about quasi bishoprics, it would have been proper to place them among the regulations concerning the particular churches. Clergy as well as lay people can belong to personal prelatures. They are presided over by a "proper ordinary" (Canon 295 § 1), so that, unlike the religious orders, there might thereby be permitted an organization coinciding with the regular structures of the church. Indeed, the verb *can be* in Canon 294, referring to the erecting of such a personal prelature, pertains to the concerned (probably better *disconcerted!*) conference of bishops, and its activity needs the approval of the diocesan bishop. Nevertheless, it cannot be overlooked that already with the experience with Opus Dei the particular churches can be cut up, even divided, by personal organizations directly subject to the pope.

The personal prelature is, by the way, a very revealing example of how the good intentions of the Council were sidetracked in the course of time. Its introduction was founded upon the decree "Presbyterorum Ordinis" (Decree on the Ministry and Life of Priests) of the Council. In Article 10, Section 2, the desire was expressed that existing norms regarding the connection of priests to a spiritual home organization should be reexamined and new forms of association sought so as to achieve a more flexible pastoral ministry. The idea of the personal prelature surfaced in this connection. The Council expressly added that this must be done "without prejudice to the rights of local Ordinaries." That the spiritual fathers of this conciliar decree were not thinking of an already existing organization like a religious order—as the "Opus Dei" was (and is)—to be invested with the additional rights of a personal prelature can be garnered from the postconciliar legislation. Thus the *motu proprio* "Ecclesiae Sanctae" of Paul IV issued in 1966 mentions the personal prelature (I,4) and precisely in the sense of a form of categorial or special pastoral ministry for specific groups or areas (missions).

A further example of the modification of traditional law in favor of papal primacy can be found in the new regulations concerning the coadjutor (Canons 403–11). A coadjutor (or coadjutor-bishop) is an auxiliary bishop. While the earlier law differentiated between coadjutors with or without the right of succession in case of the death or loss or abandonment of office by the local bishop, the new code recognized only the legal form of the coadjutor who has the right of succession. Now it is just this form which is controversial, especially in those particular churches which still recognize some form or other of participation by the local or particular church in the election of a bishop. The appointment of a coadjutor with right of succession has, on the one hand, the character of an exception,[5] and on the other, actually enables the pope to bypass all of the regulations of universal or particular law and, in a given instance, "ex officio appoint a coadjutor bishop," insofar as this suits his purposes (Canon 403 § 3). This means that the pope can not only provide a bishop with an auxiliary bishop but that he can also force a successor upon him. Just how serious is the import of this is also shown by the regulation according to which the local bishop must name the coadjutor as his vicar general, his alter ego, as the vicar general is sometimes called (Canon 406 § 1). One can gather from this what remains of the principle of collegiality as one understood it from the last council. If one simply reads the new code precisely, one recognizes behind the pleasant-sounding formulations a papal "emergency powers law" for the universal church. How can collegiality between pope and bishops continue to develop in such a framework?

THE LAITY

Important central assertions of the last council concern the place of the lay person in the church. Whoever had experienced the euphoria with which the theological revaluation of the laity and its contribution to the church was spoken and written about before and during the Council, can find in the new code some verbal repetition of corresponding conciliar utterances. Thus, the new code also underscores the mutuality of clergy and laity and speaks of both in the conciliar terminology as *christifideles* (Christian faithful). The new code also has a title on "The Obligations and Rights of All the Christian Faithful" (Canons 208–23; notice the word order!). Despite many desiderata which remain unaddressed, this section can be considered a net profit. Finally, there is in the new code a separate section on "The Obligations and Rights of the Lay Christian Faithful" (Canons 224–31) which, compared to the earlier code, likewise shows progress.

Yet here it is also worth examining the formulations more closely to determine just what does not appear in the new legal text. Because in many particular churches more and more lay people, women as well as men, have taken over responsibilities which the clergy formerly held, one naturally looks in the code for regulations governing the ministry of these lay people. One then learns that the code contains scarcely any norms on the laity as ecclesiastical ministers. It essentially covers only the degree to which lay people as volunteers (and therefore probably temporary) can take over ecclesiastical functions. In this connection we can refer to the very instructive formulation of Canon 230 which makes very clear in three paragraphs that male lay persons, "lay men," under certain circumstances "on a stable basis" may take over specific liturgical functions (§ 1). Further, lay persons, therefore even women, by temporary deputation may fulfill specified liturgical actions (§ 2). And finally, lay people "when the necessity of the Church warrants it" can obtain broader authorization (§ 3). It is like an emergency powers provision which permits even lay people to dare look after the functions of the church.

Now, in what touches upon the question of the conferring of ecclesiastical jurisdiction upon lay people, the new code, probably in the face of the situation in many particular churches, takes a much more unequivocal but also much more restrictive position than did the code of 1917. It is thus remarkable that the new code no longer employs the term *missio canonica* for the ecclesiastical mission. Because this was an overly inclusive concept embracing the ecclesiastical mission of clerics as well as lay persons it was eliminated from the new code. In its place, the new code refers to the corresponding authorization of clerics as *facultas* (faculty, see

Canon 764), that of religious as *licentia* (permission, see Canon 765), and that of lay persons as *mandatum* (mandate, see Canon 229 § 3).

If the new code now distinguishes so carefully between what clergy and laity respectively may or can do, it is the logical consequence of the new regulations of Canon 129. The content of this canon was discussed with downright animosity in the code commission. Proof of this long discussion was, among other things, Canon 126 of the 1980 draft of the revised code. This still spoke of a power of jurisdiction that was not based upon ordination. Similar formulations were contained in corresponding earlier schemata of the code commission. Cardinals Hume and Ratzinger especially argued with reference to tradition that the conception according to which there is a power of jurisdiction which is not based upon ordination is self-contradictory. In Canon 129 § 2 one now reads, as a result of this discussion, that lay people can only cooperate in the exercise of the power of jurisdiction. Not once is delegation or delegating of the power of jurisdiction to lay persons mentioned. The word now employed, *cooperari* (cooperate), was, until now, not to be found in the repertoire of juridical concepts of canon law. So, for the time being, we must wait and see just what is to be understood by it.

The new Canon 129 does raise logical problems. For the revised law also provides that some lay persons, both men and women, can be appointed as ecclesiastical judges (Canon 1421 § 2), even if only as members of collegiate tribunals and even if only one on such a tribunal. A judge, however, possesses the power of jurisdiction, that is, must personally possess it in order to dispense justice validly. Between Canon 129 § 2 and 1421 § 2 there exists, therefore, a logical discord. At the same time this discord might be viewed as exemplary of the arenas of the conciliar and the traditional parties in the leadership mechanism of the contemporary Catholic church.

WHAT IS NOT FOUND IN THE NEW CODE

Already at the outset it was mentioned that the new code has to be measured not only in itself and its contents, but, much more so, must be evaluated on the basis of its lacunae. And there are many of these lacunae, which really have no place in a book of law which should reflect the contemporary reality of the church.

One omission was already alluded to in the foregoing section: the code contains no ministerial law for lay persons in permanent ecclesiastical positions. While, in the meantime, a number of particular churches are acquainted with a ministerial law for laity that is in part completely developed, the new code not once mentions ecclesiastical offices like those of pastoral assistants (*Pastoralreferenten*).

Other legal matters which are of great importance to the contemporary church were indeed discussed at length in the code commission with parts worked out to a stage of readiness for promulgation by the lawgiver (the pope) but then nevertheless not made part of the code. The most important examples are the drafts of the regulations on the laicization of clerics and on administrative adjudication.

In the matter of laicization, the Pontifical Commission for the Revision of the Code of Canon Law had developed, already in 1977, a discerning and reasonable proposal for its juridical regulation. Besides the presently named possibilities for laicization in the new code (Canon 290: invalidity of ordination, penal reduction to the lay state, and laicization for the most serious reasons), there were, according to the commission's draft, the following additional routes to laicization: cases expressly named in law, which again and again appeared in postconciliar dispensations; severe illness of the cleric rendering the practice of celibacy impossible; release by the (simpler and faster) administrative method. The last-named method particularly would have resolved the entire matter, for the commission had proposed that the conferences of bishops should specify "pastoral reasons" for such a procedure.

In the context of our theme it should be pointed out that this draft by the commission had grown out of the many years of Roman dispensation practice since the time of the Council. And when one looks at just who the authors of this draft were, one can scarcely arrive at the conclusion that these were firebrands at work wanting to weaken the discipline of the church. No, the singular responsibility for rejection of this reasonable draft is borne by John Paul II! Instead of approving of the draft, he let the bishops and heads of religious orders be instructed by means of a secret letter from the Congregation for the Doctrine of the Faith, dated 14 October 1980, that he was of the view that a dispensation from celibacy could not be something like the automatic result of an administrative process. Furthermore, it was announced that in the future a dispensation would be granted only in exceptional cases. Accordingly, the pertinent canons of the new code were reduced to empty formulae. Since the beginning of the pontificate of John Paul II, the practice concerning dispensations has been handled restrictively. Postconciliar moderation, in Catholic canon law, also called "canonical equity" (*aequitas canonica*), is since then actually proscribed.

Another example for the proscription of a newly developed postconciliar legal attitude within the Catholic church is the rejection by the pope of an arrangement for ecclesiastical administrative adjudication. The comprehensive draft of the new code of 1980 still contained an excellent section concerning administrative adjudication. By administrative adjudication is meant jurisdiction over acts or measures of administration. Because in the contemporary state as well as in the church there is emerging a steadily intensifying trend not to regulate problems of administrative conduct by the protracted process of judicial trial, it has become even more necessary to supervise administration by means of special jurisdiction ordered to it. Many civil law systems have already taken this into account. Because similar internal problems also exist in the church—one need think only about the occasional completely authoritarian procedural methods of episcopal chancery offices in Germany—the draft of 1980 found wide approval. Concerning the reasons which were decisive for its rejection by the legislator one can, as an outsider, only offer conjectures. It apparently does not fit the image of the church held by the present pope that anyone who feels injured by the methods of ecclesiastical administrators should have the possibility of a juridical review of these methods conceded by ecclesiastical law.

Also to be fitted into this picture is the fact the new code, in which there are so many dispensable items, does not contain any norms for doctrinal examinations or doctrinal complaint procedures.

Possibly this is an indication that the present pope considers the norms, which have been in effect since 1971, in need of revision.

CONCLUDING EVALUATION

In the first evaluations, the new code of 1983 was given a much too positive assessment even by critical commentators. Upon closer examination it reveals very clearly that, behind a terminology based in part upon concepts and images of the Second Vatican Council, it conceals a tenor which has little or nothing whatever to do with the objectives of this Council. Thus, for example, in the first commentaries it was positively noted that the penal law of the Catholic church was fundamentally cleaned up; the number of penalties threatening excommunication was reduced from more than forty to only seven. Nevertheless, it went mostly unnoticed that the new code also knows about intensifying penalties and, in cases that earlier threatened excommunication, the sanction of a new kind of interdict still obtains. As far as intensified penalties are concerned, reference should be made to the fact that in the new code the penalty of automatic excommunication for abortion remains (Canon 1398). The earlier code also knew this penal sanction (Canon 2350 § 1). The 1980 draft of the code, however, considered reducing the sanction to that of interdict in its Canon 1350. Completely incomprehensible, finally, is the re-acceptance of a regulation according to which parents or guardians who permit their children to be baptized or raised non-Catholic are to be penalized with a censure or another "just penalty" (Canon 1366).

Thus, the new code in many respects will appear to be a compilation of the results of the First rather than the Second Vatican Council. Because of its retrogressive adaptation it can offer no help and direction for the course of the church in its near or farther future. This book of law was already antiquated upon its coming into force. The outlook is not good for the reception of a new ecclesiastical law in a church in which neither clergy nor laity are otherwise well disposed toward canon law. When all is said and done, one can hardly blame them.

Translated by
James Biechler

NOTES

1. K. Walf, "Lakunen und Zweideutigkeiten in der Ekklesiologie des II. Vatikanums," in *Kirche und Wandel*, eds. G. Alberigo, Y. Congar, and H. J. Pottmeyer (Düsseldorf, 1982).
2. K. Walf, "Die katholische Kirche— eine 'societas perfecta'?" *Theologische Quartalschrift Tübingen* 157 (1977): 107–18. On *communio*, see H. Müller, "Communio als kirchenrechtliches Prinzip im Codex Iuris Canonici von 1983?" *Im Gespräch mit dem dreieinen Gott: Festschrift für W. Breuning*, eds. M. Böhnke and H. Heinz (Düsseldorf, 1985), 481–98.
3. See R. Lill, *Die ersten deutschen Bischofskonferenzen* (Freiburg, 1964), 8: "With all loyalty to the pope, which the conferences have often demonstrated, the bishops have placed the greatest value upon their deliberations remaining confidential and not under direct control by Roman diplomats. They have consistently been able to avoid the participation of the nuncios."
4. This contradicts, by the way, the postconciliar efforts to abolish bishoprics immediately subject to the pope, the so-called exempt bishoprics.
5. K. Mörsdorf, *Kirchenrecht* (Munich, 1964), I, 423.

8. Defaming the Historical-Critical Method

GEORG SCHELBERT

The Second Vatican Council had aroused hopes that the so-called historical-critical method in exegesis, as applied to the New Testament and particularly to the Gospels, had attained full status in the church and would henceforth be recognized as having a rightful place there. The rejection of the prepared schema "On the Sources of Revelation" on 19 November 1962—a day that Yves Congar referred to at the time as the end of the Counter-Reformation—and especially the instruction of the biblical commission "On the Truth of Gospels" of 21 April 1964 signalled a breakthrough. These events led to the preparation of a third and eventually to a fifth, definitive version of the constitution on revelation (*Dei Verbum*), which was accepted on 18 November 1965 with 2,344 affirmative votes to only six negative. And in the intervening twenty years there has certainly been a series of positive statements from the highest levels in the church. But the Council was scarcely over before laments and warnings began to be heard. The principles formulated by the Council and the implications of the model it had accepted for the origin and character of the Gospels were not taken seriously. Instead, they were practically ignored. In fact, the historical-critical method the Council called for was quite simply calumniated. This has to be said, unfortunately, of the era of Paul VI. John Paul II, who was a professor of theology himself, has a more positive and secure attitude toward scientific theology and toward biblical scholarship. But, all the more for that, historical-critical biblical studies have been sharply attacked by the Congregation for the Doctrine of the Faith, or rather by its leader, and have been made a kind of scapegoat. We are talking about the historical-critical method as employed by Catholic exegetes, that is, by believers who are in the church and loyal to it. For we must unfortunately conclude—and this is the calumny in question—that an image of these exegetes as enemies is being created by means of denunciations (mainly blanket ones) and accusations of destructive intentions either stemming from or resulting in hostility to the church.

THE COUNCIL'S FUNDAMENTAL ACCEPTANCE OF THE HISTORICAL-CRITICAL METHOD

It is necessary to recall, first of all, that the Council really did give fundamental recognition to the historical-critical method. This is to be found in its statements on the truth of Scripture in the Constitution on Divine Revelation (III, 11b), as well as those on the principles of interpretation (III, 12) and the origins and special character of the Gospels (V, 19).

With regard to this last point, the conciliar constitution incorporated the essentials of the instruction of the biblical commission of 21 April 1964 and thus elevated this instruction to the level of a conciliar statement. The Council thereby recognized the *model* which underlies the historical-critical method, with those characteristics that differentiate it from the previous model. There are four such characteristics.

1. This model is no longer "one-dimensional" or even "two-dimensional," producing a flat picture, but "multi-dimensional," i.e., *multi-leveled.* Generally speaking, we can differentiate three principal levels or stages: the level of Jesus ("what Jesus . . . really did and taught"); the level of oral transmission ("the apostles handed on to their hearers what He had said and done"); the level of the Gospels ("the sacred authors wrote the four Gospels").

2. The model is no longer static, but *dynamic,* i.e., words and narratives do not pass untouched and unchanged through the various levels. At the level of oral transmission we find reference to the hermeneutic relevance of the Easter events and post-Easter understanding to the handing on of Jesus' words. Citations are given from the Gospel of John. At the level of the Gospels and their earlier forms, the constitution

speaks of selection, synthesis, and explanatory interpretation: "selecting some things from many which had been
handed on by word of mouth or in writing, reducing some of
them to a synthesis, explicating some things in view of the
situation of their churches."

3. The model is thus also no longer simply individualistic, that
is, the Gospels are not simply regarded as the work of single
personalities who "could, would, and must speak the truth,"
as the earlier view had argued. There is, instead, a *sociological
component* involved, "the situation of their churches," i.e.,
the *Sitz im Leben* of the Christian communities.

4. Finally, the model is no longer that of a chronicle or tran-
script, but that of a kerygma (*formam denique praeconii retin-
entes*). The Gospels, then, are no longer regarded as
historical works with a kerygmatic tinge, as was still the case
in the second draft of the document—"sometimes (*ali-
quando*) in the form of proclamation" (*Dei Verbum*, IV, 18)—
but the reverse: they are works of proclamation with an infu-
sion of history. This model of the origin and character of the
Gospels "requires critical method" for its "understanding
and interpretation," that is, the "differentiation" and "separation" of redaction and tradition (literary criticism), of recognizable levels of tradition (form criticism and tradition
criticism), of event and depiction, history and its presentation (historical criticism in the more specialized sense). In
other words, the historical-critical method is necessary for an
accurate interpretation. Thus "the exegete must take into
account the three phases of transmission through which the
life and teaching of Jesus have come down to us" (Instruction, 2). The synthesis of a history of the words and deeds of
Jesus with their transmission (tradition criticism and form or
formation criticism) and redaction (redaction criticism) is
therefore the goal of analysis.

The principles of interpretation arising out of this understanding of inspiration, which are sketched in the constitution (III, 12)
as applied to all of Scripture, are thus applied to the Gospels.
These principles include the recognition of the literary conditioning of "truth," or what the text says, at all levels, and atten-

tion to the literary forms and types, including their historical conditioning, whether in the context of profane literature, salvation history, or the history of revelation.

It was undoubtedly an important concern of the Council to maintain the historicity of the Gospels. One of the last three interventions of the conservative minority at the Council through the pope himself concerned precisely this question. This took the shape at first of the simple statement "but always in such fashion that they told us the honest truth about Jesus" (*vera et sincera*) and the citation of Lk 1:2–4, in which *asphaleia* is translated, as in the Vulgate, as "truth" (*veritas*). But the end result of this intervention was the insertion of the relative clause, "whose [the Gospels'] historical character [*historicitas*] the church unhesitatingly asserts," near the beginning of the paragraph (*Dei Verbum*, V, 19).

Certainly, the Council fathers had already given fundamental recognition to the fact that some texts are "history of one kind or another" (*vario modo historicis; Dei Verbum*, III, 12b) and that "as he used contemporary literary forms" the author was also subject to historical conditioning.

It is clear that this fundamental affirmation neither could nor should have been negated by the statements concerning the Gospels. The historicity which is asserted is, moreover, to be understood in light of the portrayal of the nature and origin of the Gospels. This is true especially of the consequence which J. A. Fitzmyer pointed out in his commentary on the instruction: "that the Biblical Commission"—this is no less true of the conciliar constitution—"calmly and freely admits that the gospels as we now have them contain neither the words and deeds of Jesus from the first phase of transmission nor even the form in which they were proclaimed in the second phase, but rather that the Gospels present the words and deeds of Jesus in the form in which the Evangelists composed and edited them."[1]

No less important in this connection is the replacement of the concept of scriptural "inerrancy" or "freedom from error" with the positive notion of "truth" and its definition as "saving truth" (*veritas salutaris;* see *Tridentinum DS 1501*) or, in the final formulation, "that truth which God wanted put into the sacred writings for the sake of our salvation" (*Dei Verbum*, III, 11b). This refor-

mulation was the result of a second point in the papal intervention, but did not alter the meaning of the passage. In Scripture it
is not simply a question of a positivist truth, that is, whether what
is said is correct or not. It is not a matter of the facticity of what is
related. Instead, it is a question of the truth of salvation and for
salvation. This alone is covered by the words "firmly, faithfully
and without error," and not, as in the first draft of the schema,
"every sort of religious or *profane matter"* (II, 12; emphasis supplied). Since God, according to the witness of Scripture, has acted
in history for human salvation, there is undoubtedly a notable
measure of historicity in this saving truth, but only as regards the
fundamental facts and their intrinsic elements. Therefore historical-critical research—"careful investigat[ion of] what meaning
the sacred writers really intended, and what God wanted to manifest by means of *their* words"—is necessary "to see clearly what
God wanted to communicate to *us,"* "since God speaks in sacred
Scripture through human persons in human fashion" (III, 12a).
This is the reason for the relevance and irrevocable necessity of
such research.

POPE PAUL VI'S POSITIVE ACCEPTANCE OF MODERN BIBLICAL SCHOLARSHIP

In his Apostolic Exhortation on the fifth anniversary of the
Council (6 January 1970), Paul VI gave recognition to the fact
that the work of the Council was founded on "the best achievements of biblical and theological knowledge." In an address to
the twenty-second Italian Bible Week on 29 September 1972 he
praised "the wonderful development of biblical scholarship,
which is able to determine with precision the historical moment,
the geographical location and the cultural milieu of God's revelation in history." Similarly, on 14 March 1974, in addressing the
newly reorganized biblical commission, he spoke appreciatively of
the establishment of the *Sitz im Leben* of tradition, form, and redaction criticism respectively, "which we have urged, together
with the necessary corrections." He referred at that time to the
instruction of 1964. In this speech he also used the terms *synchron-
ic* and *diachronic,* which in the meantime had been borrowed from
linguistic analysis and adopted as technical exegetical language.

COMPLAINTS, WARNINGS, AND DEFAMATION OF MODERN BIBLICAL SCHOLARSHIP

But less than a year after the close of the Council, the Congregation for the Doctrine of the Faith, then (until 1968) headed by Cardinal Ottaviani, sent a letter to the bishops (24 July 1966), which, though intended to be secret, later had to be made public. It complained of misuses already arising in the interpretation of the Council and detailed a catalogue of errors. The first was thus described: "There are some who appeal to Scripture and deliberately put aside Tradition, who place limits on the inspired character and freedom from error of the Bible in both scope and effect, and who judge incorrectly concerning the historical texts." Beyond this, the overemphasis on historicity—"certain people recognize almost no objective, absolute, fixed and unchangeable truth"—as well as on the humanity of Jesus Christ, were condemned. Here, at any rate, the conciliar terminology had left practically no traces. Even the pope himself seemed disturbed. In Christmas week of that same year (28 December 1966) he spoke in his general audience on the topic of "seeking Jesus." He said:

Since we did not have the privilege of knowing the Lord directly and through the senses, we must try to gain a historical knowledge of him, a reliable memory. . . . At the present time major discussions are breaking out, a great number of studies and interpretations, *that try to diminish the historical value of the gospels,* especially the chapters that speak of Jesus' birth and childhood. We only mention the depreciation of the historical content of these wonderful pages of the gospels in order that you may learn, through your studies and your faith, how to defend the consoling certainty *that these pages are not the inventions of popular fantasy, but that they speak the truth.* (Emphasis supplied)

The pope cites remarks of Cardinal Bea, "a knowledgeable person," refers to the concept of witness in the New Testament and to the conciliar statement about the redactional activity of the Evangelists, whose purpose was "always to tell us the honest truth." It is apparent that the pope is not thinking of the important achievement of the conciliar text concerning the "saving truth" of Scripture, which alone is "taught firmly, faithfully and without error." Truth is here equated with historicity. No account is taken of the variety of forms, or of the singular character of the infancy narratives as opposed to the transmission of Jesus' public words and actions. The opposition between "inventions of popular fantasy" and "truth" is a tendentious alternative. It is simply defamatory to assert, as he does, that research on the infancy narratives has as its *goal* the devaluation of their historical content. The exegetes here referred to are in fact simply trying to establish the particular character of these narratives and to determine what they are really saying. This content is obviously not at the historical level, but instead is theological-christological in character: the proclamation of Jesus as the Christ.

The Apostolic Exhortation on the occasion of the nineteen hundredth anniversary of the deaths of Peter and Paul (23 March 1967) contains a similar lament, this time with the whole church as audience. On the one hand, the pope complains of a "radical historicist direction," and on the other hand that "they go so far as to rob the testimony of Sacred Scripture of its historical character." Can anyone really speak of Catholic exegetes in that global fashion? This exhortation was addressed to the Catholic church! Did the model of the origins and character of the Gospels which the Council recognized not require a differentiation and distinction between history and the way it is presented? Even before that, is this not required by the differences in the ways the Gospels themselves present their material?— unless, that is, one continues to read the Gospels, or at least the infancy narratives, contrary to the method approved by the Council, as if they were chronicles or transcripts.

Again, if one takes into account the variety of descriptions of the Easter appearances in the several Gospels, one really dares not say—as the pope did in an Easter address in 1967—"we have received this testimony (of the Resurrection) . . . from eyewitnesses, and *with scrupulous exactness*" (emphasis supplied). If there is anything that is *not* true of the actual content of the tradition, it is this kind of "scrupulous exactness." The descriptions are too different, and too much influenced by the "theology" of the various Evangelists.

Finally, let me mention the address to the general audience of 1 August 1973.[2] The pope is talking about the problems of belief today:

We must mention another manifold obstacle that has arisen in recent years. [This results] when people rely on subtle erudition and particularly when they submit Sacred Scripture to a hermeneutic, that is, a new, destructive interpretation based on pretended but really questionable criteria, in order to rob the holy book of its authentic authority, which the church acknowledges and which makes it the motive and object of the faith that is handed down.

Again the statements, or rather accusations, about the goal or purpose of such studies are defamatory. Exegetes are not in the business of robbing Scripture of its authority; their intention is instead to reveal its true character.

Paul VI's last utterance on the subject of biblical scholarship, however, was the address of 14 March 1974 to the reconstituted biblical commission, cited above. His last word, so to speak, was a more positive one.

POPE JOHN PAUL II AND BIBLICAL SCHOLARSHIP

The present pope, himself a former university professor, as he mentioned in his address to the professors at Salamanca on 1 November 1982 ("You know that the Pope was also a man of letters and of the university"), has an unbroken relationship to scholarship, to theology, and to biblical studies. His remarks to the Papal Academy of Sciences, for example, refer to the relationship between the Bible and the natural sciences. In that speech he admitted—something that very rarely happens, given his scarcely historical, or rather "sundial" view of church history—that the church committed errors in the case of Galileo (10 November 1979) and announced that the case would be reinvestigated. He referred to this again on 9 May 1983 and at that time spoke of "imprudence, the result of misunderstandings and errors" (no. 1). Nor is it a matter of a "convenient apologetic intention, when the church turns to the discoveries of science" (no. 8). At a symposium on the theme of "Christian faith and the theory of evolution" on 26 April 1985 he emphasized that faith in creation and evolutionary theory, when correctly understood, need not impede one another.

His positive attitude toward theological and biblical scholarship was expressed in a variety of statements to the respective scholarly groups in Rome and elsewhere. At his first meeting with the theological commission, the pope underscored that "the work of the theologians . . . may not be restricted . . . simply to the repetition of dogmatic formulae," and recognized a "healthy pluralism of theological schools" (26 October 1979, nos. 4 and 5). On 6 October 1981, he cited an important passage from his address to the theology professors gathered in Altötting, 28 November 1980, and he referred to this again in his remarks to the Spanish theology professors and students in Salamanca (1 November 1982). It was evidently a statement that was very important to him as well. Max Seckler has called it a "turning-point in the teaching office's view of theology" or at any rate a "milestone in the relationship of the church to scholarship." Here the pope emphasized, among other things, the reference of all theology to sacred Scripture:

Every theology is based on Sacred Scripture; all theological tradition is founded in Sacred Scripture and returns again to it. The study of Sacred Scripture remains therefore, as the Constitution on Divine Revelation of the Second Vatican Council says, "the soul of theology." (no. 24) It continually nourishes and renews our theological quest.

He particularly underlined the ecumenical importance of this study:

If we live from Scripture we come nearer to our separated brethren, in spite of all the differences that may remain between us. (no. 2)

Twice the pope cited the important no. 3 of this address:

Theology is a science with all its potentialities for human knowledge. It is free in the use of its methods and analyses. . . . Teaching office and theology have different duties. Therefore they cannot be reduced to one another. Nevertheless both serve the whole. But precisely in this structural relationship it is necessary that they remain in constant dialogue with one another.

He also spoke expressly of many examples of good cooperation between theology and the teaching office.

John Paul II has expressed himself on the subject of biblical scholarship especially in addresses to the biblical commission. In the first of these, on 26 April 1979, on the subject of enculturation, he indicated that, among other things, it was "obviously one of your duties" to "differentiate between those things that are passing and those that are of permanent value." On the seventy-fifth anniversary of the Papal Biblical Institute he called for committed and serious involvement in research, for knowledge of ancient languages and of the environment in which the Bible originated, for untiring effort and readiness to understand a world completely different from our own in which the word of God took its literary form. He spoke of this research as a special service to the church, as a mission, an apostolate. With regard to the New Testament he exhorted:

Do not cease to examine these texts, no matter how difficult and obscure they may be, with the aid of your philological, linguistic, literary and historical investigations, for they are more useful than ever for a better understanding of the word of God. Faithfulness to the text as handed down to us must remain characteristic of your work.

Here he also cited the conciliar Constitution on Divine Revelation (III, 12c) where the purpose of research is described: "so that through preparatory study the judgment of the church may mature." Once again he indicates that sacred Scripture is the basis for dogmatic and moral theology as well: "There is no spiritual life, no catechesis or pastoral utterance that does not demand continual recourse to the sacred books." And he repeats once more that "Sacred Scripture is the soul of theology" (*Dei Verbum*, VI, 24) and emphasizes the ecumenical importance of its study, especially for Christian-Jewish dialogue. In his "catechesis" at his Wednesday general audience on 22 May 1985, the pope, in a short commentary on Vatican II's constitution on revelation, mentioned its statements on the Gospels:

This brief conciliar statement reflects the whole wealth of research that biblical scholars have continually devoted to the question of the origin of the four gospels and summarizes it in brief.

On 1 May 1985 he discussed the description of the inspired character of Scripture and its consequences (*Dei Verbum*, III, 11) and followed with a very cursory reference to the principles of interpretation (III, 12) for historical and literary, but also for "theological" interpretation and quoted the statement of purpose (III, 12c).

Of course, all this is accompanied by, or rather subordinated to, a continual emphasis on the tie to the so-called authentic magisterium. The *catechesis* also concludes thus: "For all of what has been said about the way of interpreting Scripture is subject finally to the judgment of the church, which carries out the divine commission and ministry of guarding and interpreting the word of God" (*Dei Verbum*, III, 12d). The pope added:

This rule is important and decisive for the clear determination of the mutual relationship between exegesis (and theology) and the magisterium of the church. . . . It should be emphasized once again that the magisterium makes use of the work of the theologians and exegetes and at the same time watches over their studies in an appropriate manner. For the magisterium is called to guard the complete truth contained in divine revelation. Belief, in the Christian sense, therefore means to adhere to this truth, making use of the guarantee of truth that comes from the church because of its designation by Christ himself. This is true for all believers, including theologians and exegetes. Here is revealed to all the merciful providence of God, who wished not merely to give us his self-revelation, but also to guarantee its true preservation, interpretation and explanation, by placing it in the hands of the church. [Clearly, the church has here become identical with the magisterium.]

Obviously, for John Paul II one of the most important sentences in the Constitution on Divine Revelation, which he repeatedly quotes and which he insists upon, is: "The task of authentically [*authentice*] interpreting the word of God, whether written or handed on, has been entrusted exclusively [*soli*] to the living teaching office of the church, whose authority is exercised in the name of Jesus Christ" (II, 10b).[3] This is no less true for him than for Paul VI! In his first speech to the International Theological Commission, 26 October 1979, he expressly quoted his predecessor's remarks of 11 November 1973:

From all this the difficult task and responsibility that you share in a certain sense with the church's magisterium will be clear. I say "in a certain sense" because, as my predecessor, Paul VI, wisely said, the authentic magisterium, which is of divine origin, is "equipped with a particular charism of truth that cannot be shared with others and that cannot be replaced by anything else."

Paul VI had added:

They [bishops and pope] are therefore not released from the obligation to seek appropriate means of assistance in researching divine revelation. Their authentic magisterium thus has need of the "technical" help of theologians, who work according to the rules of their own method, in order that "the judgment of the church may more easily mature." (*Dei Verbum*, III, 12c)

John Paul II said at Altötting:

The theologian teaches in the name and under the direction of the ecclesial community of faith. He should and must make new suggestions; but these are simply offered to the church as a whole. Many of these need to be corrected and expanded in brotherly dialogue, until the whole church can accept them.

His description of theology, given on the occasion of the presentation of a prize to Hans Urs von Balthasar (23 June 1984, no. 5), is a kind of summary of the subject:

Theology is a missionary service to the church. It cannot, therefore, be understood as the free exercise of a profession of just any kind. It is really a competent cooperation in the prophetic office for which the church, by the will of Christ, is responsible. The profession of theologian is a call from the church. . . . In the final analysis, theology is a service to the magisterium. In the church the office of protecting the truth of revelation, of interpreting it authentically, and of teaching it to all is, by the will of Christ, entrusted to the Pope of Rome and the bishops in union with him and under his leadership [*Lumen Gentium 5*]. The services of the magisterium and the theologians support one another, although not within the same order, and the magisterium needs theologians. A correct relationship between magisterium and theology is a decisive factor in the life of the church and for the witness that all who believe in Christ are called to give to the world. For such a correct relationship makes it possible to prevent deviations and uncertainties that seriously disturb the conscience of the faithful, who are thereby made insecure in that which is most valuable to them: the truth for which one must also be prepared to die. Theology helps the magisterium by following and accompanying it, but also when it goes ahead of it in exploring new horizons and new paths. And especially in the latter instance the theologian, who poses new questions and opens up unforeseen dangers, must be careful to unite within his heart the childlike reverence of a disciple with the desire for ever-increasing knowledge and a continually deepening penetration into the understanding of the church's living tradition of the mystery of revelation that has been entrusted to it.

From the papal speeches to theologians in Germany, Fribourg (Switzerland), and elsewhere, it is clear that the pope's ideal is as

118 / GEORG SCHELBERT

follows: New questions should first be discussed among the theologians and should reach the larger church audience after being filtered through the magisterium. The critical function of theology, especially of biblical scholarship in respect to Scripture, the special object of its research, is not considered. Joseph Ratzinger's remark about Vatican II, in his commentary on *Dei Verbum* (II, 8), is applicable here: "On this point it regrettably made no progress; the matter of tradition criticism is almost completely ignored."[4]

What is the effect of this understanding of things on papal practice with regard to biblical scholarship?

The pope's so-called *catecheses* or remarks on this subject over a long period of time (September 1979 to March 1983) reveal a particular effort to work out a "theology of the body" in accordance with Scripture. Old Testament texts including the creation accounts, the story of Paradise, and the sin of Adam and Eve were discussed, as well as New Testament texts such as the second antithesis in the Sermon on the Mount, 1 Cor. 7, and Eph. 5, among others.

In the texts published with footnotes in *Osservatore Romano*, the pope cites a series of authors, including some exegetes. He also speaks without further clarification of the Yahwist. With respect to the authorship of the letter to the Ephesians, he proposes a compromise solution as "working hypothesis": the letter is a Pauline draft completed by a fellow worker. The pope describes his remarks as a "theological" interpretation. In my opinion they are just as much philosophically and systematically influenced by the value- and essence-ethics of Karol Wojtyla, and, in fact, he cites his own work. The underlying philosophical-theological anthropology seems to be presupposed. The texts are interpreted on that basis, though also in a certain sense in a very vivid, though also re-interpretative manner. Nor is the whole picture in the documents of revelation presented. For example, there is not a word about Matthew's qualification of the prohibition on divorce.

It is no use to say that the nature of these addresses before a constantly changing group at the general audiences, people without philosophical or theological background, did not allow for such refinements. Quite a few of these talks, in fact, presume such an education, even when one reads them, and seem more like a transfer to Saint Peter's Square of material from the pope's professorial period: the authors cited come from the period between 1943 (Tanquerey) and 1977 (Sabourin on Matthew). The talks were also supposed to be "following at a distance the preparations for the bishops' synod" on the subject of marriage and the family.

In his circular letter of 22 November 1982, which was intended to present the results of this synod, nothing is said about these talks. But the notion of marriage which appears in the letter is very strongly marked by the same ideas. Note, as one example, the subject of the "beginning" (Mt. 19:4), which is of fundamental importance in both (nos. 3, 10, 13), along with the notion of "truth" as corresponding to this divinely willed "beginning." It is interpreted as a kind of "origin of essence" or "original essence," from which the strictest conclusions are then drawn.

How can anyone, for example, say that "such a society radically contradicts polygamy; the latter directly rejects the plan of God as revealed in the beginning" (no. 19), in view of the biblical stories of the patriarchs, including especially the figures of Abraham, Jacob, and David as special subjects of the promise? Is it not rather a question of an ideal which is attained only in stages? Is not the same thing true of divorce? How else could Moses, according to the Scripture, have made concessions in the name of God to the "hardheartedness" of the people, if such concessions had contradicted something "essential" in the divine plan? Finally, Gen. 2:23–25 was written by someone who lived within the Old Testament social context. Is it not more appropriate to say, with the Constitution on Divine Revelation, that "these books [of the Old Testament], though they also contain some things which are incomplete and temporary, nevertheless show us true divine pedagogy" (IV, 15)? Is it not also rather remarkable that, in the question of divorce, not a single word is said about the so-called Pauline privilege (or about the extension of that privilege, which for a long time was falsely called "Petrine"), which relaxes these rigorous conclusions?

The effort to draw as much as possible on the fundamental sources of revelation for his remarks is especially apparent also in the numerous scriptural citations in the "Circular Letter on Divine Mercy" of 30 November 1980. This also contains something unusual for such a letter, namely, a long footnote on the concept

of "mercy" (*ḥèsèd, raḥamîm*) based on the results of biblical scholarship (no. 4, n. 52). But can one, for example, speak of the *lex
talionis* (with reference also to Jesus' way of thinking) as "the then-
current way of falsifying justice" (no. 12)? Was it not rather a major step forward in ethics leading directly to Jesus' moral
teaching?

A statement on the subject of "justice" also shows to what extent these utterances are really determined before and independent of any biblical basis: "In any case the reparation of evil and
scandal, reparation of damage, and satisfaction for offence are
the conditions of forgiveness" (no. 14). The parable of the lost
son, which is the point of departure for this remark, certainly contains no such idea, nor does that of the unmerciful servant with
his enormous debt (Mt. 18:23–25), which is not mentioned. It is
equally absent from Jesus' strictures on forgiveness.

The "Circular Letter on Reconciliation and Penance" of 2 December 1984 is also based on Scripture, on the parable of the lost
son. Certain texts are discussed in particular detail, such as 1 Jn.
5:16–17 ("sin unto death," no. 17), but only to end up with the
traditional two categories; or 1 Tim. 3:15–16 ("mystery of faith")
with a note on the concept *mystêrion* and on the grammatical construction in the verse in question (no. 12). With regard to 1 Jn.
3:9, reference is made to commentaries that interpret the "one
born of God" as Jesus Christ (no. 20). On the other hand, in the
discussion of Jn. 20:22, a text that is very important in this context, there is reference to Mt. 18:18, but not to 18:17 (church
community!), and we find no hint at all of difficulties of interpreting the text. Everything is taken as a directly transmitted word of
Jesus, that is, of the risen Lord, and exclusively interpreted in reference to the sacrament of Reconciliation. The Tridentine nar-
rowing of the question is all that matters. Of course it is admitted
that the sacrament of Reconciliation has developed. But then so
much is included in the "essence of the sacrament, of which the
church was always and without deviation clearly conscious," that
is, "that, according to the will of Christ, forgiveness is granted by
the minister of the sacrament to each individual in sacramental
absolution," that individual confession in the Tridentine sense is
anticipated and, in effect, projected back to the beginning (no.
29). There is simply a leap over the whole period between now

and the origins. But are there not larger possibilities with regard to those origins, so that the structures as we now have them, while certainly legitimate, are not the only legitimate ones? Again and again we hear about "truth." On 18 May 1985, the pope demanded of the biblical commission "scientific exactness and no abridgment of the faith," "no garbled or incomplete knowledge." But is it not also in the nature of truth and completeness, veracity and honesty, to recognize that not everything is so clear, that much is still open, and that much could and can quite legitimately be other than what it has become? I would like to see evidence of a greater degree of historical consciousness.

But in conclusion one must say that, in the statements of the current pope with regard to biblical scholarship and the historical-critical method, there are no calumnies and accusations. It is reserved to others to make them.

DEFAMATION OF THE HISTORICAL-CRITICAL METHOD BY JOSEPH RATZINGER

The declaration of the Congregation for the Doctrine of the Faith issued under Cardinal Seper (1969–81)—on the mystery of the incarnation (1972), on the church (1973), on the admission of women to the priesthood (1977), on eschatology (1979), on infant baptism (1980)—are directed at "erroneous opinions of recent times," according to the judgment of the congregation. But such opinions are not especially attributed to biblical scholarship in these documents.

Since 1982 it seems to me that one can observe a different style. Differing opinions are pictured as having radically destructive consequences or as being the result of radically destructive premises, the latter including the adoption of a "rationalist" exegesis. This is the case in the declaration "On Some Questions Related to Service at the Eucharist" (1983), in the instruction "On Certain Aspects of the Theology of Liberation" (1984), and in the "Notification" on Leonardo Boff's collection of essays *Church: Charism and Power* (1985). The opinions of the challengers and the premises which, supposedly, can be conclusively deduced from them, are thereby presented as so extreme and radical that we are really confronted with hostile portraits in which these persons can no longer recognize themselves. Here we can discern the hand of the systematic theologian who, in his commentary on the declaration "On Questions of Eschatology" (1979) went so far as to write that "the way the historical-critical method deals with its object can be compared with a kind of necrophilia."[5] Although in his assessment of the postconciliar period after ten years, written in 1975,[6] he had not yet drawn a bead on historical-critical exegesis, it apparently grew to be for him more and more a principal scapegoat for the crisis of faith which he diagnosed, culminating in his thoroughly negative interview with V. Messori in which that calumnious comparison reappears: "An exegesis in which the Bible no longer lives and is understood out of the living organism of the church"—in the context, it is historical-critical exegesis that is being discussed—"becomes archeology: the dead burying their dead."[7]

This mania for drawing conclusions is apparent in the document on servers at the Eucharist. There it is stated that the rejected opinion would repudiate not only the power of office entrusted to the priest, but the entire apostolic structure of the church, and would destroy the salvific effectiveness of the sacraments (III). But prophetic, charismatic potentialities in particular situations that, as such, are not simply subject to official authority, do not destroy the normal structure. They do not take anything away from anyone; instead, they give something that is essential to life. They also make clear that God is and remains Lord of the church and that Christ alone is its head. Everything and everyone else are body and belong to the body. They also make clear that not only grace, the comprehensive breadth of which the declaration is also forced to acknowledge, but also the "means of grace" remain God's "capital." Should Acts 11:17–18 not furnish a model for God's gracious action in other situations as well, so that the "water" can be poured after the fact, as Peter did in that case?

The procedure whereby "rationalistic" exegesis is accused of proposing the most radical theses possible is obvious in the instruction on the theology of liberation and in the remarks on the work of Boff, mentioned above (11 March 1985). Here there seems to be no hesitation in editing quoted material in such a way as to falsify the intention of the author. This really amounts to defamation before a worldwide audience. "What would be the genuine Catholic attitude? Openness to all orientations"—this much is cited. But Boff continues: ". . . but without excluding even a single one *that is possible on the basis of the New Testament.*"[8]

In his interview (with Messori) the cardinal degrades historical-critical exegesis to pure archeology with no relevance for the present-day church: "Historical-critical interpretation has certainly opened up many magnificent possibilities for better understanding of the biblical text"— so much has to be admitted, willy nilly—"but from its very nature it can only understand the text in its historical dimension, and cannot explain it in its present demands."[9] But he (quite correctly) calls "the Bible *just as it is*" the rule of faith.[10] And it is precisely *the* intention of *historical*-critical exegesis to keep the Bible current and living, to give it a voice in the present, *just as it is,* with its whole richness, with its possibilities and implications, with all its variety within a basic unity, as the authoritative origin in opposition to all attempts to make capital of it or to put restraints on it; against all sorts of all-too-direct backward projections that leap over millennia to locate at the "beginning" what has since developed—all this, so that the whole church "is constantly rejuvenated" (*iuvenescit, Dei Verbum,* VI, 24), so that it remains young. It has the task of cooperation "so that the Bible in the future must first of all be seen, reflected and questioned on its own terms; only then can the unfolding of tradition and dogmatic analysis begin," as Joseph Ratzinger wrote in his commentary on the sixth chapter of the Constitution on Divine Revelation.[11] The truth is that "[the church] has always regarded the Scriptures together with sacred tradition as the supreme rule of faith, and will ever do so. For, inspired by God and committed once and for all to writing, they impart the word of God Himself without change, and make the voice of the Holy Spirit resound in the words of the prophets and apostles. Therefore, like the Christian religion itself, all the preaching of the church must be nourished and ruled by sacred Scripture" (*regatur oportet*), that is, must take its direction from it (*Dei Verbum,* VI, 21).

Translated by
Linda Maloney

NOTES

1. J. A. Fitzmyer, *Stuttgarter Bibelstudien* 1 (Stuttgart, 1965), 33. See *Theological Studies* 25 (1964): 400.
2. See also the "Exhortatio apostolica" on the fifth anniversary of the Council, in which, after a positive evaluation of the contributions of biblical scholarship, there is a lament about "devastation among the people of God" brought about by "the spreading of fantastic hypotheses and opinions confusing to faith" (6 January 1970). In the general audience of 30 October 1968 the responsibility for problems of belief today had already been laid at the door of "philological, exegetical and historical studies applied to the first source of the truth of revelation, Sacred Scripture. . . . When robbed of its complement in Tradition and the authorized support of the church's teaching office, even the study of the Bible is full of uncertainties and problems which tend more to confuse faith than to strengthen it. Left to personal initiative, it creates such a pluralism of opinions that faith is shaken in its subjective security and robbed of its social authority."
3. See addresses to the theology professors in Fribourg, Switzerland (14 June 1984), and to the biblical commission (19 April 1985). He also emphasized this before the academic community of the University of Louvain-la-Neuve (21 May 1985) with reference to his speech in Fribourg. He spoke here of a "complete agreement with the clear statements of the church in the realm of faith and morals and the pastoral directions it gives."
4. Joseph Ratzinger, "Das Zweite Vatikanische Konzil II," *Lexikon für Theologie und Kirche,* (Freiburg, 1967), 519f.
5. Joseph Ratzinger, "Fragen der Eschatologie," *International Katholische Zeitschrift* 9 (1980): 215.
6. Joseph Ratzinger, *Theologische Prinzipienlehre: Bausteine zur Fundamentaltheologie* (Munich, 1982), 383–411.
7. Joseph Ratzinger, *Zur Lage des Glaubens* (Munich, 1985), 75; see especially 75–77; 188–93. The English is *The Ratzinger Report* (San Francisco, 1985).
8. Leonardo Boff, *Kirche: Charisma und Macht* (Düsseldorf, 1985), 145. Emphasis supplied.
9. Ratzinger, *Zur Lage des Glaubens,* 174.
10. *Ibid.,* 76. In the text there is the addition: "as it has been read in the church since the time of the Father."
11. Joseph Ratzinger, "Das Zweite Vatikanische Konzil II," in *LTK* (Freiburg, 1967), 575, on no. 24. One should read the whole commentary, which to my way of thinking is outstanding, including the remarks on ch. II, 8–9, esp. 518ff.

9. Moral Doctrine at the Cost of Morality?

The Roman Documents of Recent Decades and the Lived Convictions of Christians

DIETMAR MIETH

The question in the title is neither rhetorical nor is the following essay a polemic. Rather, it is a question of the well-known conflict between the moral teaching represented by the utterances of the Holy See on the one hand and the convictions of Christians drawn from their own lived experience on the other. According to my thesis, of course, this conflict does not result simply from the banal phenomenon that people do not always adhere to that which is morally correct and that even Christians may be sinners. Nor is it simply a matter of historical consciousness that lags behind an advanced or prescient recognition of the demands of truth. It is instead a matter of differences in recognition and acceptance of what is right, that is, not the truth of what is good in itself, but rather the questions related to normative usage.

In questions of normative usage, as we know, we are dealing with mixed judgments, in which the recognition of that which is objectively right is just as important as the correct description of moral phenomena and the consequent logic of prescriptive statements. We are not concerned with a crisis of morals in the sense that people really do not know what the right thing is and what they ought to do. Instead, we are dealing with a moral conflict within the church that, as it were, is not being carried on in an open, dialogical, and communicative manner because it thwarts practical, lived convictions within the church in certain areas. In this sense we can certainly speak of a crisis.

Although there are differing moral convictions among Christians in a great many areas of life in which there is an urgent need for action, the conflict is by no means to be found in all areas where one could complain that an unequivocal Christian morality is lacking. In questions of the use of violence, of the universality of the rights of free persons, of the distribution of goods, of truthfulness—in all these matters there is certainly Christian tradition and a developing moral teaching of the church. But it is the questions relating to the fifth and sixth commandments of "natural law," which according to scholastic teaching are convergent with the commandments of the Old Testament, that cause the most conflict. Within the Sermon on the Mount as well, it is mainly the statements concerning marriage that lead to conflicts within the church, not because there is clearly a plurality of interpretations among Christians, but because of a claim that there can be only one interpretation. On that basis we are certainly justified in restricting these reflections on church moral doctrine since the Second Vatican Council to positions and controversies related to sexual ethics and questions concerning human life.

The first question that presents itself is, Why is it precisely the statements concerning interpretation of *these* commandments that are controverted on several points? This may not be, in the final analysis, unrelated to the clarity and the high degree of obligation with which these teachings are expressed and the vigor and self-assurance with which they are emphasized. It may also be traced to the fact that it is precisely in these areas that individuals, inevitably and without exception, are affected, since these questions are connected to decisions within one's personal life-history that no one can avoid. But why is it just *here*—and this is widely attested—that church teaching is so rigorously unequivocal in its interpretation and moral orientation?

THE PRIORITY OF FAMILY ETHICS IN CHURCH MORAL DOCTRINE

We are speaking of moral doctrine in which the magisterium (by which I mean the ordinary magisterium, whose teachings, according to its own interpretation, are binding but not infallible) has presented unequivocal rules of moral conduct allowing no exception. We must distinguish moral doctrine from general moral teaching (thus the distinction made in English between "doctrine" and "teaching"). A moral doctrine in this sense is an ethic of obligation that, while conscious of the problem of practical attribution of guilt in extreme cases and no doubt recognizing the invincibly dissenting conscience as binding on the individual, still sees a truth free from all error fully present in each obligation that it imposes. Church moral teaching apparently exhibits this type of ethic of obligation only in the area of sexuality, marriage, and family. In other cases it tends rather to restrict itself to basic moral truths, to indications of the ways in which these are to be applied, and to an appeal to the conscience of Christians to make an application of these basic truths in consideration of the facts and a morally correct argumentation. We are thus faced with the question why, in certain spheres of action, the church has developed its general moral teaching to the level of moral doctrine, in the sense of an ethic of obligation with concrete commands down to the last detail and allowing of no exceptions.

In essence, this question probably allows only of a historical answer. For one thing, it may be connected with a more or less sexualized concept of sin going back to Augustine. For another, the presence of the church at the critical moments in life's decisions, which are also bound up with sacramental life, plays a role. Finally, the understanding of the practice of faith has gotten mixed up with the matter of personal life-decisions which are often connected to sexual self-development. That the church here clings to its already formulated positions like a second skin, so to speak, may also be based in the fact that, besides its legitimate desire to remain the defender of the binding force of faith, it has also developed a particular tradition of "power over souls." In the last analysis we are talking about bastions within which the church has practically, over a long period of time, withstood the waves of secularism, the Enlightenment, and the scientific revolution. At the same time we have to do with marks of something that, while not meant to be exclusive, is yet seen as decisively Christian and thus as giving the idea of Christian discipleship its own concrete visibility.

It therefore seems to me scarcely conceivable that a change, in matters of sexual doctrine, for example, could come about without a shift of the center of gravity in the notion of the concrete obligation imposed by Christian faith. For simply to abandon its positions would, in this connection, cause the church's moral teaching as a whole to take on the kind of generality and abstraction that is often to be found in church social teaching. From the historical point of view it is no accident that questions of sexuality, marriage, and family have assumed such a prominent role. And it is precisely this which is problematic, for it means that a retreat from these positions would seem equivalent to self-annihilation. We must return to this question in our concluding evaluation.

THE INDIVIDUAL POSITIONS OF CHURCH MORAL DOCTRINE

BIRTH CONTROL

It is well known that the conflict over church moral doctrine both in scholarship and in practice intensified in the wake of the postconciliar decision of the magisterium in the question of birth control. But it is often overlooked that the encyclical "Humanae vitae" (1968) emphatically extends and deepens the Council's teaching about the primacy of love among the purposes of marriage. Here we can, in fact, really speak of a development in the spirit of the Council. The instruction for conduct in the matter of birth control is, on the other hand, essentially a repetition of the formulation of traditional teaching going back at least to Pius XI's encyclical "Casti conubii" of 1930. As is well known, birth control is said to be impermissible as long as it is not practiced through a combination of periodic abstinence and observation of the woman's menstrual cycle. Of course, there are admitted to be possible justifications for use of other means of birth control so long as regulation of births is not the directly intended purpose of their use. The church thus does not reject family planning. The most recent document, Pope John Paul II's "Charter of Family Rights" of 1983, distinguishes between allowable and necessary family planning on the one hand and birth control contrary to morality on the other. But in the language used, birth control is associated with the idea of an arbitrary discretion, that is, a morally repugnant manipulation of incipient life. To avoid repetition, we will discuss the foundations of this doctrine, and of those dealt with in the other individual points, in the next section.

ABORTION

The prohibition of abortion rests generally on the idea of the protection of every innocent human life that is not dangerous to another. It thus admits of no exception and is limited only by the protection of equivalent human life. This judgment includes a decision about the moment of the beginning of human life, which is identified with that of fertilization. The prohibition also includes a judgment that no person is justified in opposing some other good to that of the innocent life which endangers no other. According to church moral doctrine, there can be no valid proof of such justification.

SEXUALITY AND MARRIAGE

Again, the restriction of sexuality (that is, sexual activity, which, in this sense, should be clearly distinguished from the human sexual characteristics that are present in each individual), without exception, to the institution of marriage involves certain judgments: the linkage of sexuality to the contracting of marriage at a particular point in time and its restriction within the framework of marriage, as well as a judgment about the prescribed order of male-female partnership; then the idea of faithfulness to a living partner (against premarital, nonmarital, and extramarital sexual activity). This includes prohibition of a sexually active homosexuality.

REMARRIAGE AFTER DIVORCE

The prohibition on contracting a new marriage during the lifetime of the partner in a previous marriage follows from the norms connected with the exclusive location of sexuality with marriage, but adds a further judgment, namely, the so-called indissolubility of an existing marriage contract between living partners. Here, however, moral doctrine comes into contact with a "more flexible" pragmatism in church law, while maintaining its rigorous attitude both in the construction of canon law and in the sanctions it imposes.

The conflict over compulsory celibacy for priests is not related to church moral doctrine, since this compulsory celibacy is not connected with any judgment on the moral rightness of personal conduct. It is simply a matter of a legal convention of the church through which it exercises its jurisdiction over the qualifications for the priestly office.

SUBSTANTIATION OF INDIVIDUAL POSITIONS

In describing the church's position we are already sounding a characteristic note of postconciliar church moral doctrine, namely, a method of concretizing norms in relation to individual problems that can exist parallel to a general concept of sexuality and love and that chooses in each particular area certain proofs or forms of reasoning that are more oriented to the permissibility or nonpermissibility of individual acts than to the overall realization of the meaning of sexual life. It is now time to discuss these ways of reasoning.

GENERAL TYPES OF PROOF

There are essentially three types of proof which can readily be recognized in the positions taken by the magisterium. The first is directed to an understanding of reality as a whole and especially that of "human nature." It is taken for granted that the meaning of the creation of human consciousness as found in revelation provides the necessary certitude and assurance that we can come to a common understanding of the inherent meaning of "nature" as a whole. The recognition of this meaning within "being" carries with it, at the same time, an obligation: *agere sequitur esse* (action follows being).

A second type of proof is directed to the consequences of human action. An attempt is made once again to strengthen fundamental positions on the basis of an experience of observed consequences and a prognosis of the results that are to be expected from certain actions, independent of any judgment of the correctness of individual actions themselves.

The third form of proof rests on the authority of the church and its tradition. In this instance the argument of the consistency of the magisterium plays a primary role.

Finally, in many cases, but not always, a biblical proof will be offered. These are, however, less clearly obvious in questions such as birth control and details of modern medical ethics than, for example, in the matter of the permissibility of a second marriage during the lifetime of the partner in a previous marriage.

REASONS GIVEN FOR THE RESTRICTION OF FAMILY-PLANNING METHODS

Birth control is the perennially cited example of the types of reasoning mentioned above. First of all, a particular understanding of the "nature" of sexual acts plays an essential role; an openness to the transmission of human life is assumed to be part of this "nature." The concept includes the possible ways in which sexual acts should be carried out, as well as the prohibition of means that would restrict the significance of a particular sexual act to its expression of affection between the persons concerned and would positively exclude the possibility of conception. Certainly, sexual intercourse as an expression of marital love is always allowable, even when one knows that, in the particular situation, conception cannot occur, that is, when "nature" of itself does not allow for conception, whether because of the woman's menstrual cycle or because of age, illness, or physical disability. The particular difficulty of this argument lies in the distinction between acts in which natural conditions are simply taken into account and others in which "nature" is artificially manipulated. For the position of the magisterium includes an affirmation of the legitimacy of so-called natural family planning.

The reasoning based on effects and consequences rests, in the realm of birth control, essentially on two grounds: first, the danger of moral decay in sexual behavior if the question of the openness of the persons involved to conception of new life is reduced to a *quantité négligeable* (negligible quantity); second, opposition to social programs of population control that, especially in the Third World, might lead to manipulation of the poor—and that, in certain cases, have done just that.

The argument on the basis of consistency in the magisterium is especially emphasized. Of course, it is not a matter of a very ancient position, since the birth control methods in question are relatively new. But we are faced here with a teaching of the magisterium that, from the very beginning, was vehemently emphasized.

We are talking especially about the teaching of the most recent popes. It is not simply a matter of magisterial consistency (*ecclesia sibi suaque doctrina constat*), but also of the argument of special inspiration of the magisterium's knowledge, by which the guidance of the Holy Spirit is expressed.

John Paul II has attempted to strengthen the first line of argument by means of his personal understanding of nature. His argumentation is directed, not so much to a contradiction of nature in the sexual act as such, but rather to a hostility to persons—that is, a refusal of the obligation to the "nature" of the human person—in "artificial birth control." For the possibility of conception, or rather, the possibility of becoming a father or mother, is such a fundamental element in the personal potential of those concerned that a disregard for this personal reality would represent a reduction of the value of one's partner.

REASONS GIVEN FOR FORBIDDING ABORTION

This position holds that a life that can be called human and that is neither guilty nor in itself threatening nor dangerous to others may never, that is, under no imaginable circumstances, be terminated by another human being. To this extent we are here dealing with two elements of proof: the determination of the existence of human life at the factual level, and the determination that no condition is present that would remove the right of this life to protection, at the level of recognition that there exists no human right to kill. The primary assertion offered as foundation for the statement that human life exists from the moment of conception is that the complete and valid information necessary for this human life is present from that time on. No balancing of values between the prospective life of the unborn on the one hand and, on the other hand, the challenge posed by the demand for acceptance and care of the child by the parents, particularly the mother, is regarded as acceptable, since these are not considered to be comparable goods of the same order.

STRUCTURE OF THE REASONING WITH REGARD TO SEXUAL ETHICS

According to this line of reasoning, the created purpose of genital expression within a sexual relationship is only to be found in the framework of meaning given by marriage. This excludes masturbation, premarital, nonmarital, and extramarital sex, as well as homosexual acts. It is a question of a cultural ordering of humanity that is part of the plan of creation itself, within which and only within which the sexual act can achieve moral value. Here, too, there are some additional arguments derived from observation or prognosis of effects and results. And here, too, the consistency of magisterial tradition plays a major role. I have already pointed out that the imbedding of sexual acts within the meaning of marital partnership is also insisted upon in such an exclusive sense because in any other situation the "weakness of concupiscence" that is otherwise present in sexuality could exercise its destructive power.

REASONS FOR THE PROHIBITION OF REMARRIAGE

Although, according to the thinking of the magisterium, the indissolubility of marriage corresponds to God's creative purpose and thus is characteristic even of "natural marriage," the reasoning given here is more dogmatic in character. For indissolubility as an expression of the sacramental bond between persons has been intensified even further in the economy of salvation. In this sense the biblical words of Jesus about divorce are cited and applied. It would be justifiable in some sense to speak of a specifically dogmatic-ethical reasoning on this point.

CONFLICTS IN THE UNDERSTANDING OF MORAL THEOLOGY

THE CONFLICT BETWEEN DOCTRINAIRE AND COMMUNICATIVE APPROACHES

Here it is not a matter of a discussion of theories of truth, that is, of an argument about whether one takes truth to be an objective reality in perception or an agreement in the understanding (consensus theory). It has rather to do with the fact that concepts take on a different aspect within theological perspective when what is placed in the foreground is no longer a doctrinaire instruction, but rather the process of God's self-communication within the process of self-clarification of faith. A paradigm shift of this sort changes concepts like "revelation," "nature," "church," and "morality." Truth is then not simply a system of knowledge that only needs to be emphatically taught. Instead, it is understood within a process of self-discovery, behind which stands God's own process of self-revelation (*Selbsterschließung*). Thus it is not a matter of applying a truth that has been defined once and for all, but of understanding and discovering truth in the communicative process of the forces at work within the church (magisterium, theology, *sensus fidelium*). To the extent that this shift from the simple application of existing truth to a process of understanding and discovery of truth was set in motion by the Second Vatican Council, church teaching after the Council really dares not fall back into a doctrinalist understanding of "teaching." (See Max Seckler, "Zur Interdependenz von Aufklärung und Offenbarung," *Theologische Quartalschrift* 165 [1985], 161–73, esp. 169–70: Zur Offenbarungskonstitution "Dei Verbum" des Zweiten Vatikanischen Konzils.)

Moral teaching is a good example of what is meant here. It applies, for one thing, to the matter of biblical instructions. The instructions found in the Bible in regard to ethical matters are not simple statements that impose duties valid for all times. Instead, they are models of practical self-discovery on the part of communities, elicited in historical process as answers to challenges to the truth of practical conduct. What is here said about the scriptural tradition is equally valid for the church's tradition. This also presupposes that "morality" is not to be regarded as a given, preformulated system, but as a vital coming-to-be of the practical option of faith in dialogue with contemporary moral reason and perception of reality.

A nondoctrinaire concept of morality corresponds to a nondoctrinaire notion of nature. In view of the progress in scientific understanding of nature—and in light of the increasing depth of our understanding of the human person, which is less and less tied to concepts of substance and more influenced by the idea of identity—*natura humana* can no longer be perceived simply as a link in the chain between biological nature on one side and the spiritual substance of the angels on the other. That is, the human being appears not as a metaphysically fixed essence, but as an open capacity for meaning. The human responsibility for self-development is thus no longer to be seen as purely receptive, but rather as creative. The criticism of an excess of human creative self-determination resulting from an overly optimistic idea of progress is certainly justified, but it should not overlook the fact that human beings discover their "nature" precisely in dealing with this realm of responsibility and creativity.

THE CONTROVERSY OVER MORAL AUTONOMY

Reflection on the autonomy of morals in theological ethics during the last two decades has shown that what is at stake is not human self-glorification as a sign of disregard for the will of God, but rather a human search to recognize and put into practice the personal responsibility that is a consequence of human freedom. Such an autonomy is in no way contradictory to a self-confirmation in faith which presupposes revelation as divine self-communication. But it is confident that moral norms can be found to be in agreement with reason, because that is precisely where the positive meaning of belief in creation finds its expression.

THE CONFLICT OVER THE FOUNDATION OF MORAL JUDGMENTS

This means that moral norms must be susceptible of rational foundation. Arguments resting on authority, or the constancy of a doctrine, or on the establishing of historical rules of thumb as timeless precepts are not sufficient. The court of reason rests its judgments on various sources of moral experience (in Scripture and tradition and in the lived convictions of believers) but primarily on the rational evaluation of the consequences of human action. It is thereby obligated at the same time to the principles of empirical rationality, without wishing to make these in themselves normative. The recognition of appropriate values and their evaluation in concrete circumstances is the precondition for a moral argumentation that aims at concrete obligation. Norms are, in this sense, to be formulated as conditional statements that describe the circumstances of their validity along with the command or prohibition they contain. This way of thinking is not all new. The ideas of traditional moral theology about the circumstances of action, of the balancing of goods, of the lesser evil, of actions with double effect are all part of the development of a tradition concerning the ways of founding moral judgments that could not accept an understanding of morality based on the idea of moral teaching as doctrinaire instruction.

SOME CONSEQUENCES

Thus a reference to consistency and authority in the teaching of a doctrine cannot relieve the need for substantiation in the case of concrete moral directives. The effort made by the Papal Commission on Birth Control before 1968 to arrive at concrete moral directives in the spirit of a communicative understanding of church moral teaching was, as is well known, stopped by the encyclical "Humanae vitae" before it was able to produce fruitful results within the meaning of the conciliar understanding of truth. The majority of the commission connected the means of birth control to characteristics of responsibility of the human person in general. They found no basic arguments for the "unnaturalness" of so-called artificial means, or rather, they did not find that human persons had no right to use such means. The sharp differentiation between the possibilities of fashioning human nature could not, according to the opinion of the majority of the commission, be maintained in face of the insight that a differentiated relationship of human beings with their own nature as such belongs, in itself, to human nature.

THE CONTRADICTION OF THE ACTUAL, LIVED CONVICTIONS OF THE CHURCH

This very discussion about argumentation in the question of birth control had shown that the moral doctrine of the magisterium and theological-ethical reflection come into conflict insofar as the magisterium's moral doctrine was not prepared to accept and implement the paradigm shift contained in Vatican II's "Pastoral Constitution on the Church in the Modern World" and in other documents. In many of the individual questions that were addressed in doctrinaire fashion there thus emerged a contradiction between the factually lived conviction of believers in the church and this moral doctrine.

We now turn to a discussion of the other elements of argumentation in light of this conflict.

BIRTH CONTROL

Why is it that Catholic Christians do not follow the teaching of the church in the matter of birth control? According to church teaching, this is possible because they are following an invincibly false judgment of conscience. Under pressure of contemporary ways of thinking, they are not able to form their consciences in such a way as to correspond to the demands of the magisterium. Many believers can live with the respect that the church shows even to false decisions of conscience. But many others cannot, because they do not grasp the reasons which are supposed to prove that their consciences are false. In the choice of the means of birth control, they are well aware of the difference between responsibility and caprice, but they do not perceive the differences that are supposed to govern the choice of means at the material level. For example, they do not see why the use of birth control means that inhibit ovulation—while taking into consideration and carefully examining possible physical and psychical consequences—is supposed to be *in and of itself* a manipulation that, by contrast to the use of the rhythm method, is immoral per se. For in the final analysis one must perceive a basic difference between altering the periodic cycle and simply choosing certain times within that cycle, or one must find a criterion for the acceptance or rejection of one or another technology. For even the so-called natural family planning method is increasingly dependent on technological refinement in order to be effective. Moreover, a limitation of birth control to periodic continence is simply not possible for many people, for reasons of physiological conditions, biopsychic regularity, or pure problems of timing. The more these questions are dealt with at the most immediate level, the more likely is it that those concerned will leave a church that, on the basis of such unintelligible reasoning, attempts to make objective judgments about the existence of serious sin.

ABORTION

The attitude of church moral doctrine to the interruption of pregnancy is certainly the one that enjoys the most respect. A moral judgment formulated under very clear conditions, which extends its protection both to unborn and to damaged life, is difficult to oppose in its own inner logic. And yet there are contradictions here, as well, to factually lived convictions, in three respects.

First, there is the problem of being certain that the point in time at which the irreversible process of becoming human begins is identical with conception. It is not so much a matter of accepting this point in time as an *orientation*, for the very uncertainty about the beginnings of life can be regarded as a reason for starting to protect unborn life at the earliest possible moment. It is rather a question of the *rigor* with which this point in time is insisted upon, in view of the fact that "nature" itself has not so inevitably determined this process as to prevent that the further step of implantation of the fertilized egg might fail to take place. A rigorous equation of abortion with a prohibition on birth control methods that act by preventing implantation thus repeatedly leads to problems in borderline situations.

A second practical objection is directed to another rigorist element in church moral doctrine. Protestant theologians like Karl Barth had already pointed out this element when they both admired and detested the moral doctrine of the Catholic church because of its severity. Here it is a question of the concrete balancing of the right to protection of the unborn human being and its human future, or rather, the demands this future places on the other persons concerned. It is perhaps prudent to say that church moral doctrine is correct in disputing the general possibility of an equation in this matter. In fact, this matter of "demand" (*Zumutbarkeit*) is not a good that can be equated with the basic good of existence. But there are existential situations that are not covered by rules formulated from an objective standpoint. Especially here it would be important to differentiate between rules that tell people in advance how they should behave and what they should do and rules that judge individual human actions after the fact. Problems with the severity of the church's position in questions of abortion would certainly be diminished among Christians, and other people as well, if the church could abandon its monolithic position in the matter of birth control. World hunger and the population explosion are repeatedly cited in this connection as "signs of the times" in face of which it is problematic to bring new human persons into the world only so that they may face a quick death.

But the principal argument that one continually hears, from Christians as well, against the church position on abortion, is that of the inconsistency of the church's teaching. If the growing number of legal abortions appears to the church as "genocide," then the question repeatedly arises, why the church does not oppose with equal severity the killing of innocent and other nondangerous persons in wars and armed conflicts and through totalitarian violence. There is plenty of evidence that modern war is absolutely impossible without the killing of innocent and noncombatant persons and that people are being killed simply to give a signal of readiness to cling tenaciously to one or another fundamentalist position. Certainly, the church condemns torture, terrorism, and misuse of force, but at a much more general level. As long as this inconsistency continues, the ethical persuasiveness of the arguments against abortion will be perceived more as a sign of a one-dimensional consciousness within church moral doctrine than, as it should be, a sign of the church's decisive option for life.

SEXUAL ETHICS

In church sexual ethics primary emphasis is placed on characteristics of time, form, and action. On the other hand, in the lived conviction of Christians the degree of responsible mutuality of the partners plays a much greater role. Two things should be noted here. On the one side there is the paradigm shift in the consciousness of believers, according to which the consequences of original sin are to be sought not so much in a disordered sexual desire as in signs of a violent misuse of other persons. Evil, to put it simply, is seen less in a failure to master one's desires than in a failure to curb aggression and violence. Certainly, most people today share the insights of the social sciences that there are positive human models of "desire" as well as of "rebellion": the experience of the impact of the destructive power of sin on human existence is seen, however, less in the dangers of sexual immorality, and more in the experience of human inability to cope with new sources of aggressive potential.

In the factually lived experience of Christians there is also the conviction that there is a moment of anthropological urgency in sexual relationships that should not be confused with a pure loss of control of sexual drive at the expense of the other. Forms of sexual communication as instants of human encounter that reach into the depths of the whole person cannot simply be equated, in human consciousness, with the aim of starting a family. The more that life decisions are differentiated, in this matter, into those that follow one another and those that accompany one another, the less understandable is a fixation on a particular action at one point in time, such as the marriage ceremony, or even the form of that act itself. This is no way prevents the factually lived convictions of Christians from agreeing in *intention* with the goals of church moral doctrine. The goal of a fully valid personal unfolding of sexuality is not disputed in the church. But it seems to many people within the church that a normative casuistry is not the proper means to achieve that goal.

REMARRIAGE AFTER DIVORCE

Also in the case of the remarriage of divorced persons, the dissent is not directed to the intention expressed in church moral doctrine. Christians really do want to behave in such a way as to make their marriages indissoluble and inviolable. They want, that is, to live in such a way that their marriages will not break up. They also want to live so as to insure that marriages that come about some time after the collapse of previous marriages are not necessary. But the recognition of rules as guidelines for moral conscience should, here again, be distinguished from a judgment on conduct after the fact. And it is precisely here that the problem lies, because church moral doctrine, joined with ecclesial sanctions, makes irreversible life decisions, which are seen as necessary and which are carried out with deep conviction, the objects of judgment and ecclesial punishment. People within the church are seeking here a morality that accepts the processes of a life history in which new developments come about, sometimes on the basis of false evolutions or even wrong decisions with guilt present. Nevertheless, in these developments, human values are found and actualized for the partnership and for the children. These practical, lived moral convictions of persons in the church expect a moral instruction from the church in which the good of the persons concerned is of primary interest. They don't want the doctrine of an institutional order in which Jesus of Nazareth's struggle against the hardheartedness of the doctrine of divorce in his own time is no longer recognizable.

CONCLUSION: PROGNOSIS FOR DEVELOPMENT

Church social *doctrine* has shifted, since John XXIII and the Second Vatican Council, toward a social-ethical *instruction* of human persons. The paradigm shift from doctrinaire to communicative development of the truth of faith has certainly contributed to this development, in a dialogue with "signs of the times" and with the practical consciousness of believers. But even in social instruction there are repeated lapses back into the doctrinaire mode, as exemplified by the conflicts concerning liberation theology in Catholic social teaching. But on the whole it appears that this development is irresistible.

If we can, despite contrary tendencies, make a positive prognosis for postconciliar church development in this area, which can also be substantiated from documents of the present pope, John Paul II, in the realm of social teaching, still the situation demands a much more pessimistic judgment with regard to development of church moral doctrine in questions concerning fundamental existential decisions in the face of medical-ethical and sexual-ethical problems. Church moral doctrine in this area since the Council has displayed an inability to learn that threatens to disconnect it, not only from developments of moral consciousness (the ambiguity of which should also be taken into account), but also from the lived moral praxis of Christians themselves. The reciprocal relationship between church moral doctrine and the lived convictions of persons in the church is more and more in danger of falling apart, even when a commonality of intention is maintained and strengthened through a many-sided communication on the part of theology and the church educational institutions. There seems to be no prospect of a change in this regard. For many Christians this is a reason to distance themselves from the church. But a real change could be effected if we could come to an agreement, on the basis of a common human sense of values, that the period of doctrinaire-normative systems of knowledge is at an end and should be replaced by communicative agreement about responsibility in the various spheres of life and moments of decision. The church could open a bridge to such a positive development if it would try to place the attractiveness of values and positive models of human basic attitudes *together* in the foreground. It is not the least of the disadvantages of church moral doctrine that, in questions of sexual ethics for example, it is not in a position to sketch a positive and attractive basic scenario for a moral life. The priority of prohibitive commands in church sexual ethics, as well as in other situations in which life decisions are made, lends church moral doctrine a uniquely inflexible and negative stamp. The lack of freedom for theological discussion, at least so far as it takes place in public spheres within the church, does not provide fertile ground for a mood of spiritual awakening in matters of morality. The course of the bishops' synods, for example, the one on the family in 1980, makes it clear that church moral doctrine prefers instead to wall itself off in face of the wisdom of factually lived convictions of Christians and the rationality of theological-ethical argumentation. Such a climate certainly does not have an elevating effect on morals. It is not a climate of openness, but one of fear; it is not a climate of *communio,* but one of claims to positions of power. The authority of the magisterium suffers as much as does the concrete transmission of faith. The prognosis is bad, but that is no reason for theology to cease its efforts at mediation.

What direction could these mediating efforts take? I have already pointed out that on the level of human values and basic attitudes, or basic models of moral behavior, the agreement is greater than at the level of normative application. And here, too, the practical need for orientation is greater among Christians, who would rather learn, for example, how faithful love can be positively lived than to hear what, when, where, how often, and with whom one may or may not do this or that.

Another idea appears to me, however, even more important. Following Christ requires concreteness; faith calls for the witness of obligatory praxis. The question is, in the present moment of historical *kairos,* which concretion, which witness? Are the questions of liberation, of the just distribution of goods, of the promotion of peace not more important concretions of the witness of faith for today? In the Sermon on the Mount they are at least as important as the questions of decisions about sexual life. If the church, in the course of history, was able to shift the emphasis in moral teaching toward the fulfillment of personal life, does it not have an equal right at the present time, in face of the "signs of the times" and of the gospel, to shift the emphasis of its moral teaching in the concretizing of moral behavior in another direction (while abandoning the doctrinaire style of its teaching)?

Translated by
Linda Maloney

Source Notes

"Gaudium et Spes" (The Pastoral Constitution on the Church in the Modern World), *Das Zweite Vatikanische Konzil, Anhang zum Lexikon für Theologie und Kirche*, vol. 3 (Freiburg: Herder, 1968), 242ff.

"Humanae vitae" (On the Proper Regulation of the Transmission of Human Life), *Nachkonziliare Dokumentation*, vol. 14, 3d ed., Deutsche Bischofskonferenz (Trier, 1972).

"Persona humana" (Declaration of the Congregation for thè Doctrine of the Faith on Certain Questions of Sexual Ethics), *Verlautbarungen des Apostolischen Stuhls* [Acta Apostolicae Sedis], no. 1, ed. Sekretariat der Deutschen Bischofskonferenz (Bonn, 1975).

John Paul II, "Familiaris consortio" (On the Duties of the Christian Family in the Modern World), *Verlautbarungen des Apostolischen Stuhls* [Acta Apostolicae Sedis], no. 33, ed. Sekretariat der Deutschen Bischofskonferenz (Bonn, 1981).

John Paul II, "Charter of Family Rights," *Verlautbarungen des Apostolischen Stuhls* [Acta Apostolicae Sedis], no. 52, ed. Sekretariat der Deutschen Bischofskonferenz (Bonn, 1983).

Statements of the congregation for education: orientation to upbringing [erziehung] in human love; directives on sex education, *Verlautbarungen des Apostolischen Stuhls* [Acta Apostolicae Sedis], no. 51, ed. Sekretariat der Deutschen Bischofskonferenz (Bonn, 1983).

10. "Liberation" from Liberation Theology?
Motives and Aims of the Antagonists and Defamers of Liberation Theology
NORBERT GREINACHER

In 1973, five years after Gustavo Gutierrez had first spoken about liberation theology,[1] the study group Church and Liberation was founded. But, in spite of its name, this group, whose central figure was Bishop Franz Hengsbach of Essen, was not formed in solidarity with the theory and praxis of Christians in Latin America who were engaged in the struggle of the Latin American peoples for more freedom, self-determination, and human rights. Instead, this study group wanted to liberate Latin American Christians from the theology of liberation. Lothar Bossle, professor of sociology at the University of Würzburg and one of the chief ideologues of this study group, expressed it this way: "European Christians thus have the obligation to help deliver Latin America from the trauma of the theology of liberation, by showing how the ideas that are basic to liberation theology have failed in Europe."[2]

Bossle's formulation was, however, not original with him. In 1974, a book entitled *Liberacion de la liberacion* by G. Gulat had already appeared in Bogotá. And after a visit to Latin America, Bishop Franz Hengsbach reported: "The so-called theology of liberation leads nowhere. Its result will be communism. Revolution is not the way to improve the situation."[3]

THE CONFLICT OVER LIBERATION THEOLOGY
WITHIN THE CHURCH

To date, in the struggle within the church against liberation theology, a central role has been played by Alfonso Lopez Trujillo, who was named auxiliary bishop of Bogotá, Colombia, in 1971. From 1972 to 1979 he was general secretary of CELAM (the Latin American bishops' conference), and from 1979 to 1983 served as its president. In 1979 he was made archbishop of Medellin, Columbia, and on 2 February 1983 he was named a cardinal. During the preparations for the third general assembly of the Latin American bishops, which took place from 27 January to 13 February 1979 in Puebla, Mexico, Lopez Trujillo wrote a letter to Bishop Luciano Duarte that was accidentally made public. In this letter he said, among other things: "Get your bomber aircraft and your herbal poisons ready, then, for you will be needed in Puebla and in the CELAM meeting, in fact, more than ever before and in the best of condition. I think you had better get in training like a boxer preparing to enter the ring for the world championship, so that your punches will hit the mark and square with the Gospel."[4]

But the conflict over liberation theology visibly sharpened during the years 1983 and 1984, primarily due to the actions of Cardinal Joseph Ratzinger, prefect of the Congregation for the Doctrine of the Faith in Rome. In March 1983, Cardinal Ratzinger presented the Peruvian bishops' conference with a document containing ten critical questions directed to Gustavo Gutierrez's theology. In September of that year, he delivered a lecture, in the presence of the pope, on the theoretical aspect of liberation theology from a scholarly point of view. On 23 January 1984, the Peruvian magazine *Oiga* then published an article by Cardinal Ratzinger, "Presupuestos, Problemas y Desafios de la Teologia de la Liberacion" (Presuppositions, Problems, and Defects of the Theology of Liberation). An Italian translation of the article appeared on 3 March 1984 in *30 Giorni*, an Italian magazine, and a somewhat abridged version was published in the August 1984 issue of *Die neue Ordnung*.[5] Here we read: "An analysis of the phenomenon of liberation theology reveals a fundamental threat to the faith of the church."

OPPONENTS OF LIBERATION THEOLOGY OUTSIDE THE CHURCH

But it is not only within the church that this new theology of liberation meets with bitter opposition. It also plays a major role in international politics and has been portrayed, especially by those representing a particular trend in North American policy toward Latin America, as unusually dangerous. These politicians recognized from the beginning that the theology of liberation was a serious threat to the North American policy of intervention in Central and South America. This is witnessed by the "Rockefeller Report" of 1969, as well as by a secret paper prepared by the CIA for the Bolivian military and an analysis written in 1969 by members of the Rand Corporation in Santa Monica, California, entitled "Latin American Institutional Development: the Changing Catholic Church."[6]

Then there is the "Santa Fe Paper," which sees in liberation theology a serious menace to the economic and security interests of the United States. This document, which contains guidelines for a "new American policy for the 80s," was developed in May 1980, during the Carter administration, by the "Santa Fe Committee." It still serves as a basis for the Latin American policy of the Reagan administration. The authors of the paper proceed on the assumption that the Third World War is already in progress. Carter's foreign policy is seen as a tactical retreat in face of the growing influence of Moscow in the Caribbean. It is time to replace Carter's human rights policy with "ethical and political realism." With respect to theology of liberation, we read: "United States foreign policy must begin to oppose liberation theology, as it is used by the 'liberation theologians' in Latin America. The role of the church in Latin America is of decisive importance for the idea of political freedom. Unfortunately, Marxist-Leninist forces have used the church as a political weapon against private property and capitalist methods of production, by infiltrating religious communities with ideas that are not so much Christian as Communist."[7]

We ought not to overlook the role of the German economy in this coalition against the theology of liberation. At the beginning of October 1982 there was a conference at the papal Urbaniana

University in Rome, whose theme was "The Christian Concept of a World Economic Order as Alternative to Marxism." The conference was organized and paid for by the Hanns-Martin-Schleyer Foundation in Cologne. Between 24 and 28 July 1985 an international seminar on Latin America took place near the city of Los Andes in Chile, at the invitation of the magazine *Communio,* that issued the "Los Andes Declaration" against liberation theology.[8] Also in 1985 a "study-dialogue" was put on by the Institute for the German Economy, the National Federation of German Employers' Councils, and the Guild of German Catholic Engineers.[9] The principal speakers (Cardinal Joseph Höffner, Manfred Spieker, Heinz Joachim Held, Martin Honecker, and Otto Esser) unanimously rejected the theology of liberation. Characteristically, not one liberation theologian was invited to participate in the dialogue. Professor Gerhard Fels, director of the Institute for the German Economy, took note of this in his closing remarks: "The accused was not present, and a defender would also have had a hard time getting in."[10] Similarly, at the symposium "Church and Industry: Their Responsibility for the Future of the World Economy," held again at the Urbaniana University in Rome from 21 to 24 November 1985, a position was taken in opposition to theology of liberation in the absence of any liberation theologians. The symposium was sponsored by the Papal Council for the Laity, the Institute for the German Economy in Cologne, the Konrad Adenauer Foundation, the International Union of Catholic Universities, the League of German Catholic Industrialists, the Society for the Advancement of the Swiss Economy, plus the Austrian Society for Economics, and the International Christian Industrialists' Union.

That this controversy over the theology of liberation is not merely an academic affair, something being dealt with at the desk and the lectern, but instead is a conflict that for many of those concerned is literally mortal, is clear from the fact that in many Latin American countries anyone who commits herself or himself on behalf of an improvement in justice and human rights is branded a communist and thus made fair game. As an example of this we can mention the so-called Banzer Plan, a secret strategic paper prepared in 1975 at the request of the then-president of Bolivia, General Hugo Banzer, with the help of the CIA. According to this plan an effort should be made to deepen the division that already exists within the church so that committed Christians will be combatted by the church itself both on doctrinal grounds and through disciplinary measures. In addition, foreign clergy must be opposed through an emphasis on "the authenticity of a national church." Representatives of the committed clergy have to be connected with the "guerrillas" and made to appear as friends of international communism. The following concrete directions are given: "Priests on the 'black list' should be arrested, preferably in empty streets or in the countryside. . . . If a priest has been arrested, the Ministry must try to smuggle subversive propaganda materials or a weapon (preferably a large-calibre pistol) into his belongings or—if possible—into his dwelling; at the same time his 'story' must be put together in such a way as to put him in a bad light before the bishops and the public."[11]

WHOM DOES LIBERATION THEOLOGY OPPOSE?

It is clear that there is a broad coalition of those who despise the theology of liberation, extending from the Roman Congregation for the Doctrine of the Faith and its prefect, Cardinal Ratzinger, to, under the influence of the pope, the Roman commission for Latin America and the Latin American Bishops' Conference (CELAM), to conservative, reactionary, even totalitarian political forces. Therefore this theology of liberation must be a threatening and dangerous business.

In fact, the theology of liberation is dangerous and subversive. The question is only, for whom?

To begin with, liberation theology radically questions the validity of the capitalist economic system. The concluding document of the third general assembly of the Latin American bishops at Puebla (1979) is completely united with liberation theology on this point when it says: "The free-market economy in its purest form, which remains the economic system of our continent and is legitimated by certain liberal ideologies, has increased the distance between poor and rich because it values capital over labor and economic interests over social needs. Minority groups, sometimes joined to foreign interests, have exploited the opportunity offered them by these old forms of the free market to secure their own advantage at the expense of the interests of the greater part of the population." Such a judgment contradicts certain conservative traditions in Catholic social teaching, especially as represented in West Germany and in the German episcopacy. Thus Cardinal Julius Döpfner elaborated in a lecture to the National Federation of German Industry on 11 March 1975 on "Ethical Bases of Economic Leadership," laying special emphasis on his teaching authority as a bishop: "These largely ideological attacks on the economic structures of society are only part of a general tendency that threatens not only industrialists, but also the church and our entire free society. . . . Church and industry are thus faced with the same challenge." Cardinal Joseph Höffner also, at the symposium mentioned above on "Church and Industry: Their Responsibility for the Future of the World Economy," in November 1985 in Rome, spoke of the free-market economy as representing, for Catholic social teaching, the proper basic form of economic order.[12] Previously, on 24 September 1984, in his opening remarks at the fall assembly of the German Bishops' Conference entitled "Church Social Teaching or Theology of Liberation?" Cardinal Höffner had presented a critical discussion of liberation theology. In that talk, speaking in the style of a kind of theological neocolonialism, and completely misunderstanding the character and content of liberation theology, Cardinal Höffner said: "Properly understood, the theology of liberation is part of the church's social teaching. It is not identical with it, because church social teaching is more comprehensive."

It is evident that here conflicts of interest and theological standpoints collide. On one side stands the theology of liberation which champions the liberation of the hundreds of millions of starving, oppressed, and exploited people in whose name it speaks, and condemns the structural injustices of international and national capitalist economic systems. On the other side we find a theological tradition and an ecclesial-political position, in fact, a political theology (even if its proponents reject this designation) that defends the free-market economic system, with certain social programs tacked on—and not only defends it, but legitimizes it as the only possible Christian economic system.

THE RELATIONSHIP BETWEEN CHRISTIAN FAITH
AND POLITICS

The discussion surrounding theology of liberation thus confronts us once again with the question of the relationship between Christian faith and politics.

What does it mean when Christians say, in the creed, that "for us and for our salvation" Jesus Christ "has come down from heaven"? Liberation theology is convinced that the salvation that was fundamentally accomplished in Jesus Christ and that began to be realized in him cannot be restricted to human words, to the supernatural dimension of the human person. Nor is it limited to the saving reality of the church and its sacraments. Rather, it aims at the complete liberation of individual persons and of society in all its aspects. Jesus Christ wanted to free people, not just in part, but as whole persons in all dimensions of their existence and to save them and restore them to wholeness in the fullness of their reality.

But that is also to say that every historical act of liberation from economic, political, or any other kind of unfreedom is related to God's saving history with humanity, even though we recognize that the grace of God that is given us in Jesus Christ always exceeds any efforts or successes that, being human, are thereby limited and conditioned—quite apart from the enduring sin and basic alienation of human persons, for example, in sickness and death.

And this is also to express a fundamental *politicization of faith.* This idea loses its provocative character and liability to misunderstanding if we recall the original sense of the word *polis:* city, communality. Politicization of faith then means that the theory and practice of Christian faith and of the church have a basic political dimension, that is, a relationship to the public sphere and to society.

But it is precisely this politicization of faith, of the Christian community, and of the church as a whole that the detractors of liberation theology fear. They accuse it of identifying Christian faith with political reality or of making it an instrument to political ends; more precisely, of subordinating faith to politics. Cardinal Höffner, in the lecture already quoted above, "Church Social Teaching or Theology of Liberation?" finds the politicization of the base communities questionable. And in his book *The Ratzinger Report (Zur Lage des Glaubens)* Cardinal Ratzinger expands on the point: "What is theologically unacceptable and socially dangerous here is this mixture of Bible, Christology, politics, sociology and economics. You cannot misuse Sacred Scripture and theology in order to absolutize and sacralize a single theory about the sociopolitical order."[13] (Did Cardinal Ratzinger realize that, with this statement, he was condemning his colleagues Döpfner and Höffner, who have lent Christian legitimation to the free-market economic system?) But Cardinal Ratzinger had already written, in an earlier essay, "Christianity has been careful, in opposition to certain false initiatives, not to locate the messianic in the political. On the contrary, from the very beginning it has insisted that the political be left in the sphere of rationality and ethics. It has taught and made possible the acceptance of what is imperfect. To put it another way: the New Testament is acquainted with a political ethic, but not with a political theology. It is precisely in this distinction that we find the line of division that Jesus himself and then, very emphatically, the apostolic letters drew between Christianity and fanaticism. No matter how fragmentary and accidental the various statements in the New Testament that concern the details of political life may be, they are absolutely clear and unanimous about this line of division: fanaticism is always rejected when it seeks to make the kingdom of God a political program. It is always the case that politics is not the concern of theology, but of ethics—although the latter, to be sure, may only find its foundation in theology."[14]

I will leave aside, for the moment, the fact that these remarks do not seem to me completely logical. I do not see why politics is not the concern of theology if, in fact, politics is within the sphere of ethics which "may only find its foundation in theology." However, it is in this question of the relationship of Christian faith to politics that I sense the best possibility of contact between Cardinal Ratzinger and the theologians of liberation. Thus the representatives of liberation theology can probably recognize themselves in the following statement in the "Instruction of the Congregation for the Doctrine of the Faith on Certain Aspects of the 'Theology of Liberation' " of 6 August 1984: "The scandal of inequality between rich and poor, which cries out to heaven— whether it is a question of inequality between rich and poor nations or of inequalities among social classes within the same nation—will no longer be tolerated. On the one side a heretofore unattained excess has been reached, which encourages waste; on the other side people are still living in a condition of need that is characterized by the lack of the most basic necessities of life, so that there are countless victims of malnutrition. An absence of justice and of a sense of solidarity in international exchange works to the advantage of industrialized countries, and thereby steadily increases the gap between rich and poor. Hence the feeling of frustration among the peoples of the Third World and the accusation of exploitation and economic colonialism directed at the industrialized countries." (Here, however, one should ask, Isn't this also a *theological* statement?) And Cardinal Ratzinger was more on the side of the theologians of liberation than on that of Cardinal Höffner when, at the symposium "Church and Industry: Their Responsibility for the Future of the World Economy" in November 1985, which I have already mentioned several times, he said:

The question of business and morality has become, in our day, far more than a merely theoretical problem. Since the internal inequality of the individual major economic spheres endangers the business cycle, efforts have been made, since the 1950s, to establish an economic balance through development projects. But today we can no longer overlook the fact that this effort, in its present form, has failed, and that inequality has, in fact, intensified. The result is that major groups in the Third World who formerly anticipated great things from development aid now see the cause of their misery in the free-market economy, which they regard as a system of exploitation, as sin and injustice in structured form.[15]

On the other hand, those who attack liberation theology also emphasize that Christian faith reveals a gracious "surplus," a God-given "superfluity" that can never be attained in the political realm. But it is only because of this belief that the base communities and the national and continental churches in Latin America are able, through their Christian faith, to interpret the memory of the saving event brought to completion in Jesus Christ as a subversive and critical potential in history and society.

THE RELATIONSHIP BETWEEN THEOLOGY OF LIBERATION AND MARXISM

In connection with the question of the relationship between Christian faith and politics, however, the question of the relationship between liberation theology and Marxism also presents itself.

Cardinal Höffner was, in fact, correct in pointing out that the concepts of "class" and "class struggle," or "class conflict," are older than Karl Marx. In his lecture "The Relationship of the Theologians of Liberation to Catholic Social Teaching," Höffner says of the concept of "class division": "In 1823 the Mainz *Katholik* wrote that development was tending toward a total division of human society into two classes, 'gluttons and starving beggars, human beings and beasts of burden, rich and poor.' "[16] And in an interview with the Italian magazine *Il Regno*, Höffner pointed out that "we cannot deny that there have been class struggles and that some are still going on."[17]

And in fact, Pope Pius XI especially, in his encyclical "Quadragesimo anno" (1931) freely made use of the concepts of class, class society, and class struggle as instruments for analyzing the social situation shaped by the capitalist economic system. At the very beginning of the encyclical, in paragraph 3, we read: "Toward the end of the 19th century new economic methods and industrialization led more and more, within a great many peoples, to a division of society into two classes: the one, few in numbers, was almost alone in the enjoyment of all the comforts which modern inventions and discoveries were able to offer in such abundance; the other class, however, embracing the enormous mass of workers, suffered from the pressure of wretched need, unable, despite the most strenuous efforts, to free themselves from their lamentable situation." And the pope had no hesitation at all in making use of Marxist theory to analyze class society: "It is true that labor . . . is not a salable good; rather, here the human dignity of workers is always to be respected; nor can it circulate in the market like any kind of goods. Nevertheless, in the present situation, the law of supply and demand applied to the laboring power of people in the 'labor market' creates two classes, or two opposing 'fronts,' so to speak: and the conflict of these two parties in the labor market turns it into a battlefield on which the two parties struggle in close combat" (no. 83). Therefore it was only logical for Pius XI to speak, under certain conditions, of a legitimate class struggle: "If enmity and hatred for the other class are abandoned, the objectionable class struggle can be decontaminated and become an honorable contest between classes, carried on out of a sense of justice. It will still not yet attain to the social peace desired by all, but it can and should serve as a starting point from which the parties can work toward harmonious cooperation between themselves" (no. 114). Oswald Nell-Breuning has summarized Pope Pius XI's decision thus: "The peaceful order of society that is our aim not only can but must arise out of a militant conflict between classes."[18]

Logically, then, the General Synod of the Dioceses in the Federal Republic of Germany (1971–75) wrote, in its concluding statement on "Church and Labor":

Thus we cannot fail to recognize that Karl Marx identified a number of fundamental facts about the new social reality founded on industrialization and formulated them in a politically effective manner. Although Catholic statements on social questions began at an early date to take up these descriptive elements of Marxist teaching and to make them the occasion of social initiatives founded in Christian principles, the result of the unavoidable ideological confrontation with Marxism has been that the process has by no means been carried out in a sufficiently comprehensive manner. So, for example, the ideas of class, class society or class conflict were not yet accepted in many Catholic statements as proper descriptions of the social situation, when Pius XI in the encyclical "Quadragesimo Anno" adopted the corresponding clarifications of Catholic social scientists on the question. The resistance against accepting facts and formulations certainly had multiple causes. . . . To the detriment of our credibility, the discussion among us even today continues, in part, within the old channels, while in international Catholic and ecumenical circles the categories for social analysis introduced by Marx are used quite as a matter of course. (no. 1.5.1)

The primary objection raised against liberation theology by the Congregation for the Doctrine of the Faith in its instruction of 6 August 1984 and also, repeatedly, by Cardinal Höffner, namely, that it is impossible to separate elements of Marxist social analysis from the whole of Marxist atheist theory, thus applies to important traditions in Catholic teaching, including the papal magisterium itself. But even apart from that, this objection lacks internal logic. In the whole history of theology, especially in the area of Christian ethics, elements borrowed from non-Christian philosophies and social sciences have been critically adopted without their origin *as such* being regarded as an argument for or against the correctness of the theological statements in question. This began with the theologians at Alexandria and continued through Augustine and Thomas to Karl Rahner's grounding of faith in transcendental philosophy.

Gustavo Gutierrez, for example, shows that the theologians of liberation have assimilated Marxist analysis in a thoroughly critical fashion. In his book *Die historische Macht der Armen (The Historic Power of the Poor)*, he writes: "Here, in the midst of the historical process and not in the silence of a library or in a dialogue between intellectuals, the popular movement encounters the social sciences and Marxist analysis. Both are important for understanding the mechanisms of oppression in our prevailing social order. It is primarily this system that the exploited are questioning. They can neither live nor think their faith outside this field of conflict. So this is the place where social sciences and Marxist analysis meet theology. Of course, it is a critical encounter."[19] And in his earlier book *A Theology of Liberation*, Gustavo Gutierrez had written with regard to class struggle: "It must be real and effective combat, not hate. This is the challenge, as new as the Gospel: to love our enemies."[20]

THE QUESTION OF VIOLENCE

At this point the question of the attitude of liberation theology toward the use of violent means is always brought up. It is simply not true that, as Cardinal Höffner claims, "an impartial reading of the texts leaves one with the impression that the theology of liberation favors the use of violence by the church itself."[21]

Instead, we need to see first of all that the political situation in Latin America—to varying degrees in different countries—is all too often characterized by a repressive structural violence indifferent to human dignity, through which the state, the military, and also certain privileged social groups maintain their power. Many Latin American Christians find themselves thus in a situation of pitiless structural violence, quite apart from their own will in the matter or their theoretical convictions. They have not sought this situation, but they suffer from its violence and must try to come to terms with it in some Christian manner. Under these conditions we must also keep in mind that a nonviolent, passive attitude can lead to the consequence that the structural and institutional violence will continue to be exercised and that millions of people will go on suffering from it.

Nevertheless, the theology of liberation emphasizes first and foremost, in discipleship to Jesus Christ, that even in such a situation nonviolence is a binding principle for Christians. José Miguez-Bonino makes a careful distinction:

Insofar as nonviolent action respects the human person, makes room for an internalization of the project of liberation in the masses and fosters the sense of solidarity in the construction of a new society, it is the means most coherent with the revolutionary purpose. Moreover, when efficacy (which, as we saw, cannot be separated from Christian love) does require the use of violence for overturning an oppressive system, it creates a number of very serious problems: the exacerbation of hate, resentment and rivalries, the imposition of changes from a structure of power without a corresponding development of conscience, the acceptance of the "rules of the game" of the present oppressive system. Victorious revolutionary violence runs the risk of simply substituting one form of oppression for another and thus becoming really counterrevolutionary. It certainly makes the construction (human, economic, social, institutional, political) necessary after the takeover of power all the more difficult, almost in proportion to the amount and length of the period of subversive violence.[22]

However, despite this adherence in principle to nonviolence, most theologians of liberation do not exclude the use of physical force against material objects and against persons as the means of last resort in limited situations, when the people can no longer be asked to bear the violence of their political masters, when all other, nonviolent methods have been exhausted, and when it seems probable, after careful consideration, that the violent actions will succeed. The theologians of liberation are, in this respect, in agreement with the words of Pope Paul VI in his encyclical "Populorum progressio" (par. 31). And moral theology, in fact, has traditionally pointed out that there are certain limited human situations in which, even for Christians, the use of force cannot be

excluded: capital punishment, individual self-defense, just war, ty-
rannicide, the right to defense. Can and may we European Christians, who often proudly remember our national revolutions or
applaud the active resistance of Christians against Nazism, deny
the same right to the Christians of Latin America?

ANOTHER WAY OF DOING THEOLOGY

This, at least, must be clearly recognized: there is a basic difference between traditional European theology and Latin American
liberation theology in the way theology is done. The conflict over
theology of liberation would certainly have taken a different
shape if certain church officials and theologians in the Roman curia had not made their own way of studying and teaching theology
the single standard according to which Christians can theologize.
But if we begin from the way in which Jesus himself and the authors of the New Testament reflected on their faith, there is a
great deal to be said for liberation theology: for its method of
starting from daily circumstances, from primary experiences,
from concrete conflicts and problems, from the experience of
Christian women and men in the praxis of their community life,
and the reflecting on those things.

That much being said, we should, however, add—"apologet-
ically," in the best sense of the word—that while the theologians
of the First World can certainly learn from their colleagues in the
Third World, and, in fact, while they *must* face the challenge thus
presented to them—they still cannot return to a time before the
Enlightenment. They cannot abandon the "dialetic of Enlightenment." And, on the other hand, they must ponder the Christian
message at the level of reflection that is appropriate to the intellectual world in Europe and elsewhere.

If we take this seriously, it means that the legitimacy of a "con-
textual theology," that is, of a plurality of theological methods,
each with its roots, its *Sitz im Leben*, in the concrete lives of people
and in a particular society, simply must be recognized and
accepted.

So, when Walter Kasper makes the fundamental accusation
against liberation theology that in it a "far-reaching decision [is]
made, a decision against a metaphysics that concerns itself with

the nature of the human being and of the world in themselves,"
we ought to ask, what is the metaphysics to which a theologian is
obligated? And within this debate, Johann Baptist Metz is probably correct in pointing out that since Karl Marx attacked the
theological concept of truth, theology has lost its innocence once
and for all. For the truth about God, human beings, and the world
is always historically mediated, depending on the condition of society and also on human interests. Theologians can no longer devote themselves to abstract questions, for in that case there is
always the danger "that, for example, the catastrophic lives of the
poor will disappear behind a subjectless concept of poverty."[23]

THE CONTROVERSY OVER CHURCH OFFICE

Another important point of conflict concerning theology of
liberation is certainly the difference in ideas about the church.
Here it is not primarily a matter of different theoretical concepts
of church, that is, it is not so much an ecclesiological question, but
rather a matter of different ways in which church can be realized.
The theology of liberation has often been accused of being opposed to church office, and of creating a counter-church in the
guise of the notion and the development of a "popular church"
over against the hierarchical church. This is one the charges that
Cardinal Ratzinger made against Leonardo Boff and his book
Church: Charism and Power.[24]

In reality it is not a question of repudiating office in the church,
but of creating another style of praxis of church office, a completely different way of translating the idea of church office into
reality. And in exactly the same way, in the matter of the idea and
the reality of the popular church, it is not a question of a counter-
church: the existence of such a thing has yet to be proved. Instead, it has to do with the fact that here church is lived, experienced, and realized in a different way from what has been going
on in Latin America for hundreds of years. And that is just what
many church officials are afraid of!

As far as the praxis of church office is concerned, it is clear that
those persons in office who live in the spirit of liberation theology
do not simply talk about the notions of dialogue, of sisterhood
and brotherhood, and of service owed by those who hold office,

but actually try to put them into practice. These officials realize that they cannot exercise their authority automatically, simply by virtue of their office, but only when their Christian arguments and the example of their lives are convincing.

And the popular church shows, in its living praxis, that "church" in the New Testament means first and foremost the concrete local community, and that structures and offices that reach beyond the local level are primarily intended to facilitate the life of the primary, local community.

This new praxis of office and of church is, in fact, a challenge to certain socially developed and historically-conditioned church structures that represent, today, a structural heresy.

One of the essential points of contention in the conflict over theology of liberation is certainly founded in the fact that some church officials in Latin America and especially in the Roman curia cannot let go of a notion of the church as something that is highly centralized in its leadership, completely European in appearance, and absolutist-monarchical in government. Quite apart from the fact that such an idea is completely unhistorical, because it makes one particular, relatively new shape of the Catholic church the only valid one, this kind of absolutizing of a particular social form of church has no legitimate basis in the New Testament. What is being expressed is really a neocolonial viewpoint of the European church that, in addition, fully fails to take into account the political and economic situation in Latin America. It also fails to realize that, at least since the general conferences of the Latin American bishops at Medellin (1968) and Puebla (1979), a new consciousness has arisen of a continental church that within a few years will include half of all the Catholics in the world.

It is simply impossible today to try to shape the world church according to the model of a particular national church, be it the Polish or the German church. The universal church can survive only if it recognizes—as the New Testament does as a matter of course, and as the Second Vatican Council very clearly demanded—the legitimacy of a pluriformity of differing theologies, theologians, spiritualities, legal and liturgical forms, and organizational structures. The Europe-centered, Roman church must become a conciliar church: many-faceted and plural-centered.

POLITICAL CONSEQUENCES

It is well know that the third general assembly of the Latin American bishops at Puebla, in particular, decided in favor of a *preferential option for the poor.* No one in the church dares to criticize this decision. And, like the pope himself on many occasions, even the Roman instruction of 6 August 1984 criticizes "the accumulation of a major share of the wealth by an oligarchy of proprietors with no social conscience, the complete absence or deficiency of the rule of law, military dictatorships that despise elementary human rights, the corruption of certain powerful persons, the unbridled practices of foreign capital" (VII, 12). Obviously, here we find a major area of agreement between theology of liberation and the Roman instruction, with regard to the analysis of the situation in Latin America.

The conflict, however, begins the moment the question is posed, what *political consequences* individual Christians, church authorities, church communities, dioceses, and national churches should draw from this analysis. Here is the decisive difference: the theologians of liberation and the Christian women and men who live on the basis of this theology are prepared to deduce concrete political demands from this preferential option for the poor, to name concrete persons and groups who violate human dignity, and to engage in concrte political actions, both as individuals and as church. But it is completely irresponsible for Christians in Europe, by a simple division of labor, to leave this preferential option for the poor, including its political consequences, to the Christian women and men of Latin America, and not to accept the challenge represented by the theory and praxis of liberation theology for individual Christians and the Christian churches in Europe as well.

During the "night of solidarity" at the Catholic national congress in Munich in 1984, Cardinal Aloisio Lorscheider quite rightly said: "Every theology must be a liberation theology. We cannot subscribe to a theology that puts on the brakes. It must lead to freedom. You people in Germany have placed great hopes in us, and we in Latin America, in turn, place great hopes in you. What do we expect of you? Ask yourselves: are there no oppressed in Germany? You must begin to assist in the liberation of those here in Germany who are oppressed. When you experience liberation among yourselves, you will be able to show the greatest solidarity with us. . . . And another thing we want from you. Ask yourselves: does your country, your economy oppress other nations? That is the second question the poor in Latin America put to you Christians in Germany. It is a duty of Christian solidarity to prevent this exploitation in the future."[25]

In 1900, 77 percent of all Catholics lived in the industrialized world of the wealthy north, and 23 percent in the countries we now call the Third World. At the end of this century, 70 percent of all Catholics will be living in the countries of the Third World and only 30 percent in Europe and the United States of America.[26]

The theology of liberation seeks to reflect on the situation of exploitation and oppression of these people in the Third World, to translate the liberating Christian message into this situation, and to give a credible and authentically Christian answer. The future of the theology of liberation will therefore be decisive for the future of the church in the Third World.

But it is not just a matter of the church; it is also a question of the human future. The theology of liberation is undoubtedly an important force within the comprehensive process of liberation of the people and peoples in the Third World, who hope at last to become the subject of their own history. So what is at stake is not simply the future of the church, but also the future of human persons. For people do not exist for the church. The church exists for people.

Translated by
Linda Maloney

NOTES

1. See Gustavo Gutierrez, *A Theology of Liberation*, tr. and ed. Sr. Caridad Inda and John Eagleson (Maryknoll, NY: Orbis, 1973), xi, unnumbered footnote.
2. Lothar Bossle, *Utopie der Befreiung* (Aschaffenburg, 1976), 10.
3. Franz Hengsbach, Katholische Nachrichtenagentur, 13 May 1977.
4. Quoted in Norbert Greinacher, *Die Kirche der Armen*, 3d ed. (Munich, 1985), 94.

5. See Norbert Greinacher, *Der Konflikt um die Theologie der Befreiung* (Zürich, 1985), 133–45.
6. See Luis Zambrano, *Entstehung und theologisches Verständnis der "Kirche des Volkes" (Iglesia Popular) in Lateinamerika* (Frankfurt, 1982), 284–89.
7. Quoted in H. Frenz, N. Greinacher, et. al., *El Salvador—Massaker im Namen der Freiheit* (Reinbek, 1982), 141.
8. See J. Em and M. Spangenberger, eds., *Theologien der Befreiung, Herausforderung an Kirche, Gesellschaft und Wirtschaft* (Cologne, 1985), 139-49.
9. Institut der deutschen Wirtschaft, Bundesvereinigung der deutschen Arbeitgeberverbände, and Gilde katholischer Ingenieure Deutschlands. Cf. Em and Spangenberger, *Theologien.*
10. *Publik-Forum* (6 September 1985).
11. Quoted in R. Schermann, *Die Guerilla Gottes. Lateinamerika zwischen Marx und Christen* (Düsseldorf, 1983), 255.
12. *Süddeutsche Zeitung* (27 November 1985).
13. Joseph Ratzinger, *Zur Lage des Glaubens* (Munich, 1985), 202.
14. Joseph Ratzinger, "Der Mut zur Unvollkommenheit und zum Ethos. Was gegen eine politische Theologie spricht," *Frankfurter Allgemeine Zeitung* 4 (August 1984).
15. Joseph Ratzinger, *Frankfurter Allgemeine Zeitung* (7 December 1985).
16. Em and Spangenberger, *Theologien der Befreiung*, 11.
17. *Publik-Forum* (22 February 1985).
18. *Publik-Forum* (25 January 1985).
19. Gustavo Gutierrez, *Die historische Macht der Armen* (Munich, 1984), 157.
20. Gutierrez, *Theology of Liberation*, 276.
21. Joseph Höffner, "Soziallehre der Kirche oder Theologie der Befreiung?" address to German Bishops' Conference, 24 September 1984, 29.
22. Jose Miguez-Bonino, *Doing Theology in a Revolutionary Situation* (Philadelphia: Fortress, 1975), 127.
23. *Publik-Forum* (1 November 1985) and 35.
24. See Joseph Cardinal Ratzinger and Leonardo Boff, "Dokumente eines Konfliktes um die Theologie der Befreiung. Das Buch 'Kirche: Charisma und Macht' in der Diskussion." Ms. edited and published by *Publik-Forum* (Frankfurt, 1984).
25. *Publik-Forum* (27 July 1984), 20.
26. *Tübingen Südwest-Presse* (3 November 1982).

11. Return to the "Old" Catechism?

Roman Offensives Against the New Religious Education

WOLFGANG BARTHOLOMÄUS

Should we return to the Council of Trent? In order to confront the problems of handing on the faith to the next generation, should the Catholic church orient itself, both with regard to content and to method, to the *Catechismus Romanus* (CR) of 1566? That is what Cardinal Joseph Ratzinger called for early in 1983 in two widely noticed and strongly criticized speeches in France.[1] On overcoming the crisis of catechetics, he suggested: "It was a ... serious ... mistake to do away with the catechism and to declare catechisms in general passé." It is true that the catechism as a book became common for the first time only in the age of the Reformation. Nonetheless, the mediation of the faith in a basic structure coming from faith's own inner logic is as old as the church itself. It follows from the very nature of the church's mission and is therefore necessary. "Because of the rejection of a structured, basic form in which the whole faith of the tradition could be mediated there has been a fragmentation of the expression of faith. This has not only promoted arbitrariness, but has also called into question the importance of individual aspects, which apart from the whole to which they belong, seem coincidental and unrelated."[2]

Those are serious charges: without a catechism, a falling away from the logic of faith; without a catechism, fragmentation and arbitrariness of the expression of faith; without a catechism, no seriousness about the mediation of the faith! Bible study is to be done away with. No more religious education oriented to specific problems. This amounts to a turning away from a mediation of the faith that is close to the experience of men and women and their problems.

BACK TO THE ROMAN CATECHISM

So, it is "back to the catechism," the first example of which the German bishops already brought forth in 1985: *A Catholic Catechism for Adults.*[3] Even more, it is "back to the *old* catechism," because "in the earliest period, a catechetical structure arose which in its essence goes back to the very beginning of the church," and which is as old as, or even older than, the canon of Scripture. Luther, we are told, used this structure for his catechisms just as naturally as the authors of the CR. This was possible precisely because it was not a matter of an artificial systematics, but a collection of those matters of the faith which mirrored the life of the church and which were to be committed to memory: the Apostles' Creed, the sacraments, the Ten Commandments, and the Lord's Prayer. "These four classical 'central pieces' of the cathechesis sufficed for hundreds of years as the organizational elements and foci of catechetical instruction. At the same time they opened a way to the Bible and the living church. . . ." Moreover, they corresponded to the "dimensions of Christian existence. . . ." The *Catechismus Romanus* specifies this when it says it describes "what a Christian must believe (Creed), hope (Our Father), and do (the Ten Commandments as an interpretation of the ways of love) and where such a life is anchored (Sacrament and Church)."[4]

Thus far Ratzinger's statements are pertinent to the catechism. They press for a mediation of the faith which is interested only in the contents of the faith it passes on and seeks to secure these. It derives what it falsely perceives to be a clear logical structure (the traditional subject areas of the catechism) from the theo-logic of the contents of faith (*fides quae*). It then quickly declares this also to be an appropriate, psycho-logically informed didactic structure for the realization of faith (in the sense of the *fides qua*), without being especially concerned about the intellectual and religious capabilities of real men and women. Methodologically, this is very problematic. Such mediation of the faith has abdicated any claim to be a communicative event, which can only effect mediation when it brings those involved, both speakers and those spoken to, together into relationship. An explanation of the faith which could do just this, which understands the gospel in the context of the experiences and problems of today's men and women and which does not ignore their puzzlement and doubt with respect to traditional church teaching, is disqualified.

In the requirements and "directives" for religious education in the Federal Republic of Germany this has been evident for some time.[5] There is a call to return to the central truths of the faith as the real object of religious instruction. It is often motivated by the shock about the religious ignorance of many young people. This call and the criticism of correlation didactics, which sought to incorporate the experiences of men and women in a post-Christian epoch productively, are most clearly articulated in a document of Catholic Parents of Germany (1984):

Modern pedagogy rejects, for example, mere assimilation of material. The student should critically examine what is presented in instruction and its different interpretations and thus come to his or her own judgment. This has led to many problematic developments in religious instruction. ... Instruction according to this so-called correlation principle is a difficult task and is not always accomplished in an acceptable way. It also brings with it considerable dangers.[6]

Through an extreme, one-sided, and exclusive application of this principle, which in itself, of course, is correct and even obvious, religious instruction has degenerated into psychology and social studies or into mere information about religion in general. All of this is now supposed to be corrected by making dogma the (only) decisive focus of religious instruction and enforcing it with the authority of the church's magisterium.[7]

Ratzinger's statements are also a call *to return to a normative theory of religious education*.[8] Such a theory assumes the possibility of an exact separation of questions concerning content and method in religious pedagogical processes. Then it assigns the determination of content to dogmatics and the methods of its mediation to religious pedagogy, or the kerygmatic principles to (dogmatic) theology and their practical application to (religious) didactics. In the nineteenth century this hierarchical ordering of theology and didactic could be seen socially in the subordination of the teacher to the pastor.

Is the background to all of this the Enlightenment, which has yet to be faced? Or is it the attempt to overcome it negatively? It was characteristic of the religious pedagogy of the Enlightenment (then called "catechetics") that it oriented itself not only to the logic of faith but also to the psychology of its actualization. One can follow this in the work of J. B. von Hirscher.[9] Of course, in some extreme instances it was one-sided and out of proportion, lacking sufficient reflection upon its theological basis and the contents of the faith being mediated. All the same, attention was thus given to the human psyche, human experience in time, and to the person in his or her real experience—both in what one must undergo and in what one chooses to undertake. Since then, the human person is no longer the addressee of proclamation, an object of only methodological significance, but is a subject whose rationality codetermines the content of proclamation as well.

Thus the human and social sciences, concerned with the empirical reality of person and world, also entered into the field of religious education. They pushed back dogmatic theology with its claim to a monopoly on truth and offered themselves as partners in the search for truth. While theology couldn't learn from them what Christian faith might be, it could certainly learn what faith's truth in the conditions of empirical reality could mean and how its saving and liberating effect could be experienced. Religious education consequently organized itself as an interdisciplinary science, which brought theology and the human and social sciences together in critical dialogue. It sought to mediate the gospel with the human understanding of self and the world. In doing this, it did not wish to make the gospel conform itself to the methods of transmission or to subordinate it to the presuppositions of the addressees. The gospel should, however, be effective and fruitful for them. It ought to be conceived and mediated not as derived from human possibilities but certainly in view of them.

For this reason, in addition to the traditional materials from catechism, Bible, liturgy, and the church calendar, subjects appeared in the plans for religious instruction in the schools which thematized the secular experience of the students.[10] New concepts of religious instruction took such things into consideration and challenged the notion that religious instruction at school was simply identical with church proclamation. The fact that this no longer produced the traditional, ecclesially socialized Christian, who knew by heart what was to be believed, is now being used to do away with such a theory of religious education.

THE FOUR MAIN PARTS OF THE CATECHISM: A CLEAR DIDACTIC STRUCTURE?

Ratzinger would like the mediation of faith to be determined didactically by the traditional fourfold catechetical division, as the CR had already done. Catechesis would then find its true center again. With this requirement, he thinks that all questions relating to the material structuring of the transmission of faith would be answered.

Anyone who speaks like this understands little about didactics. Reference simply to the four main parts doesn't say anything about what kind of a didactic structure they should build. For that, it is not enough merely to indicate the parts as elements of this structure. One must, in addition, pay attention to their mutual relationship, to the order of placement and to their interconnection.[11] As a support for his demand, Ratzinger appeals to the example of Martin Luther, who "employed this structure for his catechisms just as naturally as the authors of the Catechismus Romanus."[12] He thereby overlooks the fact that Luther put together the traditional elements in a structure totally different from the CR. To mention only one aspect as an example: inasmuch as Luther places the Ten Commandments before the Creed (unlike the CR), he takes up his reforming counterposition, which is determined by the opposition between law and gospel. Luther understands the Ten Commandments as law, which allows human beings to recognize before God their lost condition, from which they can be saved by faith alone (Creed). In the CR, on the other hand, the Ten Commandments appear after the Creed and the Sacraments, as the response of love to the gospel, represented by Creed and sacraments.

Even Peter Canisius, who reworked the traditional parts, nonetheless gave his catechism a didactic structure which was not identical with that of the CR. When he discovered the discrepancy,[13] he conformed some of his catechisms to the CR. Originally Canisius had five parts, which he connected thus: Creed (faith), Our Father (hope), Commandments (love), sacraments, and "On

Christian Righteousness," the specifically Catholic supplement. The three divine virtues at the beginning and the question concerning righteousness through works at the end—that it typical for Canisius. He did not adopt the Roman structure for all his catechisms. That would become problematic and contribute to their later demise.

Not even the commentators on the CR hold to the original fourfold division and their interpretatively significant ordering. They explain the didactic structure that they form in a way similar to Canisius: "The people must know five things. First, what is to be believed; second, what is to be prayed for; third, what is to be done; fourth, what is to be avoided; fifth, what is to be hoped. The first is contained in the Apostles' Creed, the second in the Lord's Prayer, the third and fourth in the Ten Commandments, and the fifth in the Sacraments, which order men and women to the eternal beatitude for which we hope."[14] Moreover, neo-scholastic catechisms, which since the middle of the nineteenth century determined the mediation of the faith in Germany for over a hundred years, had only three main parts ("On the Faith," "On the Commandments," "On the Means of Grace"). One can see that reference to the orientation of the mediation of faith to the traditional catechetical themes alone has nothing exact to say about the specific didactic structure formed through them. It leaves the didactic problem unsolved: in what way and in what order should the gospel be brought into learning processes so that it is truly mediated in them? And it cannot do justice to the concrete, historical character of the mediation of faith. J. B. von Hirscher could even see the use of the traditional catechetical divisions as a way of foregoing a didactically sound organization.

One can separate catechisms into two classes according to their fundamental structure. Some are structured according to an idea or basic concept which is comprehensive of religious teaching as a whole, while others attempt to order a variety of material merely according to certain general rubrics which have no higher unity binding them together. For example, the Roman Catechism divides . . . its whole instruction into four main sections . . . and itself admits no deeper, underlying purpose other than bringing together all the teachings of religion according to certain rubrics. . . . In a similar way, Canisius divided his catechism into five main sections, like the Roman Catechism in four of these, but in a different order and with an additional fifth section. Moreover, as in the

Roman Catechism, these main sections are nothing other than general areas according to which Canisius thought he could divide the whole sum of religious teachings most conveniently.[15]

Ratzinger sees a correspondence between the structure of the CR and the dimensions of Christian life. The CR itself shows this when it says that it presents what the Christian must believe (Creed), hope (Our Father), and do (Ten Commandments), and when it indicates the place for a life in which all of this is anchored (sacrament and church). I will pass over the fact that Ratzinger no longer follows the order of the CR and that this catechism does not treat of the church in a separate section. The CR understands its structure differently:

Everything which the Christian faith contains in itself is related either to the knowledge of God, to the creation and governance of the world, to the redemption of the human race or to the reward of the good and the punishment of the wicked. The signs of divine grace and the means to attain it, however, are contained in the teaching on the seven sacraments. The Ten Commandments designate the laws which have love as their intention. Finally, everything which a human being can desire, hope and petition for benefit is contained in the Lord's Prayer.[16]

What the CR designates as a Christian possibility, Ratzinger makes an authoritarian regulation. The two are worlds apart.

In the history of religious pedagogy, there are ways of approaching the question and possible solutions which could be forgotten through fixation on the structure of the mediation of faith in the CR. In order to bring about a "kerygmatic shift of a material nature," J. B. von Hirscher and J. A. Jungmann each pressed for a contemporary, relevant concentration of the gospel around a central theme that could allow the unified whole of the gospel to appear in all its elements. For Hirscher it was the kerygma of the reign of God; for Jungmann it was the person Jesus Christ.[17]

These same concerns were expressed in the search for short formulations of the faith which, in a world where faith is contested, could speak to today's men and women by expounding the faith briefly, directly, and intelligibly.[18] The point is not to mediate a theological system in its entirety as faith (faith for knowing). What is important is to reflect upon the conditions of the possibility of faith in a world alienated from God and with little relation to the church, and to unfold the existential, social, and saving possibilities of the God of Jesus Christ which offer meaning and orientation for human life in this world (faith for living).[19] K. Rahner's remark is still valid: "A catechism of the future will be totally different from previous catechisms" and one "could and must express the real substance of Christian faith in a different way and from different perspectives, clarifying suppositions which previously were taken for granted."[20] The church is presently failing to take advantage of this insight.

THE GOSPEL FOR SELF-DETERMINED MEN AND WOMEN

One might get the impression that the argument about the didactic organization of the mediation of faith, as carried on in the question about the significance of the main divisions of the catechism, is mere hair splitting. Does it take into account the seriousness and range of the problems which confront the mediation of faith today? Actually, the argument in its current form makes sense only if one assumes that all the people concerned are more or less believing Christians—in other words, when it is treated as a theological argument within the church. Many of those who are presently occupied with the right form of the mediation of the gospel have just such a narrow view. What is the empirical reality referred to when W. Kasper informs us that his catechism for adults is structured according to the Creed, since all Christians are familiar with it? He writes: "In particular we have begun with the faith of the church in the form in which it is handed on to each Christian at baptism and in which we confess it each Sunday at the celebration of the Eucharist: we have begun with the confession of faith of the church."[21] As an empirical statement, this does not hold up. What percentage of baptized Christians could really say that the confession of faith was handed on to them at Baptism or that they know it from their Sunday church attendance? A minority. Looking at the population of the world, an infinitesimal minority. They do not have problems about how to transmit the faith.

But what about the great majority? The majority of men and women in the world? The majority of baptized persons? Statistics speak clearly. They indicate that at least two-thirds of all baptized

Christians concern themselves little or not at all with the things which church authorities consider necessary. To them the power of Christianity seems to have died. That certainly has to do with their religious forgetfulness and insensitivity—also with manifold disappointments with religion and church. But it also has to do with a new self-confidence and freedom.

Many people have found the ability to *determine themselves*, to choose among different religious alternatives. They reject the insinuation that they do so only because of stupidity or because they have been led astray. They are not dull fools who vegetate on in meaningless lives. They are searching for meaning in their lives, like those who seek it in a Christian community. Like those, they too suffer because of the world's pervasive need and because of the possible meaninglessness of life. That is why they are skeptical of the brash claim that such meaning is guaranteed in the church, while outside the church there is only absurdity.[22] They want to see this claim supported. Where they have not already given up expecting anything, having grown deaf to far too many empty promises of salvation, they show themselves open for individuals or groups in which they can recognize a concrete stand which can give orientation and meaning. And so they are hardly opponents of the gospel. But they wish, not only to encounter the gospel in claims about salvation, but also to experience its saving and liberating power. They would like to see, not only hear, how the God of Christians is able to give life meaning, how God leads us out of insecurity, delivers from slavery, frees from guilt, makes us alive, and gives us strength to love. They have had enough of attempts to force belief with talk of the necessity of faith for salvation. They desire insight into the faith. They look for reasons to believe—and not only on the level of language. Therefore, it is not enough for church authorities merely to talk about what Christians really ought to believe, hope, and love. They want to know what they can really count on. And they want such knowledge to be grounded in living experience. They find questionable a church which trims things up through a catechism designed to bring about the cognitive uniformity of its members. They do not need, first and foremost, to be instructed about the faith. They want to meet someone who can engender faith in them while respecting their freedom.

The diagnosis that the crisis concerning the transmission of the faith consists in *defective knowledge about the faith*, and comes from the fact that religious instruction that has given such knowledge too little attention is wrong. The crisis of faith does not consist in cognitive uncertainty. Whoever wanted to know what the church believes always had sufficient opportunities for precise theological information, even in times of nearly limitless theological pluralism. Neither a new catechesis nor a corresponding catechism is necessary.

The crisis is deeper. And elsewhere. And right now it is our own doing. Among other things, namely, it has to do with the inability of church authorities to deal with self-determined men and women. From the universal claim of (Catholic) Christianity made in an undifferentiated way, in which no trace of uncertainty intrudes itself from ecumenical and interreligious dialogues, there appears the total claim of high (Catholic) church authorities, who seek to subject all the baptized to themselves. Thus the announcement of the gospel appears in the language of regulations and even, at times, in speechless, repressive measures.

Today, the majority will not stand for that anymore; in the future, fewer and fewer will. The hominization that, in the wake of the Enlightenment, first touched nature (no longer seen as a divine mystery, but as something brought forth and destroyed by humankind) and then fell upon ethos (no longer a holy order, but a matter of social convention of determinable criteria), has continued. We have long since realized that authorities are not divinely appointed but are the result of democratic agreement or the violent seizure of power. In the meantime churches also seem to be mere social groups, without any mystery, in which one finds everything human. Their claim to be the voice of God and the place of salvation must prove itself in the face of growing skepticism. These aspects of this process of hominization are the expression and consequence of human self-determination as well. People are ready to accept direction and to bind themselves to something trustworthy but they act freely and critically, desiring to test the trustworthiness of that which presents itself as binding. In official church texts, this attitude, when acknowledged at all, is usually seen as the greatest danger for men and women. Self-determination is not acknowledged, much less promoted: a life in the modern world, which daily demanded decisions coming from the strength of critical freedom, would simply not be possible any more. It is passed off as the general cause of the progressing decline of faith and morals and as a disruption of ecclesial order.

But having become mature, men and women do not want to let their right to *self-determined use of their critical freedom* to be taken from them. As a result of the secularization of society in the nineteenth century, religion and church, once a dimension of all reality, became one area of life next to others. But people today experience this loss of power suffered by religion and church as a liberation. It is a liberation of themselves from the unjust claims of religion (or the men of religion) upon all the details of their lives. It is a liberation of the gospel, which can really only unleash its saving and liberating power in a powerless church.

The ecclesial transmission of the faith must in its relationality accept in a productive way the very thing which church superiors often have difficulty with: this self-determined freedom. People who live in a fundamentally democratic society don't like the sound of expressions like "holy father" and "mother church." Such patriarchal and matriarchal models of relationship also alienate those who believed that they could expect to find in the church the freedom and love of brothers and sisters inspired by the gospel and are now disappointed once again. The old division between those of age and those considered to be immature, long thought to have been overcome, is becoming characteristic again. The patronizing condescension of the mature to the immature continues to perpetuate immaturity. And the reason? It is the rejection of the freedom claimed by self-determined people, who allow themselves to come to alternative decisions. Their being different frightens church superiors. They can only defame it as misuse of freedom or as the inability to exercise it properly. Without any experience with adults who have become uncomfortable to deal with, they seek to put an end to freedom that they consider to have been far too generously allowed and in fact only misused. In the end, this will drive people away, even those of goodwill.

If only the church could see its way to become a sign of God's new world, a world of uninhibited freedom and radical love; a world of freedom which overcomes every form of slavery, not only economic and political, but also the slavery of egoism and

174 / WOLFGANG BARTHOLOMAÜS

power, guilt and death; a world of love, which not only loves with fascination that which is lovable, but also turns to the unlovable and so makes it lovable—then we could be calm when we meet people who experience the conditions of pluralism and secularity as a psychic easement, and who in different degrees of nearness or distance to church authorities find a totally new openness for the gospel.

Church authorities, however, are pulling on the reins again. Ratzinger does not understand the sections of the catechism as ways of expressing faith, hope, and love. He sees them as texts which contain what Christians must believe, what they are to hope, and in what manner they are to love. Possibilities are not described; rather, duties are imposed. But this is repugnant to men and women, especially in questions which concern them most deeply.

Recent official actions in the church regarding the transmission of faith seek to secure the faith, not to set it free. According to Ratzinger, orientation to the old catechism should serve to "secure the identity of the content of faith."[23] It intends to be a "compendium of the faith which ought to be known by heart."[24] What the church believes may well be secured in such a catechism. However, security alone, as meaningful as it may be for specific purposes, hinders and blocks life. It has never yet engendered it. How bitter if such were really necessary today. Religious education in the liberating power of the gospel knows that its duty is not to establish security, but to bring about life.

Translated by
John R. Sachs, S.J.

NOTES

1. Joseph Ratzinger, *Die Krise der Katechese und ihre Überwindung* (Einsiedeln, 1983). Similarly: Joseph Ratzinger, *Zur Lage des Glaubens* (Munich, Zurich, Vienna, 1985), 72–77.
2. Ratzinger, *Die Krise*, 15.
3. Die deutschen Bischöfe, eds., *Katholischer Erwachsenen-Katechismus. Das Glaubensbekenntnis der Kirche* (Bonn, 1985). Compare W. Kasper, *Einführung in den katholischen Erwachsenenkatechismus* (Düsseldorf, 1985). Also: W. Kasper, "Das Glaubensbekenntnis der Kirche. Zum Entwurf eines neuen Erwachsenenkatechismus," *Internationale katholische Zeitschrift*, 13 (1984): 255–72. A heated de-

bate has arisen concerning the pros and cons of this catechism, its contents, and function.

4. Ratzinger, *Die Krise*, 32; referring to the *Catechismus Romanus*, Prooemium XII. Also Ratzinger, *Zur Lage*, 73; here there is no reference to the church as the place for such a life.

5. Compare the forewords and introductions in the new teaching plans for religious instruction: *Lehrplan für das Fach katholische Religionslehre in Baden-Württemberg* (Freiburg und Rottenburg, 1984); *Grundlagenplan für den katholischen Religionsunterricht im 5.–10. Schuljahr* (Munich, 1984). See also the statements of the Catholic Parents of Germany (1980 and 1984) concerning religious instruction and of the Central Committee of German Catholics in 1981—also the preparatory document concerning the religious instruction (*Religionsunterricht*) for the synod of the diocese of Rottenburg-Stuttgart (see note 7).

6. Katholische Elternschaft Deutschlands, eds., *Probleme des Religionsunterrichts heute* (Bonn, 1984), 7, 12.

7. The preparatory document on religious instruction (*Religionsunterricht*) for the synod of the diocese of Rottenburg-Stuttgart in 1985 stresses, as a first concretization of its recommendations, the responsibility of the bishop as a "teacher with the authority of Christ," which he exercises in granting the canonical mission to teach and in his supervision of religious instruction. In *Materialdienst* 22 (Rottenburg, 1985), 43.

8. Compare W. Bartholomäus, *Einführung in die Religionspädagogik* (Darmstadt and Munich, 1983), 52f., 77, 112f., 117f.

9. J. B. von Hirscher, *Katechetik. Zugleich ein Beitrang zur Theorie eines christkatholischen Katechismus* (Tübingen, 1831). Compare F. Blacker, *Johann Baptist von Hirscher und seine Katechismen* (Freiburg, 1953).

10. Compare *Zielfelderplan für den katholischen Religionsunterricht der Schuljahre 5–10* (Munich, 1973); *Zielfelderplan für den katholischen Religionsunterricht in der Grundschule* (Munich, 1977). The same holds true for plans of other kinds of schools and different grade levels. Compare W. Bartholomäus, "Der bisherige Zielfelderplan für die Sekundarstufe I. Seine Bedeutung und Leistung für die religionsdidaktische Entwicklung," *Katechetische Blätter* 109 (1984): 377–83.

11. In this respect, Ratzinger has no realization of the problems. He apparently considers the individual elements as related to each other only additively. This is why he can order them in different ways: compare Ratzinger 1983 (*Die Krise*, 31) with Ratzinger 1985 (*Zur Lage*, 73). On the history of catechisms: F. X. Thalhofer, *Entwicklung des katholischen Katechismus in Deutschland von Canisius bis Deharbe* (Freiburg, 1899); W. Busch, *Der Weg des deutschen katholischen Katechismus von Deharbe bis zum Einheitskatechismus* (Freiburg, 1936); J. Hofinger, *Geschichte des Katechismus in Österreich von Canisius bis zur Gegenwart* (Innsbruck–Leipzig, 1937); F. Weber, *Geschichte des Katechismus in der Diözese Rottenburg von der Aufklärungszeit bis zur Gegenwart* (Freiburg, 1939).

12. Ratzinger, *Die Krise*, 32.

13. The first catechisms of Canisius appeared between 1555 and 1563; the *Catechismus Romanus* in 1566.

14. "Populus tenetur quinque scire. Primo quae sint credenda, secundo quae sint petenda, tertio quae facienda, quarto quae fugienda, quinto quae speranda. Prim. continetur in Symb. Ap., sec. in Or. Dom., tert. et quart. in Decalogo; quint. in sacramentis, quae ordinant homines ad aeternam beatitudinem, quam speramus." S. Cattaneus, *Explicatio in Catechismum Rom. ex decreto Conc. Trid. et Pii V. iussu editum* (Ingolstadt, 1590), 2. Compare Thalhofer, *Entwicklung*, 12 n. 3.

15. Hirscher, *Katechetik*, 124f.
16. *Catechismus Romanus*, Prooemium XII. Translation from: *Der römische Katchismus. Herausgegeben auf Befehl der Kirchenversammlung zu Trient und des Papstes Pius V. Übersetzt von Dr. Ignaz Felner* (Mainz, 1948), 9.
17. Hirscher, *Katechetik*; J. A. Jungmann, *Die Frohbotschaft und unsere Glaubensverkündigung* (Regensburg, 1936); J. A. Jungmann, *Christus als Mittelpunkt religiöser Erziehung* (Freiburg, 1939). Compare F. X. Arnold, *Dienst am Glauben* (Freiburg, 1948); W. Bartholomäus, "Erleben wir eine neue materialkerygmatische Wende?" *Theologische Quartalschrift* 164 (1984), 243–56.
18. Compare K. Rahner, "Kurzformeln des Glaubens," *Diakonia / Der Seelsorger* 1 (1970), 4–17; K. Rahner, "Reflections on the Problems Involved in Devising a Short Formula of the Faith," in *Theological Investigations*, XI, trans. David Bourke (London and New York, 1974), 230–44; R. Bleistein, *Kurzformel des Glaubens. Prinzip einer modernen Religionspädagogik*, 2 vols. (Würzburg, 1971); L. Karrer, *Der Glaube in Kurzformeln. Zur theologischen und sprachtheoretischen Problematik und zur religionspädagogischen Verwendung der Kurzformeln des Glaubens* (Mainz, 1978).
19. Compare A. Teipel, *Die Katechismusfrage. Zur Vermittlung von Theologie und Didaktik aus religionspädagogischer Sicht* (Freiburg–Basel–Vienna, 1983).
20. K. Rahner, " 'Grundriss des Glaubens'–Ein Katechismus unserer Zeit," *Katechetische Blätter* 105 (1980), 547.
21. W. Kasper, "Der neue katholische Erwachsenenkatechismus," *Katechetische Blätter* 110 (1985), 366.
22. Criticizing the new adult catechism, W. Langer observes: "There is a sort of general pathos which pervades the catechism: the conviction of faith about the necessity of salvation . . . through God. In sharp contrast, the situation of human beings in the world is characterized as completely lost. All human efforts at mastering the human condition are discounted as meaningless attempts at 'self-liberation,' which create nothing but 'new conflicts and alienations' and so can only result in a 'vicious circle.' Such a black and white picture is not necessary to make the gospel message clearer." See W. Langer, "Glaubens-Lehre. Der neue katholische Erwachsenen-Katechismus," *Katechetische Blätter* 110 (1985): 885. I would add that such a black and white picture contradicts the experience which people have of themselves.
23. Ratzinger, *Der Krise*, 38.
24. Ibid., 32; compare 33.

12. A Protestant Look at an Aggressive Papacy

ROBERT McAFEE BROWN

It is initially awkward for a Protestant to offer an appraisal of a Catholic pope. The impression is bound to be created that all would be well if the pope would just assert more frequently some of those things Protestants believe, or, in an act of supreme ecumenical goodwill, dissolve the papal office. Since I harbor no illusions that either eventuality will take place, I can approach the task less diffidently. Even so, a certain presumptuousness remains. To criticize another church than one's own is to create the impression that all is well in one's own sheepfold (which in my own Presbyterian case is manifestly untrue), since the place where one dwells is the obvious place to work for reform and renewal.

However, as I learned in the heady days of ecumenical exchange in the early sixties, what happens for the good in one branch of the Christian family redounds to the good of all, and just as clearly (maybe even more clearly), what is harmful to one branch is harmful to all. Thus I, as a Protestant, have a vested interest in the Catholic church operating at its best, since whenever the gospel is embodied clearly—whether in Rome, Geneva, or Constantinople—the purposes of the gospel are being furthered.

I discovered this while attending two sessions of the Second Vatican Council as a Protestant "observer." In a way I had never anticipated, I came to believe that, not only for Catholics but for *all* Christians, it was important not only for the Council to succeed but to succeed brilliantly. Indeed, I found that on a few occasions I was shamelessly "lobbying" for or against documents that I felt had significant ecumenical implications. In my judgment, the Council did "succeed brilliantly" (perhaps despite the Protestant lobbyists), and the conclusion of the fourth session, on 7 December 1965, began what augered well to be a renaissance in Catholic, and therefore all Christian, life.

There were a few euphoric years, not only of Catholic renewal, but of unprecedented ecumenical activity that drew many Catholics and many Protestants into extraordinarily new and close relationships. By the time of the fourth world assembly of the World Council of Churches (WCC) at Uppsala in 1968, the address on ecumenical cooperation by Fr. Roberto Tucci, S.J., was so far ahead of the already-prepared WCC report, that the drafters of the latter document had to reconvene hastily and prepare a new assessment of the state of relations between Geneva and Rome.

Much of that now seems a dim memory. Important activities still go on, such as the remarkable participation of Roman Catholic theologians in the Faith and Order Commission of the WCC, and the degree of consensus that has been achieved in the report "Baptism, Eucharist and Ministry." But on less exalted levels, things have gone downhill to a degree nobody could have anticipated. This is not to say that they are out of control, or that recoveries are not possible, but the high hopes are on hold, and people on both sides of the divide feel an ecumenical chill setting in.

This change in atmosphere is not coincident with the beginning of John Paul II's pontificate. At the end of the third session of the Council in 1964, for example, matters were at a low ebb. Pope Paul VI and many of his advisors appeared to believe that the church was coming apart at the seams, and a number of defensive curial actions were introduced to reverse the process. Happily, there were significant recoveries at the fourth and concluding sessions, particularly the overwhelming passage of the declaration on religious liberty (which had become a Protestant litmus test of the sincerity of the Council's ecumenical resolve) and the adoption of the constitution "The Church and the World Today." Three years later, however, came "Humanae vitae," Paul VI's attempt to shore up Catholic teaching on birth control by reiterating traditional proscriptions in a document that seemed to go against the spirit of the Council, since three different commissions appointed during the Council had recommended new approaches to the topic. In 1968 also, the Latin American bishops at Medellín, Colombia, produced remarkable documents on justice and peace that set a new course for the Latin American church, presaging the development of liberation theology and the emergence of the base communities. But subsequent overtures from

Rome signalled a curial desire not only to bring such new tendencies under centralized supervision, but to neutralize them if possible.

Through the latter part of Paul VI's pontificate, then, the spirit in Rome seemed increasingly cautious and reserved.

Enter Pope John Paul II in 1978. Any non-Catholic assessment of his pontificate has to proceed on two levels—his extramural dealings with the world, in which all of us have a stake, and his intramural dealings with the Catholic church, in which Catholics have a special stake. While these areas can never be fully separated, they are at least initially useful distinctions.

On social, political, and economic issues, the pope has spoken forthrightly, often prophetically, and Protestants make use of his statements in these areas. Particularly helpful as we try to develop a theology of work for the present era, has been his encyclical on labor, "Laborem exercens" (1981), although we have difficulty with the role assigned to women in the letter.

In his widespread travels, the pope sometimes fosters an ecumenical chill by constant reiteration of the primacy of Peter both substantively and ecclesiologically. But in the midst of such claims there are often forthright and powerful pleas for a reconstruction of the social order, accompanied by unexpected declarations of the inadequacies of capitalism along with expected denunciations of Marxism. In Winnipeg, Canada, for example, the pope powerfully denounced the rapaciousness of northern nations in their dealings with southern nations. After his formal speech to the Latin American bishops at Puebla, early in his pontificate, the pope spent another week in Mexico, meeting mainly with the poor, and the deepening of his understanding and compassion was noticeable almost from day to day, leading to a speech in which he declared that "a social mortgage has been placed on all private property"—hardly a sentiment to commend itself to U. S. Catholic conservatives who are upset with the American bishops' pastoral letter on the economy.

THE POPE AND LIBERATION THEOLOGY

The pope's treatment of liberation theology is an area where extramural and intramural concerns begin to overlap, for liberation theology concerns both life in the outside world and life in the church. Once more, the message is mixed. Contrary to reports circulated by the *New York Times*, the papal speech at Puebla in 1979 did not "denounce" liberation theology, as its critics had hoped it would, although it certainly contained no ringing endorsement. The pope's decision not to condemn was interpreted by liberation theologians, rightly, I believe, as a sign of quasi approval, an interpretation given more substance on a subsequent papal trip to Brazil during which, both by words and gestures, he gave at least a clear amber, if not unambiguously green, light to Christians working there for political and economic as well as inner liberation.

On the other side of the ledger, the harsh treatment by the curia (under the direction of Joseph Cardinal Ratzinger) of both Gustavo Gutiérrez and Leonardo Boff, leading exponents of liberation theology, could hardly have taken place without the pope's approval. Boff, as the world knows, was "silenced" for an indefinite period, a ban that was lifted eleven months later. And while formal charges against Gutiérrez could not stand up under scrutiny, he had to devote the better part of two years to clearing his name from the taint of heterodoxy, if not heresy. The first of Cardinal Ratzinger's instructions on liberation theology (1984) was a sharp attack in which, although no names were named, it was made clear that "certain expressions" of liberation theology were beyond the pale of curial acceptability, and strong warnings were issued against acceptance of any form of Marxist social analysis as a tool for understanding the oppression of the poor.

Even here, however, the papal track record is not single-minded. The initial chapter of the instruction, strongly defending many concerns of liberation theologians, was not only inserted into the negative initial draft on the pope's orders, but may have been written by the pope himself. And by the time the second instruction was issued (over a year later), most of the critical bite had disappeared, and the document in most of its particulars could be accepted by liberation theologians as a clear account of what they were trying to do and even as an indication that many of their concerns had now been legitimated in Catholic social teaching.

This does not mean that the struggle is over. There are many in Rome (as well as in conservative think tanks in Washington, D.C.) who will not rest until liberation theology has been brought to heel. But the pope is surely not leading their crusade.

A further nuance in the struggle over liberation theology provides a useful transition by which to turn to papal dealing with more intramural Catholic matters. In the curial polemics against Gutiérrez, the central charge, elaborated in many ways, was his presumed infection with the taint of Marxism. Despite valiant efforts, curial officials were unable, as we have seen, to substantiate the charge. In the case of Boff, however, the Marxist issue was distinctly subordinate to the main gravamen, which was that his treatment of the church and the base communities, which might undermine the hierarchical authority structure of Roman Catholicism. (Boff did not help his case by some passages comparing the procedures of the curia to star chamber proceedings in Moscow.) When the chips were down, however, it was Boff with his presumed challenge to church authority, rather than Gutiérrez with his presumed dependence on Marx, who was disciplined, showing clearly what the bottom line is in Rome. The challenge to authority, not the challenge of Marxism, was the camel's nose that Rome perceived entering the curial tent.

THE POPE AND DISSENT WITHIN CATHOLICISM

When we look in broader terms at Pope John Paul II's relation to the internal life of contemporary Catholicism, we find the same theme writ large. The central papal fear is surely not that the church is "going Marxist," though that theme is not absent. Rather, the pope appears to be doing everything within his power to reinstitute an understanding of papal authority reminiscent of pre-Vatican II days and thereby reestablish centralized control of all activities in the life of the church.

In attempting to illustrate this point, I shall assume that the barque of Peter is a tightly run ship and that there are no glaring differences between what the pope wills and what the curia does. (In this respect, at least, John Paul's managerial style differs from that of Ronald Reagan, whose main defense in the recent White

House scandals was that that he didn't know what his subordinates were doing and, so we must conclude, was not really in control. No such case could ever be made against John Paul II).

The initial papal visit to the United States was an augury. If the intention was to tell the American church to shape up, the message got through. However many millions of Americans listened to the pope, the pope listened to few Americans. He was carefully shielded from opinions that might have implied that truth can come from the bottom up as well as from the top down. It took the extraordinary courage of Sister Theresa Kane, RSM, to stand up in a public meeting and try to break the communication barrier to acquaint the pope with grievances that American women have about contemporary Catholicism. She received no papal response.

The treatment accorded to signers of a newspaper advertisement asking, *not* for Catholic approval of abortion, but only for the right to discuss the issue of abortion within the church, was even harsher. Orders came from Rome, through Cardinal Hamer, that signers who were ordained or were in religious orders must recant or risk expulsion, and heads of women's religious orders were instructed to bring their members into line. To an outsider the pressures seem cruel, since one can hardly be asked to renounce in good conscience the notion that some matters are grave enough to merit discussion. An outsider can only hear the threat: Submit or we will destroy you.

The treatment accorded to Archbishop Raymond Hunthausen of Seattle involved the use of centralized authority to intimidate a local ordinary. Without significant consultation with the archbishop, Rome removed his authority to deal with five areas of normal episcopal jurisdiction and assigned another bishop to assume those areas of responsibility. While such action can only strike the outsider as heavy-handed, it is encouraging to note that an overwhelming number of lay Catholics in Seattle, along with many of the priests of the archdiocese, have been outspoken in support of their archbishop. The issue is even more complex since Archbishop Hunthausen is one of the most important American church leaders challenging the nuclear arms race, putting his body (along with his money, which he withholds from the IRS) where his words are, acting out what the rest of us should be doing and are not. Christians need all the Archibishop Hunthausens they can get, and as a target of Rome's wrath, he seems singularly inappropriate.

When we turn from administrative to doctrinal matters, the heavy hand is again apparent. The Dutch theologian Edward Schillebeeckx, one of the most creative and respected Catholic theologians in the world, is again in trouble with the Sacred Congregation for the Doctrine of the Faith. The challenge to theologians has come even closer to home in the case of Fr. Charles Curran, professor of Catholic theology for many years at Catholic University in Washington, D.C., who has been removed from his teaching position by the sacred congregation in Rome. What is worrisome, apart from the personal harm done to Fr. Curran, is that he does not represent "extreme" positions, nor does he argue them flamboyantly, but writes from a posture that he calls "faithful dissent." He examines matters of faith and morals that have not been formally defined as dogma, a task that, until his expulsion, had been generally understood to be the job of theologians.

The fallout from his case will be widespread. There can scarcely be a Catholic theologian anywhere who, in the light of the Curran affair, is not thinking, "If they can get Fr. Curran, they can get me." Rome's action, in other words, will have the by-product, intended or unintended, of inhibiting Catholic intellectual inquiry and encouraging timidity and blandness. "Faithful dissent" will be stifled.

Papal treatment of sexual issues is following a similar course. John Paul II has reaffirmed as his own the negative position of Paul VI's encyclical on birth control, "Humanae vitae," and speaks on this topic frequently. It is clear that Christians can have differences of opinion on the matter of abortion and feel that their whole faith rests on how they deal with it. But it is not at all clear that this is true about birth control, and the papal line here will be increasingly difficult to present persuasively to lay Catholics. A recent directive on homosexuality is negative in its approach to individuals whose genetic structure renders them "aberrant" in terms of conventional teaching, and the expulsion of Fr. John McNeill, a celibate homosexual, from the Jesuit order is indication of an increasingly hard line on this matter.

Perhaps the greatest negative legacy of the present pontificate will be its resolute shutting of all doors to women who wish to play a significant role in the life of the church. There is no evidence to suggest that even within many papal lifetimes will women be able to consider themselves more than second-class citizens in the church. Catholic women who raise questions about women priests, for example, are firmly denied a significant hearing, despite their claim that there is not a single compelling theological argument to deny them ordination. There are also myriads of petty regulations that keep women subordinate in ways that not only irritate but also wound. (A friend who is a member of a religious order was some time ago given permission to preach the homily at a Mass, and discovered only shortly before the service that it would not be permissible for her *as a woman* to read the Gospel lesson on which the homily was based.)

I have not a doubt in the world that a time will come when women can not only read the Gospel lesson, but will celebrate the Eucharist, participate in priestly ministry, and do most of the other things they are presently forbidden to do. So on one level it angers me that prohibitions so manifestly contrary to the spirit of the gospel are still in force. But on a deeper level it saddens me, for I see so many people being deeply hurt by the rigid rules of an institution they desire to serve, often at great self-sacrifice. I also see the church wanting to communicate its message to the modern world, and needlessly wounding itself by denying to over half of its members roles that would radically enhance the credibility and communicability of its teachings.

CONCLUSION

What do these things mean to the outsider looking at Roman Catholicism during the pontificate of John Paul II? I can make three observations.

First, the freshness, excitement, and vitality of the Catholic church are being sapped by the need to engage in so many diversionary struggles that are far from the main purpose of the gospel. I do not deny that good things are happening as well. The American bishops' pastoral letters on nuclear weapons and the economy are landmarks not only for Catholics but for Protestants, and we will continue to appropriate them gratefully. But it is precisely such landmarks that make me wish that more Catholic effort could be devoted to such endeavors rather than having to be expended elsewhere. What a tragedy that Charles Curran will now have to occupy his time with the legal battles that he *must* wage for the sake of intellectual integrity in the church. What a waste to have the talents and energies of so many Catholic women ignored or pushed aside in leadership and decision-making power within the church. How sad that two years of Gustavo Gutiérrez's life had to be taken away from his work with the poor, simply so that he could survive in an institution that recklessly pressed charges against him that it could not sustain. How unfair that women religious who want open debate are the object of merciless pressures from the hierarchy.

Second, the atmosphere of domination from above puts a chill on reunion dreams from the Protestant side. No one has any illusions about the difficulty of realizing Jesus' prayer "that all may be one," but, during the pontificate of John XXIII, Protestants began to reassess the doctrine of authority and the modes of church government. The pope as a "servant of the servants of God," after the manner of "good Pope John," became a symbol that Protestants could take seriously for the first time in four hundred years. But the image subsequent to Pope John XXIII is not so much an image of servanthood as an image of unilateral authority exercised from the top and resistant to challenge. Perhaps I misread the signs. I hope I do. But I am not alone among Protestants in feeling that the primacy of Peter has become a greater ecumenical stumbling block in the last decade than it was in the preceding decade.

But my third observation is more hopeful. God's purposes, whatever they may be, cannot finally be thwarted by men (and here is a place where non-inclusive language is the only appropriate language). To believe in God, and to believe in the church, is also to believe in the Holy Spirit. And to believe in the Holy Spirit is to believe that no boundaries, not even ecclesial ones, can confine and thwart the creative power of the Spirit. Whatever is of God in the present papal dispensation will be picked up and used by God; and whatever is not of God will be tested, found wanting, and discarded.

I just hope that not too many more good people will be destroyed in the process.

II. THEOLOGIANS AND RELIGIOUS VICTIMS

The Context
Breaking Reform by Breaking Theologians and Religious

Theologians were the engineers of the massive reforms that were initiated at Vatican II. Reform surely did not come from the members of the curia; they fought it every way they could—fair and unfair—and are still fighting it. It also surely did not well up from the bishops of the world, though eventually most of them enthusiastically put their names to those reforms. All of the bishops of 1962 had been trained in the traditional conservative fashion. If their experience in the pastorate had led some of them to reform ideas, they were quickly reprimanded by Rome and were made to believe that they were out of step with "the church." Perusal of the lengthy reports and recommendations submitted by the bishops around the world in preparation for the Council reveal for the most part a long laundry list of some reactionary, many conservative, a few moderate, and a tiny number of liberal recommendations for the Council. No, the great motor of reform was powered by the theologians, the religious thinkers of the church, though the courageous leadership of a few prominent prelates was essential to connect that engine with the bulk of the decision makers of the Council, the bishops.

Once the stranglehold on the Council agenda maintained by the ultraconservative curia was broken by the "revolt of the cardinals," led by Cardinals Liénart and Frings, the bishops began to meet in separate language groups to set the agenda and then discuss its topics. That was where the influence of the theologians first made itself felt. Most of the bishops had either no knowledge or a very antiquated knowledge of the theology of the multiple subjects to be tackled. After all, their seminary studies had taken place in the anti-intellectual shadow of the modernism heresy-hunt triggered by Pope Pius X in 1907 (every diocese in the worldwas, in 1962, still under his mandate to maintain "Vigilance

Committees . . . bound to secrecy as to their deliberations and decisions. . . . Let them combat novelties").

Rome suddenly became a huge theological school of the most advanced sort, with the bishops attending hour after hour of updating theological lectures and reading reams of theological prose churned out in the key languages of either German, French, English, or Dutch and immediately translated into all major languages. The world's top theologians were drawn to Rome and quickly thrown into a furious work schedule, not only writing and delivering lectures and essays but also ghostwriting speeches for the bishops to deliver in Saint Peter's Basilica, and—very importantly—sitting on the drafting committees of what became the documents voted on by the Council fathers. In essence the theologians wrote the Vatican II documents that the bishops voted on and signed.

Often it was precisely those theologians who had been silenced or otherwise oppressed or restricted in their theological work who were now vindicated and brought to Rome to place their talents at the service of the bishops and the church. They were among the most influential of the theological "experts" at the Council—Hans Küng, Karl Rahner, Yves Congar, John Courtney Murray, Godfrey Diekmann, and Jean Daniélou.

These theologians also subsequently worked in the various agencies that carried out the charges of the Council to produce further documents spelling out the various reforms mandated. They were also the ones who advised their bishops on the implementation of the reforms back home. They were in massive demand to teach, lecture, and write about the reforms to all manner of people, young and old, lay, religious, and clerical, Catholic and non-Catholic (for example, when, in the spring of 1968, Bernard Häring taught a course on Vatican II and ethical issues at Temple University in conservative Philadelphia, 650 sisters, priests, and lay people signed up for the course). In short, it was the theologians who again continued to power the reform movement of Vatican II in the years following 1965, up to and including today.

Of course, the theologians were not the only group in the church that promoted the Vatican II reforms. Theologically retooled bishops, priests, religious, and laity also took up the cause, but it was the theologians who retooled them and provided the reflective inspiration.

Nevertheless, a special case can be seen in the stance of the sisters of North America. As is detailed below by Madonna Kolbenschlag, the sisters had already undertaken their own upgrading when Vatican II urged them to accelerate and accentuate the process; they did so with vigor. Because they did this so successfully and were highly organized and very numerous, they too quickly became a second engine of reform in the Catholic church in North America.

Therefore, if a decision is made to break the march of reform, it is those two engines—the theologians and the sisters—that must be disengaged from reform. That decision was made by Pope John Paul II, and the attempt to break theologians and sisters has begun. The following are the more celebrated cases. The prosecutors hope that these *causes célèbres* will make the others "fall in line." But others hope that all Catholics will continue to remember that the church is always an *Ecclesia semper reformanda*.

Repression of theologians and religious, of course, did not begin with the pontificate of Pope John Paul II, but it has greatly and systematically intensified since this pontificate's beginning. An egregious attack on the French Dominican theologian Jacques Pohier was launched during the waning years of Pope Paul VI's pontificate, but it was consummated with breathtaking speed in the early summer of 1979, a few months after John Paul II's accession to the papal throne. Later that summer the Jesuit general in Rome, Father Arrupe, was forced by the pope to issue a letter to all Jesuits around the world, restricting their reform efforts and forbidding them to speak in dissent from any position taken by the Vatican (this was later followed by the pope's forcibly choosing Father Arrupe's successor).

But then almost immediately the news broke that Edward Schillebeeckx was under severe pressure from the Vatican to recant several of his positions on Christology (spelled out below). In the following months, support for Schillebeeckx grew—partly in the form of petitions, letters, and TV statements by Cardinal Willebrands—as the pressure on him mounted. Eventually he went to Rome for interrogation, which ended on 15 December 1979. Three days later the sudden Vatican declaration against Hans Küng was issued, and resistance went up all around the world— documented in detail in my book *Küng in Conflict* (New York: Doubleday, 1980). One of the results was the founding of the organization *Christenrechte in der Kirche* in Germany, *Droits et libertés dans les Eglises* in France, and the Association for the Rights of Catholics in the Church (ARCC) in North America and Australia. ARCC subsequently produced a *Charter of the Rights of Catholics in the Church*, which has been translated and published in French, German, Spanish, and Polish.

A relative lull followed, presumably as a result of the fierce resistance that had been evoked by the mounting series of repressions. Probably the lull was also a period of consolidation and reorganization for the Vatican—in 1983 Cardinal Ratzinger was made the head of the Vatican Congregation for the Doctrine of the Faith—until 1984.

As Dr. Kolbenschlag outlines below, the American sisters already began to come under fire after Sister Theresa Kane's TV request to the pope during his September 1979 visit to Washington, D.C., that women be ordained to the priesthood. Their embattlement intensified during the 1983 Sister Agnes Mansour case in Detroit and reached a crescendo in the aftermath of the multiple episcopal attack on the 1984 Democratic candidate for United States Vice-President, Geraldine Ferraro. Cardinal O'Connor of New York and several other prelates attacked Ferraro during the campaign for her position on the law and abortion. Consequently, during the campaign a large number of Catholics signed a statement in the *New York Times* stating that there are differing positions among Catholic theologians and reflective Catholic laity on the questions surrounding abortion. Among the signers were twenty sisters. For over two years, these sisters have been systematically harassed by the Vatican, demanding a recantation.

Then suddenly in 1985, Pope John Paul II announced that he was calling an extraordinary synod of bishops to consider Vatican II. A tremendous uproar ensued in the fear that the pope intended to roll back the Council. Given his papal track record and the highly regressive public statements made by his first lieutenant, Cardinal Ratzinger—which are discussed in detail elsewhere in this volume—the conclusion was ineluctable. Fortunately, the bishops going to the synod resisted this attempted *démarche* against Vatican II, and so it failed: the synod strongly reaffirmed the Council.

L.S.

13. A Continuous Controversy
Küng in Conflict
LEONARD SWIDLER

In the year 1957, the year he received his doctorate in theology from the Institut Catholique in Paris, Hans Küng's dossier 399/57/i was, as he later remarked in a letter to the Vatican, "to judge by the number, already started by the Index" department of the holy office in Rome. He was then twenty-eight years old, and from that time forward he frequently, at times constantly, had to defend himself vis-à-vis the Vatican and/or the German bishops.

"JUSTIFICATION"

Küng was born in 1928 in Switzerland and studied seven years at the Gregorian University in Rome (1948–55), after which he was ordained to the Catholic priesthood. In 1951 he wrote a thesis for his licentiate in philosophy on the atheistic humanism of Jean-Paul Sartre and in 1955 a thesis for his licentiate in theology on the doctrine of justification in Karl Barth, a fellow Swiss and the most influential Protestant theologian then alive. In this latter work he was supported by his professors at Rome and by another Swiss, a well-known Catholic theologian, Hans Urs von Balthasar (also an expert on Barth's theology), who urged Küng to expand his work on Barth into a doctoral dissertation. This he did during his year and a half at the Sorbonne and Institut Catholique in Paris (1955–57) with the title "Justification, La doctrine de Karl Barth et une réflexion catholique" under Louis Bouyer. The dissertation appeared simultaneously as a German book, published by von Balthasar in Switzerland (1957). The book, which argued that Barth's doctrine of justification and the Council of Trent's were fundamentally the same, caused a sensation in Protestant and Catholic theological worlds. (I can recall a seminar being offered on it by Heinrich Diem of the Protestant faculty at the University of Tübingen while I was studying there during the summer semester of 1958.)

DOSSIER

It was precisely this bridging of the presumably unbridgeable that brought immediate and manifold delations (technical term for tattling) to Rome. At the time Küng judged the chances of the book's being placed on the Index of Forbidden Books about fifty-fifty. However, the support of his teachers, especially Sebastian Tromp, Franz Hürth, Louis Bouyer, and Guy de Brogile, fended off that effort. But that move started his dossier 399/57/i—and it has been active ever since.

Under the influence of the newly announced Council (in January 1959 by John XXIII) Küng began an intensive study of the whole conciliar tradition, which resulted in the publication in 1962, the year Vatican II began, of *Structures of the Church*. All of the seemingly settled problems of authority, decision making, etc., were laid open again in the simple presenting of the historical evidence. This apparently made the Vatican so uneasy that Küng was called to a proceedings against the book. It took place in 1963, during the second session of the Council (Küng was an "expert" appointed to the Council by the pope), at the temporary Roman residence of Bishop Leiprecht of Rottenburg (in whose diocese Tübingen, where Küng was teaching, lay). Fortunately for Küng, the great ecumenist Cardinal Augustin Bea (who, despite his name, came from Swabia—Tübingen's province) was put in charge of the proceedings. Küng later recalled:

Well, it was the period of the Council, and so I was forgiven a certain amount. At all events a solemn session took place in Rome with Cardinal Bea in the chair along with the Bishop of Basel [Küng's home diocese] as well as professors from the Gregorian. I had to answer various questions that had been drawn up by the Holy Office. Later I had to repeat my answers in writing in Latin. Without a doubt it was thanks to Cardinal Bea, whom I had got to know during my first years in Rome when he was Visitator at the German College in the days when he was a simple Jesuit priest and Pius XII's confessor, that the proceedings came to a happy conclusion and were terminated without any obligation of any kind being laid upon me.[1]

FREEDOM AND UNFREEDOM IN AMERICA

Earlier that same year (1963) Küng made the first of what might be described as his "triumphal tours" through the United States. Again, restrictions by church authorities—this time episcopal rather than Roman—played a significant role. It all started with the so-called Catholic University affair. Küng's name was struck from a list of proposed speakers for the Lenten series at Catholic University, Washington, D.C. Usually such an action would have remained a secret, but in those heady days it was reported to the national press and loud protests spread across the nation. In the midst of the outcry Küng arrived in the States for a previously scheduled lecture tour. He was forbidden to speak by the archbishops of Philadelphia, St. Paul, Los Angeles, San Diego, and others, but wherever he did speak, the crowds ranged up to six thousand! He spoke on freedom and unfreedom in the church. Hans Küng had suddenly become the symbol of the new freedom of the Catholic church.

THE INQUISITION

Shortly after Vatican II, Küng published his next major book, *The Church* (1967). The holy office, which had its name changed to the Congregation for the Doctrine of the Faith (it was earlier called the Congregation of the Index, and before that, the Congregation of the Holy Inquisition), was displeased enough with the book to reprimand the diocese of Rottenburg for having given the book an Imprimatur and to order that further distribution and translation of the book be halted until after the author had had a discussion with representatives to be named by the doctrinal congregation. Küng received the Vatican notification two days after Christmas.

On 4 May 1968, Küng received a letter from the doctrinal congregation telling him to appear at 9:30 A.M. at the palace of the holy office for a "discussion" four days hence! Küng wired that it was impossible to keep the appointment, but that he was "in principle . . . prepared to participate in a discussion," that he looked upon "the invitation to a discussion as significant progress compared to the procedure customary in the past. . . . You can be assured of my cooperation."[2] He added five conditions he felt were essential if a fair discussion were to be held: (1) he should have access to the documents in his Vatican dossier; (2) the congregation should give him a written statement of the problem areas ahead of time; (3) because of the scholarly nature of his book, the congregation's discussants should be competent experts in exegesis, history, and dogmatics, and Küng should be informed who they would be; (4) the discussion should be in his native tongue, German; and (5) Küng would be financially reimbursed for the expenses involved. Eventually, numbers two through five were more or less granted but never number one—secrecy was to be maintained. Küng also eventually had extended discussions with both Vatican officials and committees of the German bishops— quite contrary to the myth that Küng stubbornly refused to go to Rome.[3]

INVESTIGATIONS OF "THE CHURCH" AND "INFALLIBLE" ENDED

Not only did the investigation of Küng's book *The Church* drag on for years, but it was added to after 1970 when, on the centenary of the declaration of papal infallibility at Vatican Council I, Küng published *Infallible? An Inquiry.* A year later, in the summer of 1971, Küng was notified by the Vatican that his new book was under investigation and he was given a number of questions to answer. The documents of this dispute fill 135 pages in *Küng in Conflict.* It was an intense, at times acrimonious debate between Küng and the Vatican and a certain conservative portion of the German bishops. Through it all, Cardinal Döpfner of Munich, the president of the German bishops' conference, effectually served as Küng's "protector" vis-à-vis Rome—though between him and Küng very frank, even vigorous, but always deeply friendly, exchanges took place. The case finally "ended" in a compromise declaration by the Congregation for the Doctrine of the Faith (5 February 1975) whereby Küng was admonished not to advocate his teachings on infallibility, but there was no question of his having to recant or suffer any censure: "With this declaration, the proceedings of the Congregation for the Doctrine of the Faith in this matter are ended for now"—the last two words proved to be ominous.[4]

ATTACK ON KÜNG'S BEING A CHRISTIAN

However, for Küng it was out of the fire into another frying pan, for the German Bishops' Conference also issued, two days later, a declaration in which it not only greeted the termination of the proceedings against Küng's two books (*The Church* and *Infallible? An Inquiry*), but also delivered to him a set of instructions on how to proceed theologically and issued their first statement against his new book, *On Being a Christian* (German edition, 1974; English translation [New York: Doubleday, 1976]). This book quickly turned into Küng's best seller, over 160,000 German copies alone being sold, besides the hundreds of thousands of copies in English, French, Spanish, Italian, Portuguese, Dutch, and Japanese. Because of the book's popularity, controversy over it spread quickly—not so much because of what it said, but because of what it supposedly did *not* say. At the height of the controversy, Cardinal Döpfner suddenly died and was replaced as cardinal archbishop of Munich by Joseph Ratzinger (after 1982 the head of the Vatican's doctrinal congregation), who had once been one of Küng's colleagues and collaborators but later turned in a conservative direction and became his opponent. More ominous was the replacement of Döpfner as president of the German Bishops' Conference by Cardinal Joseph Höffner of Cologne, who in single-minded fashion led a relentless attack on Küng.

The debate peaked when, on 22 January 1977, Küng met with a number of German bishops and theologians for a day in what became known as the Stuttgart Colloquium. The theological issues of *On Being a Christian* were thoroughly discussed. However, every time an agreement was about to be reached, Cardinal Höffner broke it up with steely demands on Küng that he give simple yes answers to catechism-simplistic questions. The controversy simmered on through the time of the publication of Küng's next magnum opus, *Does God Exist?* in 1978, and the election of two new popes, John Paul and John Paul II, the same year. However, all seemed on the surface basically resolved, for the German bishops had made a public declaration on Küng's *On Being a Chris-*

tian, and the requested christological clarifications would seem to have been made in the latter part of *Does God Exist?* That calm, of course, turned out to be deceptive.

ATTACK ON KÜNG'S CATHOLICITY

On 18 December 1979 (three days after the close of the Vatican hearings with Schillebeeckx—see elsewhere in this volume for details), Küng was the object of a previously unheard of Vatican document, a declaration that he "can no longer be considered a Catholic theologian or function as such in a teaching role." In the past, Catholic theologians who fell into severe disfavor with Rome were either censured, silenced, made to recant, suspended from priestly office, excommunicated, burned at the stake—or all of the above. Küng suffered none of them. Why this *novum?* To those familiar with the relationship of German universities, the German state, and Rome, the answer is obvious. If authoritative evidence could be presented that Küng was not a Catholic theologian and therefore could not function as one in teaching, then the local Catholic bishop of Tübingen, where Küng teaches, would have legal grounds to request the state to replace Küng as professor of Catholic theology at the university. This was to be done on the basis of the concordat between the Vatican and Hitler's Germany in 1933. It was all carefully planned out and executed in a series of secret meetings by key Vatican and German hierarchs that reads like the plot of an international intrigue—which it was.[5]

Why this extraordinary effort on the part of so many to diminish the stature and influence of Hans Küng as a Catholic theologian? I would like to suggest four basic reasons: (1) his effectiveness in communication; (2) his absolute honesty; (3) his dynamic, historical, critical understanding of truth statements; (4) his placing of the historical person of Jesus at the center of Christian belief and practice. But of course the ultimate goal was to reduce significantly Küng's popularity and influence.

CLARITY OF COMMUNICATION

Almost no matter what Küng wrote, if only a few thousand scholars and educated laity read his books, Rome and the German hierarchy would hardly have concerned themselves with him. However, as noted, his books have sold hundreds of thousands of copies in many languages all over the world. Moreover, people read and understood them because they made sense to them, spoke to them in their modern idiom, addressed their real problems, and made the idea of being a Christian come alive for them.

But there's the rub. In 1977, Cardinal Höffner complained to Küng that because his books were selling so many copies, the bishops were compelled to call him to task. Why? Cardinal Volk of Mainz, at the same 1977 Stuttgart Colloquium, explained: "Your book [On Being a Christian] is for me too plausible!" (Ihr Buch ist mir zu plausibel!)

But this "plausibility," this clarity of style, does not come trippingly on the pen. It is the result of an immense amount of hard work. One of his close assistants, Dr. Karl-Josef Kuschel, has described in detail how Does God Exist?, almost nine hundred pages long, was written in three years. He wrote that the mere physical strength which Küng invests in writing books demands respect. Küng's workday is eighteen or nineteen hours long, and when it is a matter of finishing a book, his last reserves are mobilized. In this Küng demands much of his co-workers (three academic associates and one secretary) in their daily contribution, but he demands most of himself.

In writing Does God Exist?, the following plan was usually followed. Before a large chapter was begun, the entire concept was deliberated upon and the design, execution, and construction of the chapter analyzed and discussed by the circle of co-workers. Then Küng began to write. For many months—from spring 1975 until the end of August 1977—Küng constantly worked from nine in the morning until late at night. Even before the first typed draft, Küng had written out for himself two or three handwritten drafts in which he gave the first shape to the material, which was based on primary and secondary literature. Here lay the real creative process of writing. Küng then dictated this handwritten draft into a dictaphone so that the secretary could produce the first typed draft.

For Küng, dictation is not only a technical expedient in the production of a manuscript but also has an important function in relation to language and content. The flowing style of Küng's books (and the ease with which they can be understood) is due not least to the "oral testing" of the text by reading aloud. Again and again Küng and Kuschel read the manuscript aloud to one another and, through that very process of "listening," were able immediately to pick out complications of both a stylistic and a substantive nature.

This first typed copy was then thoroughly revised and discussed by Küng and Kuschel for content and language, with Küng deciding which corrections he would adopt. Then the secretary made the second typed copy. This copy as a rule went to the other two academic co-workers, who were also in constant personal contact with Küng. After this, if necessary, a third typed copy was produced. Yet even after all this revision procedure, Küng was still not satisfied. In certain chapters where the systematic theologian ventured into a specialized area foreign to him, the counsel of specialists was sought. After this, and after several rereadings by Küng himself, the manuscript was sometimes typed for a fourth time (this, before the days of the word processor).[6]

After such herculean efforts to attain clarity, it must have been a bit stunning to hear the accusation: Ihr Buch ist mir *zu plausibel!*

"HONESTY IS THE BEST POLICY"

Another reason for Küng's difficulties is his total honesty. For him it is a virtue that cannot be displaced by other considerations—he says as much in the book titled *Truthfulness: The Future of the Church* (1968). A number of other Catholic theologians are aware of the results of historical and other critical studies, but at certain crucial points they "fudge" their application to Christian doctrine. In many cases it is a matter of having a fundamentally different ecclesiology. They start out with what the church has traditionally taught on some matter through some authoritative expression, for example, a conciliar or papal document, and assume that it cannot be faulted, not "essentially," although they will nowadays allow for "development." The difficulties come when the "development" moves from, for example, Gregory XVI's and Pius IX's solemn condemnations of religious freedom to Vatican II's solemn approbation of religious freedom. Küng, and others, would say that in such instances one cannot meaningfully, honestly, speak about "development," but would have to admit the possibility of error in at least one of the two contradictory positions. Such probity precipitates papal problems.

HISTORICAL AND DIALOGICAL UNDERSTANDING OF TRUTH-STATEMENTS

Probably the most important reason why Küng has difficulties with church authorities is that his understanding of truth-statements is formed within the horizon of the historical and dialogical methods. He is of course far from being the only Catholic theologian to hold such an understanding, but he does so with a consistency that is not matched by all. Fundamentally, Küng's method of doing theology is historical and hence dynamic, unafraid of the idea of change. This worldview is completely at odds with the traditional static one. As Thomas Kuhn has shown in the history of science, the shift from one "paradigm" by which reality is understood to a new one is always fraught with resistance and turbulence before the new paradigm is accepted—one thinks preeminently of the agonies of Copernicus, Kepler, and Galileo in moving from the geocentric to the heliocentric paradigm. Given the acceleration of change in the contemporary world, one hopes that Küng will be functioning as Copernicus, Kepler, and Galileo and beyond, all rolled into one.

The second creative—and trouble-causing—characteristic of Küng's method of doing theology is dialogue. Dialogue, specifically interreligious dialogue, has been officially and unofficially mandated and practiced by Catholics for over two decades now. There has been wide experience, reflection, and writing on the subject. Anyone at all conversant with these knows that what makes such dialogue possible now is the "deabsolutizing" of the human perception of statements about the truth. In the past hundred years the wide acceptance of the findings of historicism, sociology of knowledge, and language analysis has made critical thinkers see all statements about reality as "relational," related to the time and culture, the sociological class and circumstances, and the language of the speaker. This perception of the relational character of all statements is a *sine qua non* of authentic dialogue, for it assumes that no person or group can, by the nature of finite knowledge and the statements of it, know everything about a topic. Rather than being certain about having the full "truth" about a matter, such critical persons claim that one is certain it is impossible ever to have the full "truth" about something expressed by one person or group. We come to dialogue not primarily to teach but primarily to learn. As a result dialogue always entails risk: we might be persuaded by our partner's position on an issue, and thus if we would act with integrity, we would have to change. That can be painful; it challenges the static notion of truth. Küng is ready to "bite the bullet"; his opponents are only too ready to fire it.

THE HISTORICAL JESUS AT THE CENTER

Küng speaks of two "poles" of Christian theology—the living Jesus of history and our own human experience—and of how there needs to be a critical correlation between the two so that Jesus in fact can affect the lives of Christians; It is this end that tradition and the church are to serve. As Küng states it:

The source, standard and criterion of Christian faith is the living Jesus of history. Through historical-critical research into the life of Jesus the Christian faith is historically responsible in the light of the contemporary consciousness of problems and is protected from faulty interpretations arising from within or outside the Church. Schillebeeckx is correct in affirming that, "It is not the historical image of Jesus but rather the living Jesus of history who stands at the beginning and is the source, standard and criterion of that which the first Christians interpretively encountered in him." . . . Christianity is not founded on myths, legends or tales, nor solely on a doctrine (for it is not a religion of a book). Rather, it is based primarily on the historical personality of Jesus of Nazareth who was seen as the Christ of God. . . . No contradiction can be permitted between the Jesus of history and the Christ of faith. We must be able to identify the Christ of faith as the Jesus of history. . . .We can make it clear that the center of Scripture, the Christian message, the Gospel, is the living Jesus.[7]

THE ATTACK BACKFIRES

If the ultimate goal of the Vatican and the German Bishops' Conference's attack was to reduce significantly the popularity and influence of Küng, it backfired spectacularly. Before the December 1979 attack, Küng normally had about 150 students in his lecture classes. As a result of the attack, Küng is no longer a member of the Catholic theology faculty of the University of Tübingen, but he remains professor of ecumenical theology and director of the ecumenical institute of the university and can sit on doctoral committees in the Catholic theology faculty. (He of course also remains a priest in good standing.) In the succeeding years his lecture courses regularly drew first 1,000, then 1,300, then 1,500, and then 2,000 students! Further, he has also arranged to teach every fourth semester in America.

INCREASING DIALOGUE AND INVOLVEMENT

From the beginning of his public life, Küng has been committed to ecumenical dialogue, and there has been a steady progress in the process of his opening ever more fully to the dialogue, to an ever widening circle of dialogue partners. This can be seen most clearly in his attitude toward non-Christian religions. He evidences an increasing openness to them, moving from his book *The Church* (1968), to *On Being a Christian* (1974), to *Does God Exist?* (1978), to—in a quantum leap forward—*Christianity and World Religions* (1986). For Küng, the non-Christian religions have now become, along with the modern critical world, fully equal dialogue partners with his Christianity.

At the same time his involvement with feminism and other liberation theology issues has become even deeper, as illustrated by his establishing a special section of his ecumenical institute devoted to "Frau and Christentum." He has also been heavily engaged in research and reflection around the topic of the paradigm shift and how it affects religion and theology, as illustrated by the international conference he organized at Tübingen in conjunction with the Chicago Divinity School in June 1983, and subsequent publications. Theology and literature is another area which has also drawn Küng's intense attention, as reflected in his hugely popular lecture series with his friend and colleague Walter Jens, professor of rhetoric at the University of Tübingen (two thousand regular attendees during the winter semester 1984–85) and the publications to follow.

In short, Hans Küng has been, not only a lightning rod, drawing the fire of the purveyors of the passing paradigm, but also a sensitive antenna of the contemporary Christian movement, probing and pioneering the points of contact with the future.

NOTES

1. Hermann Häring and Karl-Josef Kuschel, *Hans Küng: His Work and His Way* (New York: Doubleday, 1979), 160.
2. Leonard Swidler, *Küng in Conflict* (New York: Doubleday, 1981), 11.
3. Ibid., 129–32, 180, 226, 314.
4. Ibid., 164.
5. Ibid., 383ff., 401ff., where the secret plot is described by Bishop Moser of Rottenburg.
6. Leonard Swidler, ed., *Consensus in Theology? A Dialogue with Hans Küng and Edward Schillebeeckx* (Philadelphia: Westminster, 1980), 152–58.
7. Ibid., 6, 7, 17.

14. Jacques Pohier
A Theologian Destroyed
JEAN-PIERRE JOSSUA

Jacques Pohier professor of moral theology on the Dominican faculty of Saulchoir since 1959, had since then published a number of books and engaged in several activities which showed some reservation with regard to official teaching of the Catholic church in moral matters. However, no one had attacked him—even though the authorities reaffirmed their positions—whether because the prestige of theologians (produced by the Council's need of them) was still too great, or whether because these moral problems seemed ill-suited to public debate. We may venture to think this precaution was not unrelated to events which occurred some months after publication, in October 1977, of the book *Quand je dis Dieu (When I Speak of God)* in which the theologian engaged in reflection relating somewhat to the confession of Christian faith—the classical field of dogmatic theology.

THE CONFLICT WITH THE DOCTRINAL CONGREGATION

On 26 April 1978, the master general of the Dominican order conveyed to Jacques Pohier the gist of a letter which had been addressed to him by the Congregation for the Doctrine of the Faith on 21 April. They informed him therein that, "given the gravity and urgency of the matter" in regard to this book, the congregation had resorted to extraordinary proceedings because of the presence of a "clear and certain" error in faith, and that this er-

Editor's note: Jacques Pohier, a French Dominican priest and a moral theologian, is best known in France and Western Europe. Hence his investigation and silencing by the Vatican in 1979 went relatively unnoticed in the English-speaking world. However, it was the opening shot of the greatly intensified Vatican attack on progressive theologians and still remains an unresolved scandal today.

ror involved "an immediate danger for the faithful."[1] This procedure dispensed with all juridical rules established since the Council to make it possible for theologians to defend themselves. Recent examples showed they could use these rules to draw out or even to stop the process of condemnation. Hence, the congregation was proceeding directly to the charge and the order to retract without the author having been consulted or interviewed; neither he nor his colleagues, nor his superiors had had knowledge of the preliminary actions. A one-month delay was given to Pohier for a public retraction of six specific points (the redemptive passion, the resurrection of Christ, the resurrection of Christians, the objective meaning of Scripture, the permanent meaning of definitions of faith, and infallibility); three sets of ambiguities (the transcendence of God, the real presence, the role of the priest in the Eucharist); and one vague point (the divinity of Christ).

On 17 May, the theologian answered the master general and, through his mediatior, the congregation, that the extraordinary procedure did not seem necessary, considering the slight distribution of the book and the standard interaction, well underway, of the critics; that on several points he could already show his positions were quite different from those they attributed to him and that other points did not diverge from contemporary theological consensus; that he hoped an ordinary and honest discussion might take place with the congregation—whose competence he did not deny. No response was given to this letter nor to a second of 7 July outlining the discussions which were taking place on the work, showing its positive effects and the reserve its readers were able to maintain.

It was only when the proceedings were started up anew (canonically required because of the change in pontificate from Paul VI to John Paul I) that the congregation on 16 September took note of the information received. They asked the theologian to send a statement of the points on which he thought he was misunderstood and to make an "explicit profession of faith according to the teaching of the church." As early as 23 October, Pohier wrote to the cardinal prefect, explained himself thoroughly on eight of the difficulties raised, and expressed his faith. On the resurrection of Christ and of Christians he asked for a delay, arguing that his thought had developed since publication of the book and promising publication of an in-depth article. When the proceedings were started up a second time (required because of the accession of John Paul II), the congregation on 13 December made no mention of these clear efforts at engaging in the discussion but merely pointed out the difference between the requested profession and (Pohier's own) formula "confessing my Catholic faith." They reproached him for having announced a publication. He could not "be unaware of the seriousness [of such a] public act or of the . . . clear violation of the procedure." (Which procedure?) Without the required fresh start of the proceedings, would even this meager exchange have taken place?

On 8 January 1979, Jacques Pohier answered that it was not for him to determine whether his faith was or was not the faith of the church; he could do no more than to confess it and hope for acceptance. He did not understand why they had not taken account of his explanations on the other points, or why there was such an urgency to require him to forgo a maturation period. He renounced the planned publication. And now on 2 April he was summoned with his provincial to the nuncio's residence in Paris where an undersecretary of the congregation handed over to him a letter stating that the proceedings had failed because of him and that a declaration would be published, without making its contents known to him. He was assured verbally that, as far as the congregation was concerned, the procedure was closed. The declaration was published 3 April (although they had come to an understanding on 6 April for the date). The declaration again took up in full almost exactly the points of the first letter, as if no explanation had been given. Further, the personal sanctions—conveyed to Pohier only orally by the master of the order on 5 April (to refrain from preaching, from public celebration of the Eucharist, and from all teachings in matters of faith)—were presented "as a consequence" of the declaration, although the congregation had been insisting on them for several months.

The sanctions were seen as unjust and harmful, and numerous and varied efforts followed to have them rescinded. But these attempts were a total failure, even when carried out by authorities of the order or by well-known and respected theologians—some of whom in their own positions were far removed from Pohier's positions. From all quarters people vouched for the fruits of Jacques Pohier's priestly ministry and the quality of his preaching, which never treated the debated topics. The only permission the master general could grant him was to participate in eucharistic celebrations without presiding. It is certain that this restriction came from the congregation, and it remains in effect until today. As for Pohier, he complied exactly with the measures taken against him and with the regulation to submit all texts for publication to a preliminary examination—at least until his subsequent book, *Dieu, fractures*,[2] in which he was led to relate the destructive results of these sanctions in his own life—but that is another story.

ANALYSIS OF THE CONFLICT

There is nothing extraordinary in all this if we consider church history, but we could have hoped to see no more of this kind of thing after Vatican II. As the situation is, it is no doubt more helpful to reflect than to become indignant, although both reactions are called for. Here, then, are some paths which seem to me to be open for analysis.

First, in rereading the book and confronting it with the criticisms made by the congregation, in examining Jacques Pohier's responses in the preface of the the German edition of the book,[3] and in making inquiries into other more recent cases, we can't help being struck by the lack of understanding and the inability to read on the part of the authors of the declaration. As far as the two "resurrection" points are concerned—on which the theologian never gave a satisfactory answer—we are dealing with unambiguous negations on a topic whose seriousness Pohier may very well not have calculated. On other matters, if his positions departed appreciably from classical theological perceptions—the meaning of the Passion, interpretation of Scripture, the permanence of dogmatic statements—they were indeed akin to the general state of theological work. But above all, why these false problems on the transcendence of God or the divinity of Christ when there is no wavering on these points if one knows how to adapt to a language different from one's own? Why these problems raised on subjects barely approached in the book, such as the real presence, the role of ministers, and infallibility? Why, unless because the Roman censors are *theologians*, who are neither better nor worse than others, but with a particular mindset, and because they link together their concepts, understanding, and lack of understanding, their fears and conjectures with their exorbitant powers—by the power of their office they are also judges. Hence, their limitations have considerable consequences. Those who do not set up their opinion as a norm are indeed obliged to try to enter into the thinking of theologians who differ from them.

Second, let us acknowledge that all service includes a certain authority, all "pastoral" responsibility a concern for "doctrinal" safeguarding of the faith. Let us accept then that in some cases the central jurisdiction can warn against certain possible tampering with the *confessio fidei*. But why, in the case of Jacques Pohier? Norml regulations had been operative before any threat of Roman intervention: fraternal reflection, oral or written, of readers, of colleagues; numerous and detailed critical book reviews; a public statement of the doctrinal commission of the French episcopate (May 1978). Of that the congregation was informed. As soon as the investigation became known, new regulatory actions were initiated, notably a commisson including eminent Dominican theologians. Concerning them Jacques Pohier could say: on certain points no one is in agreement with me, and they don't leave me in the dark about it. But then the proceedings unfolded without consideration for the rule of subsidiarity. No local investigation was made of the effects of the work or of the frame of mind of those whose faith experienced this "grave peril" which warranted the great haste of the condemnation process. One can't help but wonder, Why this insistent determination to intervene at the highest level? Was it a matter of discharging duty or of maneuvers of an authority which sought to assert itself and, more specifically, to reassert itself by discrediting the prestige of theologians who, in the postconciliar era, were seen as encouraging scholars and laity in a certain aloofness from and relative resistance to Roman centralism?

Third, the subject of the "rule of faith" is serious, and no Christian can take it lightly. Doubtless we can find in Jacques Pohier's book a position on the resurrection that causes difficulty in this regard. However, this was not the first question to ask, and it is only one aspect of the book. We must begin by asking, How are we to conceive of and express faith today so it will be meaningful and remain faithful to the past, in fact, by becoming different in its formulation in a different human and cultural context, in completely different theoretical systems of reference? One of the most important elements in this context is the criticism of religion by psychoanalysis which, though not linked essentially to this discipline, nonetheless holds many men and women from the faith. All effort to live, to think out, and to express faith within this area of research is difficult and risky. It can succeed only by trial and error, by detours, indeed by errors within a feasible plan for moving forward. Others who come later will correct or will aim more accurately, thanks to the path we will have opened up. In this connection, *Quand je dis Dieu* contributed much, and Jacques Pohier was prepared to continue developing, reexamining his positions. Why was the procedure so hurried, imperious, even bitter, and why did it fail to take account of the laws of such research? Must we think that those in charge could not concede any value to his contributions because they did not even imagine—isolated as they are in their closed world—the very different questions being faced in such research?

Fourth, if we want to ensure transmission of the faith, all control involves certain limitations. Ideally it is less a matter of excluding the one who persists in difference of opinion than of inviting him or her to draw inferences from that opinion. Even thus defined, such a limitation raises difficulties in view of the gospel. Jesus essentially devoted himself to a reintegration of the rejected, a rejection of harshness—and that without any "doctrinaire" criterion, but solely on the basis of trust in God's mercy. Let us admit that this contradiction is unsurmountable and that the historical social reality of the church requires a more solid structure of the believing community. Nevertheless, a certain practical resolution is possible in the question of the manner of proceeding. Is it not true that the exercise of authority in the church must seek to prove itself by adjusting to what is said about it in the gospel rather than by trying to legitimate itself by a less certain sacral system? Does not the classic criticism of a lack of gospel spirit aimed at Roman authorities seem to be rather grievously justified in this case? Why this administrative impersonality, this brutality, these lies, this pressure? Why these sanctions against a man who received from all a testimony of goodwill, of his qualifications as a presider over the Eucharist and as a preacher? Why not strive, as Paul VI had expressly asked in other cases, for the utmost humanity and kindness?

And fifth, it is perhaps not impossible to clear up a little more of these incomprehensible, even scandalous sanctions. How could the authorities so rigorously link these measures with a doctrinal admonition? By a hierarchical, pyramidal structure which at the same time is wrapped in the garment of official "representativeness." One is regarded as speaking *in the name of* . . . because one is commissioned for this purpose. To allow a priest whose opinions are judged false to officiate, to preach, to teach is to risk letting the faithful think that what he states represents "church doctrine," which he is obliged to repeat *ex officio*. The prior censure of writings, which presumes that a broad theological orthodoxy is improbable, and the reproaches against the theologian for confessing only *his* faith instead of expressing the faith of the church, is tied up with the same complex of ideas. In France, at any rate, such a view of representativeness does not hold up in the face of reality. No one is considered anything but one voice among others. It is important for one's statements to be *received* in the church, but their weight and importance will depend exclusively on the quality of evidence and of thinking. One never commits anyone but oneself. This great agitation, these protective sanctions, seem once more to come from a milieu not only cut off from reality, but lacking in curiosity to find out about it.

These points in history and these reflections were intended only to inform and to give food for thought. To see such dysfunction is a source of sadness, indeed of dejection, because of a clear inability to change things. But to shed light on the matter institutionally guards against personal bitterness. It is the system that is perverse. And hope remains that even in this morass the Spirit is building the church.

Translated by
Rosemary Jermann

NOTES

1. A.A.S. LXIII (1971): 234–36.
2. English translation, *God—in Fragments* (1986).
3. *Wenn ich Gott sage* (Freiburg, 1980).

15. The Endless Case of Edward Schillebeeckx

AD WILLEMS

Since the announcement of the Second Vatican Council, Edward Schillebeeckx has been pursued by an unabating distrust out of Rome. It is especially Schillebeeckx's hermeneutical method, which Roman officials fear will relativize central church authority, that was and is the reason behind all their efforts to discredit his theology. Thus far they have not succeeded. On the contrary, the more the public learns about the clandestine Roman designs against Schillebeeckx, the more his international reputation grows and the more his method is appreciated. Clear proof exists that it has not been any argument brought up in the debate but precisely his international reputation that has held church authorities back from an official condemnation. In the meantime, it remains our task to explain the arguments clearly and to keep the international public alerted, above all because of the patent efforts now being made to interpret the Second Vatican Council restrictively. The facts evincing Rome's distrust of Schillebeeckx can be assembled chronologically.[1]

A PASTORAL LETTER BEFORE THE COUNCIL

On 24 December 1960, a pastoral letter by the Dutch bishops appeared concerning the forthcoming Council. Already in this "preconciliar" letter, central church authority was situated *within*

Editor's note: Edward Schillebeeckx is a Flemish Dominican priest and professor emeritus of dogmatic theology at the Catholic University of Nijmegen, the Netherlands. He was a prominent Catholic theologian even before the Second Vatican Council, in which he played an influential role, and since that time he has become one of the premiere theologians in the whole Christian church. All his books have been quickly translated into English, German, French, and other languages. Among his most influential books are: *Jesus; Christ;* and *Ministry.*

the church community and not *above* it. With reference to the Council of Ephesus and the theology of Thomas Aquinas, it was explained to the faithful of Holland "that the infallibility of the papacy may not be disengaged from the totality of faith into which it was placed by Christ. . . . Factually, the personal infallibility of the Pope is situated in the infallible office of the world's bishops, which is itself upheld by the infallible faith of the whole faith community." Thus, it is to be expected "that the Council, confronted by new life-problems, will seek to make contact with the faith-consciousness of the universal church and with public opinion." At the end of this detailed pastoral letter, the Dutch bishops expressed their thanks to Professor Schillebeeckx and to the Commission for Collaboration in the Apostolate "for the distinguished and valuable service which they provided us in the preparation of this text."[2]

Translations of this letter appeared in 1961 in French, German, and English, and in 1962 in Italian. But this latter translation was withdrawn from circulation in June of that same year. The copies already circulated had to be returned to the publisher. After contacting the pope, Cardinal Alfrink explained (17 June 1962) that these measures were taken on account of an unsatisfactory translation and because in certain passages of the letter "a clearer formulation and more complete argumentation was desirable."[3] After that, it came as no surprise to "insiders" when Schillebeeckx was not officially named a *peritus* at the Council, even though, considering his competence, it would have been appropriate.

THE THREAT IN 1968

Paris-Nanterre, Prague, Berkeley, and Medellín are all places where history was made in that remarkable year, 1968. For Schillebeeckx too, it was a year of turbulence and disquiet. To *Le Monde*, the French daily, goes the credit for making public the threat of official Roman proceedings against Schillebeeckx. The 24 September edition reported that the Congregation for the Doctrine of the Faith suspected Schillebeeckx of heresy and was thus initiating proceedings. Several theologians (Dhanis, Lemeer, Chiappi) had been asked to make a careful investigation of his collected articles. From this investigation of the literature, it was apparent that Schillebeeckx's idea of revelation, as expressed in his interpretation of the Eucharist and elsewhere, could not be reconciled with the traditional conception. It was also their opinion that Schillebeeckx had too optimistic a view of the phenomenon of secularization, and that this caused his concept of the church to be one-sided. Also considered in this investigation were various complaints that had come to Rome from Holland and the United States (where he had made a lecture tour toward the end of 1967). It was probably at the personal initiative of the just named prefect of the doctrinal congregation, Cardinal Šeper, that Karl Rahner was asked to defend Schillebeeckx's case in Rome.

The news in *Le Monde* let loose a worldwide storm of protest against the Roman accusations. On 7 October 1968, as Rahner first had to listen to the consultors' criticisms of Schillebeeckx and then give his own view of the matter, several voices were raised in Vatican circles calling into question at least the opportuneness of the action. Rahner's defense of Schillebeeckx concentrated on the need in our secular age to reflect on the old dogmas and to proclaim them in a way that they could be credible to people today too as truths that *save*—as he himself had done. But Rahner defended not only the substance of Schillebeeckx's theology. Rahner's knowledge of the dossier prepared against Schillebeeckx and his own earlier experiences with Rome led him to criticize strongly, as totally inadequate, the method of those who were prosecuting him. To string together questionable quotations, taken out of context, together with poorly translated remarks about lectures and interviews was an injustice to someone like Schillebeeckx.

The end of this affair created a sensation. According to the official communiqué by the Vatican press secretary, Monsignor Vallainc, the whole uproar was based on a misunderstanding. "No doctrinal proceedings had been conducted against Schillebeeckx. None would be conducted, and there was no reason why any should be. . . . It was true that Fr. Karl Rahner's opinion had been asked. Not, however, as Fr. Schillebeeckx's defender but as a friend who on various issues shared his views. His thoughts were invited and explanations requested so that Schillebeeckx's ideas could be better understood."[4]

THE PROCEEDINGS BETWEEN 1976 AND 1980

In early 1974, a lengthy study by Schillebeeckx appeared, which he himself regarded as a believer's reaction to Rudolf Augstein's sensational work *Jesus, the Son of Man*. Schillebeeckx called his book "a Christian interpretation of Jesus," which would be followed by a "New Testament Christology," and concluded with a theology of the church and of the Holy Spirit. The doctrinal congregation could not wait for the whole work to be completed. Cardinal Šeper, as prefect of the congregation, wrote to Schillebeeckx (20 October 1976), that he was convinced that Schillebeeckx "had certainly written this impressive work in order to contribute to the development of Christ's kingdom. Therefore the Congregation for Doctrine which must investigate it because of the reactions it has generated, approaches its task not only with concern but also very genuine good will."[5]

Thus, once again, an official investigation was underway. The first phase resulted in a detailed letter (October 1976), in which Schillebeeckx was asked to give further information about a considerable number of points. The points were divided into three topics: questions about method, questions about the historical Jesus, and questions about systematic theology. Clearly up for discussion in the first section were Schillebeeckx's hermeneutics. It was strongly emphasized that in the realm of faith and dogmatic theology, the absolute norm "lies in Scripture, tradition, and the so-called definitive decisions of the church's teaching office."[6] The meaning of the faith assertions of sacred Scripture and of the "definitive" declarations of the magisterium are basically to be explained and are "simply true and precisely for that reason unchangeable."[7] In the second section, the fear is expressed that Schillebeeckx had contradicted the definitions of the Council of Chalcedon and of the Fourth Lateran Council. At the end of his book, he had spoken with some nuances about the human person of Jesus. The congregation then asked whether Schillebeeckx could not be brought "once more simply to agree with the Christology, which the church had taught its faithful?"[8] Obviously, Schillebeeckx's view of Jesus as the eschatological prophet was not acceptable or his relativizing of the traditional concept of redemption as satisfaction. His evaluations of the Gospel narratives about the empty tomb and the appearances in connection with the resurrection were also not acceptable. In the third section, Schillebeeckx is requested to confess unequivocally "the eternal existence of the Trinity" together with the "normal meaning" which the church's tradition ascribes to the Bible's teaching about Jesus' immaculate conception.[9] Finally he is asked: "Can you give an unambiguous reassuring explanation regarding the hierarchic structure of the church?"[10]

Schillebeeckx addressed all these questions in detail. In a letter dated 13 April 1977, he devoted much attention to the questions of method above all, since it was on this point that the fundamental differences between him and the congregation were the greatest. If a consensus could be reached on this point, it would then be easier to agree on many details. Of greatest importance, Schillebeeckx believes, is the thesis that "objective revelation" becomes a "formal revelation" in the faith-filled listening to what, with Thomas Aquinas, he calls the *auditus fidei* or the *assensus fidei*. Appealing to his medieval Dominican confrere, he protested to the congregation that, for there to be a formal revelation, it is "always imperative" that there be a necessary answer of faith to an objective revelation.[11] Schillebeeckx makes use of these rather general remarks in his answers to the various points of the complaints Rome raised against him. Regarding the *person*hood of the man Jesus, Schillebeeckx asks whether the modern reader of the Bible and of the teachings of the Council of Chalcedon "must first be converted to a particular philosophy, before being brought to apostolic faith?" That would certainly not be necessary, says Schillebeeckx, and therefore "Chalcedon should be explained in appropriate language."[12] To insinuate that he treats the teachings of this council casually is an insult to Schillebeeckx. "If Chalcedon were only an empty word for me, how could I have mustered the courage and passion to write two books on Jesus, comprising altogether more than 1,400 pages?"[13] With a view to his methodology, Schillebeeckx patiently explained once again all of the difficulties of detail perceived by the congregation.

On 6 July 1978, the congregation answered Schillebeeckx's detailed letter of April 1977. Apparently not quite convinced, they had asked an assistant to the congregation to make a painstaking analysis of the letter. This analysis completely bypassed Schillebeeckx's thorough account of his hermeneutical method and fixated time and again on the time-worn particular questions. This remarkable 6 July letter was sent to him with the express request that he defend his case in Rome personally, in conversation with persons to be determined by the congregation. Their names were not disclosed. A kind of agenda was drawn up for the conversation. It would be concerned with the following points: (1) the extent of revealed truth; (2) the normative character of ecumenical councils and the infallible teaching authority of the pope; (3) the pre-existence of Jesus as the Son of God; (4) Jesus' death as satisfaction; (5) Jesus' messianic self-consciousness; (6) Jesus and the founding of the church; (7) the institution of the Eucharist; (8) the immaculate conception; (9) the objective reality of the resurrection.

The death of Pope Paul VI (6 August 1978) and then of Pope John Paul I (28 September 1978) prevented the engines of Vatican officialdom from operating at peak efficiency at that time and in early 1979. By the end of 1979, however, the conversation between Schillebeeckx and his opponents was pressed to take place. Probably as a result of worldwide reaction,[14] the doctrinal congregation issued a press communiqué the first day (13 December 1979). There it was stated that this was not a so-called juridical inquiry, but rather an attempt to obtain new "elements for judgment" which would then be passed on to the cardinals who comprise the doctrinal congregation.[15] At the same time, after repeated protest against Vatican secretiveness, the names of the conversation partners were officially communicated: A. Descamps, A. Patfoort, and J. Galot, the last of whom had declared publicly on radio Vaticana (5 December 1979) that Schillebeeckx's Christology must be condemned. The Nijmegen exegete, Professor Bas van Iersel, had accompanied Schillebeeckx to Rome at his request, but was not allowed to be present at the conversation. Later he gave a detailed account of his impressions, among them, once again, why in his opinion the matter was not a "conversation" but a "judicial hearing."[16]

One after another, all the announced nine topics came into consideration during the conversation. Although it lasted approximately eight hours. From the highly abbreviated minutes,[17] it is clear that only seldom was the most important of the controverted topics explicitly mentioned, but it was constantly implicit. The congregation maintains that the faith involves "eternal un- changeable truth." Schillebeeckx: "What I reject is that there ex- ists a truth in 'itself,' that would be palpable in its unchangeableness. The unchangeable truth is attained in her- meneutical translation, in the interpretation of the ecclesial com- munity. It is the church that does the interpreting, ultimately the magisterium; theologians contribute their 'specialized service' too."[18]

So long as the significance of these hermeneutical-methodolog- ical questions is not recognized, any conversation about particu- lar aspects of charges is senseless. So long as theologians employ terms and concepts other than those formulated in tradition, there will always be questions and accusatory insinuations. But Schillebeeckx and a great number of other theologians cannot limit themselves to repeating old formulas. Time and again they will try to translate the old salvific truths "into the language of our believers," as Schillebeeckx has put it.[19] He has received no thanks for his efforts. Worse yet, precisely because of them he has been persecuted relentlessly. Cardinal Seper wrote to Schille- beeckx (25 November 1980), that the conversation in Rome had resulted in useful clarifications but that there was still doubt on certain points. Cited again were above all the divinity of Jesus, the virgin birth, the resurrection, and the validity of church teach- ings. No condemnation resulted, but neither was there an acquittal.

ORDAINED MINISTRY IN THE CHURCH

Hardly had this yearlong investigation of Schillebeeckx's Chris- tology reached a vague and yet menacing conclusion, when the doctrinal congregation found a new reason to importune the dog- matics professor from Nijmegen. In 1980, a collection of essays by Schillebeeckx appeared under the title *Ministry*. After all that had transpired, Schillebeeckx's ideas about it were viewed, as could only be expected, with particular criticism. The congrega- tion is an organ of the reigning ecclesiastical order. All the posi- tions of power in this ecclesiastical order are clearly defined. The most important and highest authority, empowered to make final decisions, resides in Rome. All other positions in the church—

anywhere else in the world—are dependent upon Roman authority. If someone begins to poke holes in the presently existing power structure, there arises the danger, from the Roman perspective, that the entire hierarchical edifice will begin to totter. Viewed from these established positions, everything depends on being able to demonstrate that the presently existing organization of ordained ministries in the church goes back to the Lord and his apostles. That is why the structures—like the doctrines guaranteed by the proper authority—are "eternal and unchangeable." That is why, therefore, *no* ordained ministers (elected) "from below," *no* laymen or laywomen as pastoral assistants, *no* room for women in ordained ministry, *no* experiments with married priests in active ministry, since none of them could be fully loyal to the vicar of Christ on earth.

Church order and the organization of ordained ministries built upon it was not sacrosanct for Schillebeeckx. That became evident in the twenty-five years Schillebeeckx occupied himself with this problematic, even before the 1980 collection of essays appeared. This time the difficulties with Rome began in 1981. The doctrinal congregation put pressure on the master general of the Dominicans in Rome. He turned to the Dutch provincial for information about the nature and contents of the book. As a result, a mixed commission of Flemish and Dutch Dominicans was organized in January 1982 to investigate the suspect book. After several months, this commission came to the conclusion that the book did contain a few historical inaccuracies, but that the revision of ordained ministry and church order, demanded and substantiated by Schillebeeckx, "was dogmatically possible and pastorally necessary." This detailed commission report stated at the end "that the pastoral situation of the church generally, but above all in the Netherlands and Belgium, is not being served, if a new 'Schillebeeckx affair' would arise. Negative publicity regarding the church and magisterium would increase once again."

A new "Schillebeeckx affair" did arise, however. As was to be expected, the considerations of the Dominican commission could not convince the doctrinal congregation. On 18 October 1982, the request came to Schillebeeckx to respond in writing himself. On 27 November, he gave a provisional answer, which was rejected by Cardinal Ratzinger, acting in the name of the congregation

(9 May and 21 July 1983), and a new complete explanation of all misunderstandings was demanded. In the meantime, the public still had no inkling of the matter, as the correspondence in 1984 dragged on. The inquiries of the congregation touched upon several points, but this was the main issue: Schillebeeckx irresponsibly accepts the possibility that, under certain circumstances, someone not officially ordained could preside at the Eucharist. Related to that, serious misgivings were raised at the way Schillebeeckx sought to inflate the apostolicity of local church communities. For the congregation, the apostolicity of such church communities is almost completely dependent on the presence of a minister who is validly ordained and thus stands in the line of "apostolic succession." Schillebeeckx, however, emphasizes that apostolicity has not only a juridical-organizational dimension, but also an inner dimension that is at least equally important. A faith community that perseveres in the teaching of the apostles and, like the apostles, desires to live as Jesus' disciples, is certainly also apostolic, even if sometimes, because of certain circumstances, no validly ordained priest is present.

The correspondence did not lead to the desired outcome, so that, on the advice of the Dominican master general, Schillebeeckx went to Rome once against to plead his cause. Without any publicity, a conversation took place (24 July 1984) between Schillebeeckx, Cardinal Ratzinger, and Damian Byrne, O.P. A substantial agreement did not materialize, but Schillebeeckx was able to refer to an article he had published in the meantime in *Tijdschrift voor Theologie* (1982) in which he corrected a number of the misunderstandings occasioned by his 1980 book. He could also inform the congregation that he had begun a detailed treatment of the whole question which would result in a new book by the end of 1984, the beginning of 1985. Impatient, however, the congregation demanded a clear declaration that he regarded it as theologically erroneous that, under extraordinary circumstances (e.g., lack of priests), a nonordained person could preside at the Eucharist. Schillebeeckx wrote Cardinal Ratzinger on 5 October that, unfortunately, the task of the new book had somewhat detained him (it appeared in January 1985), but in it he emphasized "that it would be pastorally opportune to change some provisions of canon law. Furthermore, the book advocated either instituting a 'fourth order' (with laying on the hands and an appropriate *epiklesis*) or a substantial reorganization of the diaconate."[20] Schillebeeckx explicitly informed them, moreover, that he had "taken into consideration the criticisms raised against his earlier book by historians, some theologians, and especially your Congregation." Then, on 11 January 1985, *Osservatore Romano* reported that Schillebeeckx had "recanted" his critical theses, whereupon Schillebeeckx at a press conference at Nijmegen (22 January) declared that "taking criticism into consideration" was not the same as "recanting." Clearer yet: "I have recanted nothing in the new book that I said in the first book."[21]

It is worth noting in connection with this question that the doctrinal congregation wrote Schillebeeckx (13 June 1984) that it had spoken the "last word" on the questions related to presiding at the Eucharist in its letter to the world's bishops, "Sacerdotium ministeriale" (6 August 1983). Therefore, Schillebeeckx should have known when he wrote his book (in 1980!) that these problems no longer belonged to "open theological questions." Apparently, the congregation tacitly assumes that the Schillebeeckx they so disdain had unprecedented command over the gift of prophecy . . .

On 15 September 1986, Cardinal Ratzinger wrote a letter to Damian Byrne, the master general of the Dominican order, with the information that the doctrinal congregation had ended its investigation of the book *Pleidooi vor mensen in de kerk* (1985). The results were contained in the enclosed notification of the congregation, which Father Byrne was to forward to the author of the book, Pater Schillebeeckx, and which would be published in the *Osservatore Romano*.

In the *notificatio* it is stated that in his last book Schillebeeckx unfortunately again critically analyzed the letter "Sacerdotium ministeriale" (from August 1983), that "he considers apostolic succession through sacramental ordination not essential for the exercise of ordained ministry," and finally that his hermeneutical method is not in agreement with the statements of Vatican II because he has not sufficiently attended to the authority of the church in the interpretation of the Holy Scripture. Apparently the last named difficulty is the most weighty for the congregation.

From what can be verified publicly, the discussion between

Schillebeeckx and Rome makes many things disturbingly clear. One of the most important points is that Rome is desperately trying to preserve the *depositum fidei* (deposit of faith) as an eternal and perfect, unimpeachable object of faith. Ultimately, therefore, the most that any later councils can do is to clarify further what has already been dogmatically fixed. The Second Vatican Council could not have produced anything new. And whoever thinks so, only demonstrates having a heterodox concept of revelation and church authority. One can only hope that the world's bishops have the courage and intelligence not to raise this restrictive interpretation of the Second Vatican Council to the level of a dogma.

Translated by
Ronald Modras

NOTES

1. For the documentation see: R. Auwerda, *Dossier Schillebeeckx* (Bilthoven, 1969); P. Hebblethwaite, *The New Inquisition?* (London, 1980); T. Schoof, *De zaak Schillebeeckx, Officiele stukken* (Bloemendaal, 1980), English translation: *The Schillebeeckx Case* (New York, 1984); and "De zaak Schillebeeckx," *Tijdschrift voor Theologie* 20 (1980): 339–426.
2. *De bisschoppen van Nederland over het Concilie* (Hilversum, 1960), 16, 19, 31.
3. *Kath. Archief* 17 (1962): 625–28.
4. "Verwikkelingen rondom prof. mag. dr. E. Schillebeeckx," *Kath. Archief* 23 (1968), 1050.
5. T. Schoof, *De zaak*, 19.
6. Ibid., 25.
7. Ibid., 29.
8. Ibid., 35.
9. Ibid., 49.
10. Ibid., 50–51.
11. Ibid., 70.
12. Ibid., 77.
13. Ibid., 88.
14. "De kwestie Schillebeeckx," *Archief van de kerken* 35 (1980): 649–74.
15. Ibid., 448.
16. B. van Iersel, "De onder zoeksprocedure van de congregatie voor de geloofsleer," *Tijdschrift voor Theologie* 20 (1980): 3–25.
17. T. Schoof, *De zaak*, 157–85.
18. Ibid., 163–64.
19. Ibid., 65.
20. B. V. Iersel, L. Kaufmann, A. Willems, "Schillebeeckx, der dritte 'Fall,' " *Orientierung* 49 (1985), 20.

16. Summons to Rome*

LEONARDO BOFF

In 1981, Editora Vozes brought out my *Igreja: carisma e poder: Ensaios de eclesiologia militante*,[1] a collection of thirteen essays on various aspects of the church, written during the fifteen years of my theological activity to date.

A polemical reaction to my book ensued. Under the date of 15 May 1984, through the Franciscan superior general, Friar John Vaugn, O.F.M., Cardinal Ratzinger dispatched to me a six-page letter criticizing "not a few positions that are less than fully worthy of acceptance" in my book. His eminence made two series of observations. The first concerned theological method. The second dealt with questions referring to (1) the structure of the church, (2) the conception of dogma and revelation, and (3) the exercise of religious authority. Finally, the cardinal prefect extended to me an invitation to hold a conversation with him in Rome in the coming months of June and July, adding: "In view of the influence the book has had on the faithful, this letter will be published, along with an indication of any position Your Reverence may see fit to adopt in the matter."

Cardinal Ratzinger's letter, dated 15 May, arrived in father general's hands only on 28 May. In it his eminence solicits the general's intervention in the affair, with a view to securing a "favorable attitude toward [these] observations" on my part and my "prompt reply" to his invitation to a "conversation" in Rome.

I received Cardinal Ratzinger's letter in Brazil only on 16 June. On 18 June I sent him my acceptance of the invitation. I asked for a clarification of the nature of the "conversation"—whether it would be an official interchange, and hence subject to the norms spelled out in the congregation's *Ratio Agendi* (that is, whether it

---

*This report and the following one by Clodovis Boff were excerpted from their book *Liberation Theology From Dialogue to Confrontation* (San Francisco: Harper & Row, 1986).

would be a juridical proceeding) or whether it would be exempt from these norms. I requested that the members of the Brazilian bishops' commission on doctrine, whose president was a cardinal and a theologian, Aloísio Lorscheider, be allowed to participate in the "conversation." I suggested that, in case the meeting could not be held in Brazil, it be held in Rome only in early October.

Under the date of 16 July, Cardinal Ratzinger replied that the conversation would be with himself and one other person only, who would accompany him, and that it would have to be held in Rome, since, "in conformity with the decisions taken, based on the *Ratio Agendi*, it would not appear to be possible to hold the conversation jointly with the Doctrinal Commission of the Brazilian Bishops' Conference."

The "conversation" was to be official, then. His eminence designated "September 7 or 8" as the date for the meeting, remarking that no postponement was possible.

THE CONVERSATION WITH CARDINAL RATZINGER IN ROME

I arrived in Rome on 2 September 1984. I went into seclusion at the Franciscan headquarters, near the Vatican. I had no contact with anyone whatsoever outside the Franciscan headquarters, but busily prepared my responses to the theological questions that had been raised.

Dom [Cardinal] Ivo Lorscheiter, president of the Brazilian bishops' conference, and Cardinal Aloísio Lorscheider had been in Rome for several days, paying visits to various Roman offices. They were also received in audience by the Holy Father, with whom they discussed my case, and he averred that he had read, with gratification, a number of works of mine, but not *Igreja: carisma e poder*, at present under adjudication. Our prelates also visited Cardinal Ratzinger, seeking permission to be present at the "conversation." But, as such participation was not provided for in the *Ratio Agendi*, and lest a precedent be set, their petition was denied. Cardinal Aloísio cited the fact of his presidency of the Brazilian bishops' doctrinal commission as justification for at least his mute presence at the conversation. Cardinal Ratzinger declined to render a decision on this new petition, forwarding it instead to the secretary of state, Cardinal Casaroli.

From this conversation at the sacred congregation, I could see that my "conversation" would be an official colloquium, held according to the official rules of procedure of the congregation. There was to be a stenographer, in the person of Argentinian Father [later, Bishop] Jorge Mejia. I would be permitted to take the minutes of the meeting to my quarters, study them, recommend modifications, and sign them. Finally, the "conversation" was not to be a simple conversation after all, as Cardinal Ratzinger's emissaries had promised it would be on 30 September. So I spent an entire day studying Father Schillebeeckx's colloquium, which had been published in the periodical *Il Regno* in 1979 and 1980.

On 6 September, Cardinal Arns of São Paulo joined the other prelates in Rome and earnestly sought to be allowed to assist at the colloquium, since he wished to offer his support to a former student, a friend, and a fellow Franciscan, as well as to testify to the ecclesial nature of the reflection being carried on in Brazil, since this reflection was conducted in strict communication with and dependence on the bishops and in strict respect for the pastoral orientation of the church.

Our prelates obtained an audience with secretary of state Cardinal Casaroli, who showed himself to be very receptive to their request to be allowed to assist at the colloquium. In spite of some reluctance, he acceded, thereby altering the nature of the meeting. Now it would no longer be subject to the formal rules of the sacred congregation, but indeed would be a simple explanatory conversation. And now our cardinals could be present.

The meeting would be divided into two sessions. In the first, I would be conversing with Cardinal Ratzinger. In the second, the Brazilian cardinals would join us.

Cardinal Ratzinger received me all smiles. I greeted him in German and was immediately led to the conference table. The cardinal prefect opened the conversation by offering me ample opportunity to say anything I wished. I might even read the whole of my prepared text (50 pages). I read a long introduction on the historico-social reality of Brazil, the position of the church in the situation, and the matter of theological reflection on the church and on society. I then selected a number of points in the six-page letter that his eminence had addressed to me and responded to them from my prepared text. The cardinal followed my remarks with the utmost attention and interest.

After two hours of conversation between Cardinal Ratzinger and myself, Cardinals Aloísio Lorscheider and Paulo Evaristo Arns entered the room, along with the secretary of the Sacred Congregation for the Doctrine of the Faith, Bishop Alberto Bovone, and the discussion continued. The most important intervention was on the part of Cardinal Arns, who suggested to the congregation that the promised new document, on the positive wealth to be found in the theology of liberation, should, first of all, be prepared in consultation with the "engineers" of that theology, the theologians who for years have been constructing this theological current; second, that it should be prepared in consultation with the episcopate, as it is they who perform the pastoral activity among the people, walking with the oppressed along the highways and byways of liberation, so that the ecclesial and pastoral dimensions of this new theological current could enjoy adequate emphasis in the new document; and third, that the document should be actually prepared in the Third World, in Africa or Latin America, for instance, amidst the actual reality of the poverty and oppression in which the theology of liberation has its point of departure, since this would tend to bring the text of the new document straight to the heart of things, and do justice to the cause of the oppressed. Cardinal Ratzinger timidly agreed with all three of Cardinal Arns' points.

Finally, a joint communiqué was carefully drawn up:

On September 7, 1984, at 10:00 A.M., in the offices of the Sacred Congregation for the Doctrine of the Faith, the Reverend Father Leonardo Boff, O.F.M., was received by His Eminence, Cardinal Joseph Ratzinger, Prefect of the same Congregation, for purposes of a conversation. The Cardinal Prefect was assisted by Monsignor Jorge Mejía. The subject of their conversation was the letter written by the Cardinal Prefect to the Reverend Father Leonardo Boff, under the date of the fifteenth of May of this year, on certain problems arising from a reading of his book, *Igreja: carisma e poder*. The intent of the conversation was to afford Father Boff, in view of the previously determined publication of the said letter, an opportunity to explain certain aspects of the book that were cited in the letter and that had created difficulty. The Sacred Congregation will take under advisement, via its customary protocol, suitable ways of making public, along with the publication of the letter itself, any germane results of the conversation. The conversation was carried on in the spirit of brotherhood. The present communiqué is a joint one.

The major significance of the presence of the two Brazilian cardinals was, surely, that of testifying to the ecclesial character of the theology being developed in Brazil. That theology may contain ambiguities. It may even contain errors. But it strives to be a theology within the church and to the benefit of the church. Ambiguities can be explained and errors corrected: neither deprive theology of its legitimate place in the pilgrim journey of our church. This point was amply established. A happy precedent may have been created for the handling of similar situations by the Sacred Congregation for the Doctrine of the Faith.

LESSONS TO BE LEARNED

A summons by the highest doctrinal office of the Roman Catholic Church is no commonplace event in the life of a theologian—still less in that of a theologian of the "periphery," whose theology is produced in conditions so unlike those of the great metropolitan centers of reflection. It is surely memorable—in fact, shattering—suddenly to find oneself in the public gaze. I learned from a member of the congregation itself that in May a Brazilian prelate, whose full name my informant was unable to recall but who once had been connected with Caritas Catholica, had been in Rome seeking the condemnation of my *Igreja: carisma e poder*, and seeking it so persistently that he became an annoyance. From another Vatican source I learned that the Holy Father himself, who in matters of doctrine of course always has the final word, upon reading the 15 May letter written to me by Cardinal Ratzinger, with its criticisms and even condemnation of my book, asked whether these matters had ever been discussed personally with Father Boff. On hearing that they had not, he forbade publication of the letter and requested that I be summoned for a colloquium. Had it not been for the Holy Father's personal intervention, then, the letter would have been published without previous consultation, written or oral, with me.

There are lessons to be learned from this story. In the first place, I could feel a mighty current of solidarity with thousands of my fellow Christians the length and breadth of our land—from the bishops to the simple members of the base communities—as well as from many other parts of the world, from Poland to New Zealand. These expressions of solidarity were less for me than for the cause of the value of a local church and the status of the theology it develops. It is totally baseless, indeed it is insulting, to understand this solidarity—of the highest ecclesial value as an expression of communion—as a disparagement of the office and person of the Holy Father or of the Apostolic See.

Second, the event and the discussion that was held meant that a genuine process of evangelization was under way, not so much via ecclesiastical channels, but via the secular channels of the media. The latter understood perfectly well what the real question was: commitment to the poor, to the profound societal changes that are so necessary, and to the liberation of the oppressed. This is a question transcending the frontiers of the churches. It is of concern to all; it affects conscience.

Finally, the whole affair evinces once again the limitation and finitude of all things created, including the organs of church authority, necessary as these are for the proclamation and promotion of the Christian faith. Surely we ought not to view these human beings as performing their task in the spirit of the Grand Inquisitor, but rather in that of brothers in faith with ourselves, persons seeking to discharge their arduous task and mission of zealously preserving the basic tenets of our faith and the mainstays of our hope. This task is done sometimes correctly and properly, sometimes incorrectly and improperly, but always with the intention of being faithful to that Word that ultimately will judge us all.

I went to Rome as a Catholic theologian. I returned from Rome as a Catholic theologian. I hope to be able to continue with my ministry of reflection, within the pilgrim process of our church, in a communion open in every direction, learning as I go, and giving of the little I shall have learned, with humility and courage.

The Value of Resistance:

An Addendum by Clodovis Boff

Disciplinary measures taken against Friar Leonardo Boff prevent his speaking openly or publishing for at least a year. Accordingly, he may not recount to the world what has occurred in his regard since his summons to Rome and his meeting with the cardinal prefect of the Congregation for the Doctrine of the Faith on 7 September 1984. I shall take the liberty of speaking for my brother, then, and recount the events of the eleven-month period in question, succinctly, and with an eye only to the public, objective aspect of the case.[2]

Leonardo Boff's summons to Rome stirred enormous public interest in the theology of liberation. Of a sudden, this theology seemed to "hit the streets." One could hear it discussed even in cafes, the marketplace, everywhere.

In response to this interest, Leonardo spent a great deal of time after his return to Brazil, in mid-September 1984, presenting and discussing liberation theology in response to invitations by popular groups, universities, labor unions, and various radio and television stations. Invitations arrived from all over the world. It seemed as if everyone in the universities suddenly wanted a talk or a course by Boff: in North America, Europe, and Latin America. Faithful to his theological opinion, however, Leonardo chose to remain in Brazil, and there strive to consolidate a theological reflection undertaken in solidarity with the Christian communities.

One wonders whether liberation theology would have made the waves it has today had it not been for the wide debate provoked by the Ratzinger-Boff dialogue, along with the publication by the Congregation of the Doctrine of the Faith of the "Instruction on Certain Aspects of the 'Theology of Liberation.' " The instruction was officially promulgated on 4 September 1984.

On 19 March 1985, a representative of the apostolic nuncio to Brazil, Archbishop Carlo Furno, formally handed Friar Leonardo Boff, in Petrópolis, Brazil, where Leonardo lives and works, a "Notification Concerning the Book, *Igreja: carisma e poder.*"

The document stated, "The Congregation feels itself under obligation to declare the options of Friar Leonardo Boff, here analyzed, to be of such a nature as to imperil the sound doctrine of the Church, which this same Congregation has the duty of fostering and safeguarding."

In a press release 20 March, Leonardo repeated what he had said earlier: "I had rather journey with the church than walk with my own theology and walk alone." But Leonardo also called attention to the fact the Roman document had not appeared in the form of a *monitum*, an "admonition," but bore the simple appellation of "notification." It did not, then, involve any sort of condemnation. It was simply a notification of certain reservations regarding what Leonardo seemed to the congregation to be teaching, without qualifying any of it as "heretical, schismatical, or impious." It labeled these supposed teachings with the qualification corresponding to the lowest degree of dogmatic censure: "dangerous to the sound teaching of the faith." Leonardo accepted the Holy See's intervention in the spirit of religious loyalty and obedience.

The Freckenhorster Kreis, a group of some two hundred laity, priests, and theologians of the diocese of Münster, Germany, issued a minutely detailed study of the notification, calling attention to its erroneous quotations and other misrepresentations. "With methods like this," it concluded, "it would not be difficult to denounce passages from Ratzinger, the popes, and Scripture itself."[3]

Under the date of 26 April 1985, cardinals Joseph Ratzinger, of the Sacred Congregation for the Doctrine of the Faith, and Jérôme Hamer, prefect of the Sacred Congregation of Religious and of Secular Institutes (SCRIS), dispatched a letter to Father General John Vaugn of the Franciscans, imposing three disciplinary measures on Leonardo: (1) "a period of silence under obedience," unspecified in length, but "of sufficient duration to afford him a space for adequate reflection," and also suspending his various activities as speaker, retreat director, and consultant at conventions and meetings; (2) the renunciation of his responsibilities on the editorial staff of *Revista Eclesiástica Brasileira*, which Leonardo had edited for many years; and (3) submission to previous censorship, to be applied with "particular care, including conformity with the prevailing norms of the Church and if need be of the Constitutions of the [Franciscan] Order that this means may have its effect," on any theological writing that Leonardo might do. In a letter to Leonardo dated May 1985, Father General Vaughn, as Leonardo's religious superior, charged with the implementation of the disciplinary measures taken against him by the two Roman congregations, while expressing profound solidarity with his Brazilian confrere, and being under constraint, asked Leonardo to abide by the decisions of the Holy See, and specified the period of "silence under obedience" to be of one year's duration. Exempt from the ban, Father Vaughn further specified, would be homilies at the Eucharist and lectures in theology to Franciscan seminarians in Petrópolis, these latter not being open to the public.

These measures provoked loud public outcry, in Brazil as throughout the world. Leonardo accepted the decision. The measures taken by the two Roman cardinals caused a great deal of scandal in Brazil, in view of the political context of the early months of 1985, when the country was emerging from a military dictatorship characterized by all manner of arbitrary procedures, the abolition of the right of free speech, and the most severe censorship. The church had performed its prophetic role, criticizing this state of affairs and helping to create a spirit of democracy. Then, at the very moment that the church had at last won back its liberties, it had to witness the painful spectacle of Rome's utilization of the very methods used by the military and criticized by the Brazilian bishops. Ten bishops, with an archbishop at their head who had been considered the patriarch of the struggle against the military dictatorship, Dom Fernando Gomes dos Santos, of Gioâna, some 130 kilometers from Brasilia, publicly criticized Rome and defended Leonardo. Thousands of letters and signatures arrived from all over the world in support of the Franciscan theologian, especially from the base communities of Brazil.

Two eminent attorneys, Dr. Helio Bicudo and Dr. José Queiroz, of São Paulo, celebrated for their defense of political prisoners and their campaign against the death squads, in the name of hundreds of centers for the defense of human rights and of justice and peace action groups, mounted a juridical appeal to the Holy See for the rescission of the punitive measures taken against Leonardo. Subsequently they took the same action in the courts of Geneva and The Hague. With great difficulty, they finally succeeded in having their petition filed with the president of the Pontifical Commission for Justice and Peace.

On 11 June 1985, the president of the National Conference of Brazilian Bishops, Dom (Cardinal) Ivo Lorscheiter, held a long conversation with the Holy Father in Rome concerning the perplexities being occasioned in Brazil, in church and civil society alike, by the behavior of the Congregation for the Doctrine of the Faith. It had taken its disciplinary measures without any previous contact with the Brazilian bishops' conference or with the bishops' commission on doctrine, thus undermining the meaning of collegiality and ultimately doing a disservice to evangelization. He handed the pope a thick dossier of newspaper reports, along with copies of letters received by the bishops' conference, expressing astonishment that such usages should still prevail in Rome. He conceded the right, and under certain conditions the duty, of the Holy See to intervene in these matters. This was beyond all question. In question was only the authoritarian manner in which this intervention was occurring. The popular consciousness had by now been raised to a level that no longer tolerated disciplinary tools like these. The people expected such procedures to have been relegated to utilization by Latin American military regimes.

The upshot of Dom Ivo's audience with the Holy Father was the decision to arrange a meeting between the Brazilian bishops' conference and the Roman Congregation for the Doctrine of the Faith. The agenda would include future procedures, as well as the significance of theology in a local church that, by reason of its pastoral liberation practice, stands in need of serious theological reflection.

The meeting was held on 4 and 5 July, in Rome—eight hours, in all, of debate and a sharing of experience, in which the "reference manuals" were the documents of Vatican II and the new Code of Canon Law. Some of the conclusions emerging from these conversations were later published in the *Boletim Semanal* of the Brazilian bishops' conference (25 July 1985, no. 790). The "Boff case" implied no new judgment rendered on the theology of liberation; by the end of 1985 a new document would be published in which the positive aspects of that theology would be emphasized; the document would have the benefit of previous consultation with the national Bishops' Conferences—as Cardinal Arns, it will be recalled, had explicitly requested—[the document, "Christian Freedom and Liberation," was issued 5 April 1986]; the restrictions on Boff did not mean absolute silence, since, as we have seen, he was still permitted to preach at Mass and lecture in theology to the Petrópolis friars; the Vatican would take increased account of the principle of subsidiarity in its relations with the Brazilian bishops' conference, and problems would "go to Rome" only after the church of Brazil had exhausted its internal resources; the Brazilian bishops' doctrinal commission would continue to function in a positive, and not inquisitorial manner.

On 29 July 1985, the Vatican secretary of state, Cardinal Casaroli, acting in the name and at the behest of His Holiness Pope John Paul II, wrote a letter to Leonardo in which he sought to construe the measures taken by the Holy See in a positive manner, in an evident effort to deprive them of their punitive character.

It would be premature to attempt to make a conclusive assessment of the Boff case and its repercussions on church and society. One thing, however, is altogether clear: that it has served as a powerful factor for conscientization, for consciousness-raising, in the sense of an ever more deeply felt need to get beyond authoritarian forms of relationship within the church to an awareness of the importance of "human rights for Christians too," and a new courage on the part of the national conferences to defend the legitimacy of a theological thought accompanying a pastoral practice as a right of the local church itself. Finally, the behavior of the Roman authorities has served fully to justify the criticism leveled in *Igreja: carisma e poder* against the mechanisms maintained by the central authorities of the church.

What remains open is the challenge to conversion, not only of persons in the church, but of the structures through which power in the church is distributed and exercised.

NOTES

1. English translation: *Church: Charism & Power: Liberation Theology and the Institutional Church,* trans. John W. Diercksmeier (New York: Crossroad, 1985).
2. Leonardo Boff's silencing began 26 April 1985 and was removed somewhat before the year was up. Clodovis Boff wrote this on 20 August 1985, while the silencing was still in effect.
3. "Die Lesehilfe des Freckenhorster Kreis," *Publik-Forum,* Sonderdruck, v.

17. The Curran Case
Conflict between Rome and the Moral Theologian
BERNARD HÄRING

Since July 1979, the Vatican has been conducting a formal investigation into the teachings of the well-known North American theologian Charles Curran. I have followed the case from its beginning up to the bitter end in August of 1986. Curran, like other theologians who have recently been under investigation, has sent me copies of all the pertinent documents as the case has progressed. The public first became aware of this investigation in March of 1986, after a "concluding conversation" took place with the three highest officials of the Congregation for the Doctrine of the Faith. As a result of its harsh verdict, by which Curran is no longer able to teach at a Catholic university because of his dissent on some teachings, he has unwillingly found himself in the public limelight. Because of the publicity, many are now asking: Who is this Professor Curran and what is the issue that has proved to be so controversial in the public discussion in the United States?

WHO IS CHARLES CURRAN?

The fifty-two-year-old scholar is a priest of the diocese of Rochester, New York. Before the Council, he received a licentiate degree in theology at the Gregorian University in Rome and later specialized in moral theology at the Academia Alfonsiana of the Lateran University where I was one of his professors. Curran stood out not only because of his extraordinary talent but also because of his winning modesty. His doctoral dissertation concerned the role of conscience in the work of Saint Alphonsus Ligouri, a work which left a lasting impression on him. Curran was astonished to discover the deep reverence in which that doctor of the church held the majesty of conscience, even the erring conscience of the person honestly seeking after the truth.

In 1961 Curran began to lecture in moral theology at the major seminary in his home diocese of Rochester and was received enthusiastically by the students as well as by the priests of the diocese. Beginning in 1962, together with other former students of mine, he arranged numerous conferences in which I have been able, over many years, to speak to thousands of American priests and laity. On those occasions I was able to witness anew the extraordinary popularity of this youthful priest.

When the Catholic University in Washington offered me a position as professor there in 1964 and I was unable to accept, I was asked to recommend someone else. Curran was my choice and he was, in fact, hired. There, too, he quickly won the admiration of both colleagues and students because of his untiring availability and openness. Understandably he also encountered opposition from circles which were stamped by the preconciliar, strongly law-centered moral theology. As a result the trustees of the university (composed primarily of conservative bishops) refused to grant him tenure. The spontaneous reaction was a strike of almost all the professors and students, who demanded that Curran not only be granted tenure but also be promoted. That is what then happened, though with great reluctance on the part of some of the bishops. It is important to keep this first conflict in mind in order to better understand subsequent conflicts.

Upon the publication of the encyclical "Humanae vitae" by Paul VI, Curran, together with numerous other theologians, signed a statement seriously questioning the absoluteness of the norm prescribing total or partial abstinence from sexual intercourse as the only morally permissible method for the responsible regulation of conception. They argued that there were certainly cases of the conflict of values or of conscience in which artificial birth control was morally justifiable. The stir which this caused among conservative bishops, priests, and laity diminished somewhat as others, including entire bishops' conferences, though in very carefully worded statements, came to similar conclusions. Curran and his colleagues who had signed the document were later cleared of charges that they had violated their responsibility as theologians through their public dissent. A specially appointed committee concluded that not dissent as such but only improperly expressed dissent with respect to a noninfallible teaching of the ecclesiastical magisterium would constitute such a violation of the theologian's responsibility. This is precisely the question which lies behind the present long investigation and which must now be reexamined.

FUNDAMENTAL ACCEPTANCE OF THE TEACHING AUTHORITY OF THE CHURCH

Curran has never given the slightest cause of doubt that he fundamentally accepts the teaching authority of the church, even in the area of noninfallible, reformable teachings. With the entire sound tradition, Curran, of course, also emphasizes that in the area of fallible teaching statements, an assent of faith—an irrevocable *yes*—cannot be demanded. To require a total assent to fallible teaching would contradict the once-and-for-all nature of the act of faith and stand in open contradiction to the teaching of the First Vatican Council. The draft concerning papal infallibility was adopted there only after the bounds of infallibility were clearly delineated. It is also a fact that, at the time, curial and other circles were disappointed since they wanted papal teaching authority as such to be seen as unquestionable. Ever since the First Vatican Council there has been no lack of attempts to stretch the infallibility of the pope to such an extent that no dissent, even in the realm of fallible teaching, would be permitted. This is all the more astonishing in light of the fact that the numerical minority of bishops who were able to advance this idea had been presenting as infallible a long list of papal teachings that were not only fallible but some of them actually incorrect.

The theology which we studied long before the Second Vatican Council provided the applicable qualifications for any authoritative teachings discussed so that any intelligent student could see where an act of faith was required and where a true faith assent was not possible.

Another question discussed again and again in the period before the Second Vatican Council concerned the safeguards which were built in or should be built in so that no false or unbalanced teaching of the Vatican could simply be promulgated. The most radical of those who emphasized authority solved the difficulty with the position, historically unverifiable, that at the proper time the Holy Spirit gives the person in authority the necessary insight to make the proper corrections. At the other extreme there were some, even well-known theologians, that taught that the proper corrective lay rather in the nonacceptance of such untenable teachings by the faithful and theologians, thus keeping the way open to fuller insight into the truth.

Official magisterial texts do not require an assent of faith in the area of noninfallible church teaching but rather a *religiosum obsequium* of intellect and will. The German translation of this phrase in the new Code of Canon Law is with "religious obedience of intellect and will" (*religiösen Verstandes—und Willensgehorsam*, Canon 751). I consider this translation unfortunate. What does obedience of the intellect mean in regard to official teaching based on natural law when one can find no convincing foundation for the matter in nature? Sound theology understands the Latin expression *obsequium religiosum* as that religious loyalty which prepares the intellect and will of the faithful to receive such teachings honestly and sincerely, to endeavor with honest reasoning to understand them and to appropriate them. But it should also prepare them to examine the teachings critically and, should the situation arise, to assert those reservations which seem necessary without rebellion against the authority. This, of course, must always be done in the spirit of shared responsibility with the pilgrim church which, in so many areas of newly emerging problems, is sometimes only able to give provisional answers and must continue to search for a more complete response.

Since "Humanae vitae," Charles Curran has come to view dissent as an expression of honest loyalty to, and co-responsibility with, both the church's magisterium and the entire People of God. He is genuinely concerned with that loyalty and honesty which alone can truly honor the church and church authority.

Thus when the press reports, as it did last spring, that "Curran refuses to submit to the magisterium," it is grossly misleading. The report should rather read, "Curran has declared that he, with all due respect to the ecclesiastical teaching office, cannot recant in certain questions of sexual ethics, as long as he is unable, after great effort, to see his own positions as false and the official teachings of the church as undoubtedly correct." In this long process of investigation Curran has continually asked the Congregation for the Doctrine of the Faith to clarify whether it considers dissent, whether from infallible or noninfallible teaching, to be a punishable offense in itself or if the congregation considers as punishable only improperly expressed dissent.

THEOLOGIAN OF THE UNTIRING DIALOGUE AND OPENNESS TO REVISION

Curran is the author of at least fifteen widely read books, which in large part, similar to those of Karl Rahner, consist of collected essays organized thematically on burning questions of the day. Typical titles of his books are *Catholic Moral Theology in Dialogue* and *Ongoing Revision in Moral Theology.* He deals primarily with fundamental questions of hermeneutics, methods of reappraising the tradition, evaluation of modern historical and social-scientific insights, and with the resolution of conflict situations. He is impressed with Gandhi's view of the "open-ended compromise," which never abandons the possibility of fuller realization of truth in the future. He gives a certain priority, as I do, to the "goal commandments" grounded in the Bible and the human sciences rather than the more confining norms that forbid or require particular actions. The most important question for him is whether the Christian and the Christian community are continuing to strive toward the goal commandments, living lives consistent with the Sermon on the Mount and the great commandment, "Love one another as I have loved you," thereby treating with an appropriate seriousness the "boundary-defining" norms which serve as mileposts along the way.

As a moral theologian with a great deal of pastoral sensitivity, Curran knows that an over-abundance of these "boundary-defining" norms, often poorly understood, confuse the conscience and can discourage the search for holiness, especially when they are all presented as absolutes despite the fact that, in many cases, they are very difficult to harmonize with one another.

His most vocal opponents and sharpest judges are, to a large extent, caught up in a purely normative ethic, in which the goal commandments and the Beatitudes never appear and there are only boundary-defining norms, or at least they predominate. They are missing the broader theological perspective of the theologian they attack. Not only by his words but also by his example of peaceful dialogue, his utter availability, and his life-style oriented to the Beatitudes, he points the way for his fellow Christians to the goal of a life oriented to the gospel and to grace. Again and again he has made clear the foundation of his moral theology: as complete a vision as possible, though not without tension, of the doctrine of creation; the captivity of sin and solidarity with evil; redemption—which is the more decisive term in any discussion of sin; and the eschatological tension between the "already" of salvation's accomplishment and the "not-yet" of its final fulfillment and freedom.

If Curran's statements are taken out of the context of this broad overview and dynamic, and over-simplified in addition, then they certainly can become dangerous. But the opposite question presents itself immediately: Is not the purely static, norm-based teaching, a morality which is simply concerned with setting limits, even more dangerous—and theologically unacceptable as well?

THE SPECIAL NATURE OF CURRAN'S DEVOTION TO THE CHURCH

Because of his image of the church and because of his own character, Curran is deeply convinced that the first thing a theologian owes the church is the complete honesty and uprightness of his thinking and speaking (and this includes writing). He will have nothing to do with the so-called diplomatic methods of those who through casuistic "watering-down" and hair-splitting interpretation of church teaching in fact change the meaning of that teaching without the appearance of deviation. Curran is scrupulously honest in the presentation of what the church's magisterium really says and means, even when it doesn't correspond to his own way of thinking. The primary thing for him is absolute loyalty in the presentation of the official position. If that teaching is based on arguments in the area of natural moral law, then he asks his reader what images of God and of humankind, what historical experiences are behind the arguments. Then comes the inevitable question: Are the arguments convincing? If they don't seem convincing to him, another question follows: Are there perhaps other convincing arguments that could be put forward that would support the official teaching? If, after all these considerations, he is of the opinion that the norm presented by the church is in need of some refinement or in some cases a change, he says so frankly, assuming then the difficult burden of a partial dissent. Very seldom is there a total dissent. Curran is a straightforward, undiplomatic person, which is probably another reason that he has so many admirers. He has doubtless helped many to love the church even though they have found themselves in situations in which they cannot accept certain norms of the church's sexual ethic in its bare wording and in a strict interpretation of it. Such people find in Curran a priest and a fellow Christian who obviously loves the church and works for it and, when necessary, also suffers for and in it.

DOES CURRAN GO TOO FAR IN ADAPTING TO THE AMERICAN CULTURE?

Curran is suspected and even openly accused by his opponents in Rome of wanting to adapt Catholic morality to the average North American "consumer." What can be said of this claim?

There is no question that Curran conducts theology in full consciousness of the North American scene. He knows that the reflective North American, the educated Protestants, and, since the Council, at least the decisive Catholic elite are not much moved, to put it mildly, by a claim to authority when patient dialogue has been refused. In a typically pluralistic society there is no progress without continuous, patient dialogue with the goal of convincing rather than demanding compliance. He lives in an environment in which constantly new discoveries or at least seemingly new discoveries are being made, not only in the areas of science and medicine but also in the social sciences and historical research. He wants to win a hearing in precisely this culture for the church's morality—yes, even for the church's magisterium—by arguing according to a principle which he himself has emphasized: "It is not true merely because authority says so; rather it can be asserted and taught authoritatively only to the extent that it can be proven to be true." In that area where strict faith is required, it is necessary to demonstrate that a teaching comes from divine revelation. But in the area of natural moral law, it is necessary to present the teaching convincingly in the light of an accurate image of humankind. A church that, in an area in which it has no explicit divine revelation, allows reexamination—in fact, conducts that examination itself—gains trust and is a respected partner in the continual search for the truth. This is true even when the church has the courage to admit openly that some of its answers have only a provisional quality and, in fact, some answers which it gave in the past are no longer satisfactory.

This approach applies elsewhere, but it is especially urgent in North America. I fear that some of those in the Vatican as well as some American bishops who studied all of their theology before the Council and are very authority-conscious are not able to understand and value Curran's position sufficiently.

If one considers the living witness of the man himself and the totality of his writings in moral theology, then one would have to be very advanced indeed in the life of perfection and in the radical living out of the gospel to entertain even a suspicion that Curran wants to conform morality to the American slogan, "Take it easy!" If one allows oneself to be challenged by the goal commandments and the Christian virtues, as Curran proposes, then one will quickly dismiss any temptation to accuse this man of permissiveness.

IS IT ONLY A QUESTION OF SEXUAL ETHICS?

Many ask, since all the complaints against Curran in the present investigation have to do with sexual ethics, if it is only a question of sexual ethics. In my opinion, the central concern is not so much the particular positions the church has taken in sexual ethics or even Curran's deviation from those individual positions. Rather it is the unquestioning, integral acceptance of all of the Vatican's statements in this area. Yet it does remain also a question of the very difficult area of sexual ethics.

The decisive point in this regard, however, is the following: besides the understanding of authority which the church officials bring to this question, there is also a great divergence in approaches to morality, that is, between a classical approach that emphasizes norms and tends to ignore historical developments and the more contemporary approach that is based primarily on historical consciousness. The Bible is not an abstract textbook but dynamic and changing history, the report of a continuing event in which the householder brings forth from his or her treasury things both old and new. Revelation makes humankind aware that humanity is both formed by history and able to form it. One cannot speak of the "nature" of humankind without taking into consideration both of these dimensions: that it is both a product and a maker of history. Consequently, Curran and the spokespersons for contemporary evangelical and Catholic moral theology have departed radically from the temptation to absolutize one particular culture or one particular moment in history. One must keep this in mind when speaking of natural moral law: different cultures approach the truth differently.

The church's social teaching as well as its sexual ethics—the statements of individual theologians, theological schools, and also the magisterium—require a hermeneutic. One must consciously and systematically inquire into the *Sitz im Leben*, or life context, "at that time" when the teachings were formulated; and into the life context of a church which seeks to preach the gospel to all cultures. Thus one cannot look for old answers in the archives of the Roman Inquisition and the holy office when one seeks to speak meaningfully today with the people of Rome or Europe, not to mention those of North America, Latin America, Africa, Asia, or Oceania.

A static insistence on formulations which were developed under very different historical conditions makes the proclamation of the gospel to other cultures and times very difficult, if not impossible. If we proclaim these formulations as though they were constant and inflexible norms, although they previously meant something quite different and had a very different context, then we will not be listened to even when we proclaim the revealed truth in a timely fashion. Both the speaker and the listener become mired in a neuralgic impasse.

I would like to illustrate this with an example from one of the most heated points of this already heated conflict. In two of the documents pertinent to the investigation, the Congregation for the Doctrine of the Faith emphasizes a well-known formulation as a concrete point of difference between official teaching and Curran's position, namely, that "every conjugal act must be open to the transmission of life." I have no quarrel with the matter of concern behind this statement; the problem lies in its nonhistorical, "classical" formulation. What does it mean in the long-prevailing Augustinian sexual ethic? Clearly, it means what the average person, trained in a casuistic school, would understand by it even today: conjugal intercourse is not morally permitted unless one desires to beget new life here and now, so far as it depends on the couple and the type and time of the intercourse. In the Augustinian tradition, which has long been dominant, it is stated very concretely: In the marriage act the couple must have as their goal the begetting of children, for only this goal can fully justify the marriage act. Thus sexual intercourse would have to be strictly avoided in times when conception is obviously not possible, such as pregnancy, after menopause, etc.

If these matters had been presented to Curran and other moral theologians who are under investigation in a more understanding way—as, to use an analogy, in the practice of medicine, one doesn't resort to an operation or dangerous medicines if the crisis can best be resolved through a healthy life-style and healthy human relationships—one would have undoubtedly encountered complete openness.

However, if one expects contemporary moral theologians who are historically conscious to use as their starting point formulations which are no longer understandable or communicable today, then one hinders their service to a pilgrim church which seeks to approach people of all times and places. If Curran had been asked, for example, whether he could accept the teaching of "Humanae vitae" as it is presented in the Königsteiner Statement of the West German bishops and the general synod of West German dioceses, I doubt whether he would have had any problem giving it his full assent.

Another charge is that Curran is not true to the church's teaching on the indissolubility of marriage. I admit that some of Curran's formulations are difficult for the Roman mind to understand; perhaps, too, they are too "unguarded." But basically, Curran's position is no more and no less than that which was presented by the Roman Synod of Bishops on Marriage and the Family (1981) and approved by a large majority: that one should at least carefully study the possibility of the Roman church's acceptance of the longstanding practice of *oikonomia* in the Orthodox Church, that is, the merciful application of the plan of salvation for someone whose first (canonically valid) marriage fails irreparably, though he or she has not been the cause. One cannot equate the malicious or irresponsible destruction of a valid marriage with the situation of spouses who, in spite of their goodwill, are abandoned.

In the newspaper *Rheinische Merkur*, a short well-written essay about the Curran case carried the title "When One Person Says What Many are Thinking." What is there to say when one man says and writes what almost all respectable theologians are saying and what a majority of the members of a Roman bishops' synod has approved? Can he still be penalized because of dissent? Not at least on this point.

UNCOMPROMISING STANCE—OR ADHERENCE TO PRINCIPLE?

Is an uncompromising stance the same as a healing adherence to principles? This question presents itself now in light of the final decision of the Congregation for the Doctrine of the Faith in Curran's case. How was this decision reached? The official process actually concluded around the end of 1985 with the notification that, in light of his dissent, Curran could no longer be considered a "Catholic theologian." At that time it was suggested by the congregation that it was open to holding a concluding conversation if Curran himself requested it. Before that time no meeting with Curran had taken place. Thus, there had never been a face-to-face encounter with the experts whose work, in my opinion, would have been much more careful and nuanced if a personal encounter with the accused had been a part of the process. Also, an open confrontation would have been able perhaps to throw some light on the obvious tension between a classical, static view of norm-based teaching and the pronounced historically conscious view of Charles Curran. One could say more about this, but let less suffice.

Curran took advantage of the offer, with the request that I be able to accompany him and eventually to defend him. The meeting took place on 8 March in the palace of the holy office. Besides myself, Curran was accompanied as far as the outer office by Monsignor George Higgins, a highly respected former official of the National Conference of Catholic Bishops, and by William Cenkner, the dean of the School of Religious Studies of the Catholic University of America, where Charles Curran is a professor. We used the time of waiting before the meeting for spontaneous prayer among ourselves, and just as Cardinal Ratzinger entered the outer office we were praying that God might help us to seek not our own victory but only the good of the church, the furthering of the reign of God. I told this to Cardinal Ratzinger and invited him to join us in our prayer. He nodded approval.

The meeting itself was difficult because we were reminded that it was not part of the official process, which had already been completed. However, we agreed that both sides should be open to the possibility that the discussion could lead to new results. One of Curran's questions was, "Why am I being singled out when many have said the same things?" Cardinal Ratzinger challenged Curran to support with specific names his assertion that many moral theologians are saying similar things or going even further. Curran was bewildered at first and then said, "Surely I am not expected to report on my colleagues!" The subject was not pursued. Then together we presented again, this time more clearly, the "compromise" which Curran had already presented through the chancellor of the Catholic University, the archbishop of Washington. The compromise was not accepted, though it was considered very seriously in our discussion, especially when Curran openly rejected as unjust and theologically very dangerous his disqualification as no longer being a "Catholic theologian" simply on the basis of dissent in the area of reformable teaching. Cardinal Ratzinger answered without long hesitation that this precise formulation was open to revision. Thus we inferred that the process might no longer be completely finished and we had some hope that the compromise proposal might yet be considered.

What was the compromise proposed by Curran? Here I want to point out again that the phrase, "open-ended compromise" plays a significant role in Curran's moral theology and that he feels obliged by deep conviction to accommodate the Congregation for the Doctrine of the Faith as far as his honesty and integrity would allow. Curran offered to continue his practice of not teaching sexual ethics at the Catholic University of America. In addition he promised to continue to examine these questions further. He asked that he not be required to recant, because fidelity to his conscience and the honesty he owes to God and the church would not allow him to do so. I emphatically endorsed this compromise, especially in light of the fact that Curran, on his own, had refrained from teaching courses or seminars in the area of sexual ethics, so that his partial dissent in this area would not cause difficulties for Catholic University. The meeting was conducted with full openness and without rancor on either side.

I had great hopes that the compromise would be accepted. Curran was asked to submit again a final position paper, which he did before the prescribed deadline. In that paper he emphasized that, while he couldn't recant, he did not see his positions as apodictic. Rather, they were tentative and open to revision. In other words, he wanted fully and completely to be a responsible member of a church on pilgrimage, seeking more light.

At this opportunity I expressed by own deep concern for the unfortunate pastoral consequences of a disciplinary action, particularly in light of the fact that Curran had submitted humbly as far as his conscience would allow him. With Curran, I pointed out the danger that an action which stripped him of his teaching position could lead to a lessening of respect for Catholic education and the church's magisterium in the United States. Not least important, one should be very careful of the implications of such an action on the ecumenical dialogue and the ecumenical atmosphere.

I must say openly that when I learned of the "last word"—though I still hope that it is "next-to-the-last"—I was very disappointed and saddened. However, perhaps it is worthwhile not to be pessimistic now. And so I want to cautiously share some optimistic considerations which have crystallized within me in recent days.

DANGERS AND RELEVANT OPPORTUNITIES AFTER THE CURRAN AFFAIR

First I want to mention a short-term and unpleasant danger. In some—though not many—organs of the press and other media, Curran's dissenting views are presented in an over-simplified or crude manner. In light of the popularity that this man enjoys, one worries that some uncritical people will all too gladly take this simplistic version of his views as a justification for their own laxity. We must do all we can to limit such damage. I hope by my contribution here to serve this purpose.

I see a great opportunity in this for Curran, guided by his deepest convictions, to conduct himself in accordance with the gospel value of nonviolence and the example of Ghandi. His faith and the strength he gets from his love for the church have provided him with a great deal of inner peace and self-discipline. He has appealed to all of his supporters not to let anger or anti-Roman feelings take root in them because of the outcome of his case. He wants, precisely in this situation, to give proof of his love for the church and for the cooperative search for a better understanding of the truth.

If we look more closely, we see that what is actually at stake here is not so much a "Curran affair," but rather a field of conflict that has burdened the church for two hundred years: a conflict between a majority of the leading moral theologians who are taken seriously by contemporary Christians and the representatives of the official magisterium. This conflict already became apparent when the threatened sanction was first made public. Five former presidents of American theological societies (the College Theology Society and the Catholic Theological Society of America) and over seven hundred theologians and canonists declared their solidarity with Curran, without concurring with each of his positions.

If Curran is able to persevere in the *satyagraha*—that is, the strength-loving search for, and practice of, truth—and draw his many admirers into his example, then it is possible, though after some suffering, that a reconciliation of both sides might be the result. Besides, it is valuable in itself when a man of the stature of Curran sets a standard for nonviolent perseverance in a conflict.

I would be especially pleased if Rome concludes from this whole affair that the threat of punitive sanctions in the case of dissent—and because of dissent alone—in areas of reformable teaching should again be abandoned. At the end of this long and, for scholars, very aggravating process, the congregation has applied Canon 1371 Par. 1 for the first time and to a particularly harsh degree. (It might be noted that this section of the new canon law did not come from the Committee for the Revision of the Code of Canon Law but was inserted just before promulgation by higher authorities.) The canon states: "The following are to be punished with a just penalty: . . . a person who pertinaciously rejects the doctrine mentioned in canon 752 and who does not make a retraction after having been admonished by the Apostolic See or by the ordinary." The referred-to Canon 752 reads: "A religious obedience [the American translation of the code reads "religious respect"—translator's note] of intellect and will, even if not the assent of faith, is to be paid to the teaching which the Supreme Pontiff or the college of bishops enunciate on faith or morals when they exercise the authentic magisterium even if they do not intend to proclaim it with a definitive act; therefore the Christian faithful are to take care to avoid whatever is not in harmony with that teaching." If the sanction of punishment were to be dropped again, one might translate the canon differently. Instead of "obedience of intellect and will" one could translate the Latin phrase something like, "religiously grounded obedience." Its intent has to do with a sincere willingness to prepare the intellect and will to be open to the content of such teachings, and, in case full agreement is not possible in spite of all goodwill, to exercise concern for the good of the church in one's dissent. The final decision of the congregation makes one wonder what is expected of educated theologians and laity when, in light of all the sad incidents in which the Roman Inquisition or the holy office missed the mark and brought unspeakable suffering on some good theologians, they are required to render an uncritical "obedience of intellect and will."

I would like to conclude with a wise word from Karl Rahner concerning this problematic, which has become so acute in our day:

The representatives of the magisterium must explicitly say and practice, in the name of the magisterium, "We are human beings when we make our decisions; people who should not be rash or full of prejudices, yet this is unavoidable. Aside from the fact that the Spirit protects the church from error through the ultimately binding decisions of the pope and a council, we can—and so can the pope—err in our decisions, and we have often done so in the past and up to our own day. This is a self-evident truth, which the legitimacy and function of a magisterium does not abolish. It is our duty to work under this risk because we still have a task and a function, even when the conditions and requirements of an ultimately binding decision are not present; just as a physician is not constrained from making diagnoses unless he has absolute certainty."

To us theologians, however, Karl Ranner lets the magisterium also speak:

Neither do you theologians have the right to assume arrogantly from the very beginning that our decisions must be false because they contradict the opinions which you, or at least a good number of you, have held.[1]

I believe that Curran can honestly agree with this appeal.

Translated by
Benedict Neenan, O.S.B.

NOTES

1. Karl Rahner, "Theologie und Lehramt," *Stimmen der Zeit* 198 (1980): 364–65.

18. John Paul II, U.S. Women Religious, and the Saturnian Complex

MADONNA KOLBENSCHLAG

It is sad to contemplate a lost moment of grace and possible transformation. John Paul II might have been the first pope to harvest the gifts of women for the church. The critical mass was there—in 1978, when he was elected to Peter's chair, women were entering the public sectors in unprecedented numbers, particularly in North America.

In 1978, John Paul II had access not only to the energies of increasing numbers of laywomen prepared for leadership in church and society, but also to the extraordinary capabilities and human resources of religious women in community. In the wake of the reforms and socialization that the Second Vatican Council generated in religious orders, women in religious communities in the United States—by 1978—had reconstituted their way of life with remarkable developments in consciousness, life-style, and mission. They were being described by some sociologists as the largest single group of educated, articulate, bonded women the world had ever seen. A new social dynamic, fostered by the rising liberation ethos, was evolving among them and around them. And the same bonds and connections forged in the homeland or in the mission outposts were fast becoming international—a new solidarity was emerging among women-in-church across continents and cultures.

In one sense, the Vatican could have taken some credit for the emergence of this unique group of United States women that exhibited such extraordinary catalytic power and social charism. The contemporary phenomenon of Catholic women in community probably had its roots in the forties when the sisters themselves began to assess their own professional deficiencies.[1] But certainly the sister formation movement owed much of its impetus also to the repeated urgings of Pius XII in the early fifties. The programs, workshops, planning, and publications that the sister formation movement generated produced a quantum leap in the personal and professional development of thousands of United States sisters by the mid-sixties. Along with greater intellectual skills and social awareness came an eagerness to deal with the realities of a twentieth-century urbanized population. The enclosure that had been imposed on women's religious orders in 1298 A.D. was finally disintegrating. When the church issued a call for renewal and *aggiornamento* to religious orders at Vatican II, the sisters were ready.

Perhaps more than any other single group in the church, the sisters internalized the theology and ecclesiology of Vatican II, particularly those teachings related to the church in its relationship to the world, to social justice, and the church as the People of God. A significant number of United States communities of women plunged into the task of renewal with enthusiasm and a characteristic thoroughness in their commitment to change. The Vatican provided helpful guidelines, primarily through the Vatican II Decree on the Renewal of Religious Life ("Perfectae caritatis"), subsequent pastoral documents, and through its encouragement of a period of experimentation. Looking back, it is doubtful if anyone ever regarded the changes of the post–Vatican II years as "experimental." They were far too integral, too intimately owned after a long internal process of dialogue, study, reflection, and action to be considered "experiments." The very principles which the church recommended as the basis of change were to prove so fundamental and revolutionary that, once the hand had firmly grasped the plow, there would be no turning back—in spite of the reservations, even shock, of many hierarchs and faithful.[2]

The period of renewal resulted in dramatic changes in two areas in particular. Internally there were substantial changes in the process of discernment and shared decision making in governance and enculturated developments in the concept of authority. Externally there were changes in the understanding of the sister's public identity and innovations in the concept of mission and appropriate ministries. The experience of these new ministries led to an awareness of the structural nature of many social evils and inequities. By the mid-seventies the rising sensitivity of Catholic sisters in the United States to social conditions and political issues had resulted in the first Catholic social justice lobby in the United States (NETWORK) and a variety of other ministries related to justice. By 1978 the transformation of consciousness and praxis was so evident that the conferences of major superiors of men and women felt compelled to issue a report which clearly revealed the extent to which these changes were fed and nourished by the pastoral teachings of the pope and bishops.[3] SCRIS (Sacred Congregation for Religious and Secular Institutes) followed this report with a pastoral letter of its own in 1980, which—while it contained several cautions—placed the new consciousness and praxis of religious demonstrably within the pastoral teachings of recent popes and bishops' synods.[4]

This was the "critical mass" from which emerged the small group of conscienticized women who gently confronted and surprised John Paul II on his first visit to the United States in October 1979. Some believe that the respectful but unexpected plea that Mercy Sister Theresa Kane, then president of the United States Leadership Conference of Women Religious, delivered on behalf of a greater role for women in the ministry of the church, when she greeted him at the National Shrine in Washington, was the "original sin" that cast United States women forever in the role of upstart "Eve's" reaching for forbidden fruit. Some believe that this quiet, but threatening tableau in Washington set the scene for everything that has happened since, for the clear pattern of patriarchal repression and—at the very least—wariness and mistrust that has marked the relationship between the Vatican and many United States communities of women since 1979. In all fairness, however, certain United States bishops and a significant number of Catholic right-wing voices deserve some of the credit for the estrangement that ensued.

A case in point is the effect of a small article that appeared in the *Catholic Register* in November of 1979, a few weeks after the pope's visit to the United States and Theresa Kane's intervention. The author of the article, Rev. Wm. Smith, was clearly hostile to Kane and hastened to add the information that a "leadership group" in her community was advocating direct sterilization procedures in the Mercy hospitals (a distorted assumption based on a misreading of a confidential, unrevised discussion paper which a Mercy study group had circulated to their health care administrators as a "critical pastoral issue"—rather than a statement of a policy). The ensuing concern of the United States bishops led to an investigation, a "committee of verification," and months, years of scrutinies, testimonies, and justifications. The issue was resolved only after a retraction and a series of loyalty oaths on the past of the leadership of the Sisters of Mercy. In retrospect, the chronology of this particular matter followed a tortured course. In the end, the sisters submitted, in compliance with Vatican directives, by withdrawing their questions about tubal ligation and cancelling the discussion by issuing official policy opposed to such measures. Even then, Rome was still not satisfied that the sisters had submitted their "hearts and minds" to the magisterium.[5]

Another pollutant was added to the atmosphere when Cardinal Sheehan revealed in late 1982 that he and several United States cardinals had alerted the pope to the "decline in faith" in United States women religious.[6] This opinion was based on the exodus of women from religious life, declining numbers of applicants, changes in community life, and other ambiguous "facts" (phenomena which affected communities of men as well, but apparently did not alarm the cardinals).

When the Agnes Mansour case erupted in the spring of 1983, it was against this backdrop of waxing hierarchical concern about United States religious women and a constant preoccupation with moral regulations related to sexuality. Again, right-wing elements were influential in giving Mansour's position notoriety in Vatican circles, exacerbating the fears of an insecure archbishop—who washed his hands of his own decision and threw Mansour to the wolves in Rome. This led to an unprecedented Vatican intervention which severed Mansour (and, subsequently, two other Sisters of Mercy) from a thirty-year commitment to religious vows and community. The protracted scenario between the Vatican and the Sisters of Mercy seemed to the public and to many American sisters to be a gross abuse of power on the part of Roman authorities, who indicated at several junctures that John Paul II was personally involved in the decisions that were summarily executed. Most disturbing to religious women was the lack of "fair process," the overriding of the appropriate autonomy of religious superiors, the refusal of the Vatican to allow the Sisters of Mercy to pursue legitimate canonical appeal, and the punitive treatment of Agnes Mansour, Elizabeth Morancy, and Theresa Kane—even to the point of canceling canon law itself in order to prohibit the future readmission of the sisters in question.[7]

A few weeks after the dismissal of Mansour from her community, the Vatican Sacred Congregation for Religious and Secular Institutes (SCRIS) issued its draft on "The Essential Elements in the Church's Teaching on Religious Life," accompanied by a pastoral letter from John Paul II addressed to the United States bishops, asking them to conduct a pastoral investigation of United States religious orders. Archbishop John Quinn was appointed to head a special commission to prepare a report for the Vatican. Although it followed closely on the events related to the Mansour case, the planned scrutiny had been in preparation for several months—ever since concern about United States women had surfaced in Rome. The tone and substance of significant portions of the "Essential Elements" document seemed to demand that religious return to the theology, life-style, and apostolic mode of the pre–Vatican II church. Women in United States religious orders were shocked, alarmed, and outraged—particularly since only United States religious communities had been singled out for this unprecedented scrutiny.

Fortunately, Archbishop Quinn assembled a judicious and balanced group of church men and women to conduct the study. As the "pastoral initiative" proceeded, its original purpose—vaguely perceived as inquisitorial and punitive—was modified into a "dialogue" between sisters and their bishops. In the end, it became one of the most effective processes for educating the hierarchy to the realities of life and mission in women's religious orders today and to appreciating the authenticity and vigor of the fidelity and gospel commitment of their members. Nevertheless, the "Essential Elements" instruction to the bishops hangs ominously over the future of women's communities in the United States. The Quinn Commission report remains unpublished except for selected portions, and, more recently, in his message to the United States conference of bishops, Pope John Paul II urged the bishops to exercise their pastoral mission to religious women in accordance with the "Essential Elements," the pastoral which summarizes "the church's teaching on religious life."[8]

By this time American sisters could be expected to have persecutory feelings—they were not delusions. The dust from all these events had barely settled when another storm erupted in the fall of 1984, growing out of the national election campaign and the candidacy of a Catholic women, Geraldine Ferraro. The now-famous ad in the *New York Times*—defending the right of Catholics to differ on public policy and calling attention to the fact that there was a diversity of opinion in the Catholic community on certain noninfallible moral teachings of the church—drew forth an unprecedented response from the Vatican, threatening the sisters who had signed the ad with dismissal from their congregations if they did not "recant." By now religious women in the United States were developing reflexes for "tender, loving defiance" in the face of what seemed to be disproportionate, mean, and obsessive responses to the way in which Catholic sisters participate in a pluralistic society. This time there were several sisters involved and several religious orders—the sister signers and their superiors formed a phalanx that simply stood still. No one was dismissed, no one left, no one retracted, no schisms occurred. Once again Rome sent emissaries, this time for the purpose of "dialogue" and resolution. The end result was an ambiguous process of "rectification" and compromise that "cleared" all except two dissenting sisters (whose cases are still pending)—and gave American religious women another massive injection of powerlessness and mistrust.

Another unfortunate piece of "fallout" from this process was the breakdown of the growing solidarity between lay women and men and members of the religious communities involved. The price of "saving" some of their members reasserted some of the canonical fences and elitism that United States religious women have struggled to eliminate in the post–Vatican II years.

Another ongoing experience that transcended all of these particular incidents, affected many more women religious, and reinforced growing tensions with Rome, was the process of revising constitutions, a task that was imposed on religious orders in connection with the Vatican II mandate for renewal. As the initial drafts that were labored over and discerned so faithfully over many years were submitted to Rome—and more often than not, returned as unacceptable—it became clear that there were not only bad feelings between United States sisters and Rome, but also some fundamental disagreements in regard to the understanding of authority and obedience, nonhierarchical structures of governance, and appropriate cultural expressions of their way of life. Many constitutions were returned with, among other things, insistence that a vow of absolute obedience to the Holy Father be included—a vow which, in practice, had never been explicitly demanded or articulated in women's communities before. The "corrections" suggested by Rome have generated a variety of responses and strategies among American religious women— most have owned their way of life with too much integrity to allow, as one sister put it, a few student canonists and patriarchal cardinals "an ocean away" to compromise it.

And if the foregoing events enumerated thus far were not enough, there has also been a steady flow of hearsay evidence of John Paul II's attitudes toward women, particularly United States sisters, from various conversations he has had with American bishops on the occasion of their *ad limina* visits to Rome. The purging of women from Catholic seminaries, the almost hysterical warnings about "secular feminism" (beginning to sound much like the fundamentalist cries over "secular humanism"), the closeted meetings of the National Conference of Catholic Bishops where bishops warned about "dangerous" feminist scholarship, etc.—it all suggests a need to control women, and an irrational fear of their power.

Women committed to the church in the bonds of religious community are easy targets of this patriarchal paranoia. Indeed, that is perhaps why religious women in the United States today seem to be "riding point" for the United States church. One thoughtful reflection on this by a former general superior who experienced many years of general aggravation, anguish, and harassment in dealing with Rome, suggested that sisters were becoming "the battered women" of the church.[9] Indeed, there are many undocumented, unpublished scenarios enacted between the Vatican and women's communities—the Benedictines, the Franciscans, the Dominicans, the Carmelites, to name a few—that follow the same pattern of the Mercy experience, but have not been as "newsworthy" as some of the cases that have caught the public eye. In retrospect, it will surely seem a sorry chapter in ecclesiastical history.

Coercive and punitive abuse of power—some have named it "moral terrorism"—has been sanctioned under this pope. What have been the effects of this on the women who live closest to the official church? We can enumerate a few.

1. The primary effect of the repressive atmosphere of this papacy upon many religious women is fear, a sense of powerlessness, and overwhelming mistrust. "What will they try to do to us next?" is an implicit, if unexpressed anxiety. Inevitably, these emotions undermine respect for authority and the moral suasion of ecclesial power—thus accomplishing the very opposite of what papal authority intends.

2. Right-wing extremists in the Catholic church have taken their cue from the pope and interpret Vatican attitudes as a license to go "hunting." Communication media have created impressions with a velocity and saturation that are distorted and deadly. The Vatican has not been a sophisticated interpreter of such influences.

3. Prophetic action and inquiry have been compromised. Caution and self-preservation have more influence now in decisions made about health care, public policy, ministry, intellectual dissent and discussion, even the choice of what is to be studied and how. "Thought police" are no longer a fictional fantasy.

4. Solidarity, on the other hand, has been one of the positive effects of the repressive atmosphere—a solidarity that transcends the boundaries of the religious community and includes all women and men who are disempowered or stand in jeopardy under patriarchal authority. Clearly, however, Vatican interventions that reinforce lines of demarcation between laity and religious (certainly part of the agenda of the "Essential Elements" instruction) threaten this tenuous solidarity. Moreover, Vatican interventions have also encouraged polarizations within and between religious congregations, anywhere that anxiety feeds on reactionary and nostalgic regimentation. Thus the oppressed are doubly

victimized—by abuse of power and by the divisions among themselves which authoritarianism begets.

5. Nor can we even begin to estimate the effect of perceived repression and control by the Vatican in discouraging young women from seeking a life of service in the church. If the reactions of some Catholic parents are any indication, this may prove to be a serious deterrent to many of the best candidates.

6. Related to this is the phenomenon of "patriarchal flight." Over the past four years I have conducted many interviews, held many informal conversations, and gathered considerable data from surveys in preparation for two studies on religious women in the United States.[10] I discovered that one of the most crucial effects of the events of the past few years vis-à-vis American sisters is the "p-factor" ("patriarchal flight"). It is perhaps the factor most likely to impact on the future of the church in the United States. In growing numbers, sisters are seeking ministerial/service positions in organizations and situations unrelated to the officially sponsored ministries of the Catholic church. One of the primary motivations is "escape from clericalism," and the necessity to find a "safe" haven from the threat of ecclesiastical intervention.

There may be another, indirect positive effect of this "flight." It may take the form of flight to the "grassroots"—efforts to build church at some distance from the highly visible public and ecclesial sectors, in the "outback," on the periphery. This focus of attention on the local, indigenous church may—as it has in Latin America—ultimately be the seedbed of a new ecclesiology over time.

Thus, John Paul II, in this papacy, was presented with a unique moment in the history of the church in North America. Unfortunately, he and his advisors, the "church fathers," have chosen to use the emerging influence of religious women as the lightning rod for a neo-orthodoxy rather than free the energies of women to nurture a new ecclesiology. There is a terrible irony in this, since it was the hierarchical church in the pastoral and social teachings of recent popes and the Second Vatican Council that called the sisters forth from their convents to the world, to the poor and powerless, and nourished their consciences to justice.

Now that awareness, vision, and zeal have become a mirror reflecting back to the hierarchical church the neurotic fear of women and patriarchal violence that appears to be a growing characteristic of this papacy and magisterium. The hierarchical church seems to be affected by a kind of "Saturnian complex"—reminiscent of that Greek deity who swallowed the children of his own loins, fearing they might displace him one day.

Finally, a personal afterthought: I have been scandalized by this pope or his minions several times in the past few years—perhaps never so painfully as when he forced my friend Agnes Mansour to leave her religious family. No human being should have that power. But I believe there was an earlier moment when the die was cast for American women. In the weeks following the brutal rape and murder of four American women in El Salvador in 1980, I was deeply involved in the congressional investigation of the murders, immersed in the details, evidence, and politics of that awful crime. We waited for the official voice of the church to express outrage, perhaps to intervene as it had so often done in other human rights cases of international significance—particularly in this case, since these women were the most visible victims out of some 30,000 less visible Salvadorans who had preceded them in similar atrocities. It did not come. The voice of the Holy See—which has so often eulogized the service of someone like Mother Theresa—was strangely silent. Was it a judgment on these women, so representative of North American sisters? They were a true sisterhood, these four—unique, and at the same time, so typical of United States women in community—a nun who was a member of a traditional order that had once been cloistered, two members of a missionary congregation, and a young laywomen. In the eyes of their murderers, the four women were subversives, "Romero's whores." In the eyes of those who knew them, they were sisters in solidarity, ordinary saints and heroic martyrs, women who had given their lives to the gospel, to the poor, to the church, to justice. Did the pope know the truth then? Can he possibly understand the truth about any of us now?

NOTES

1. In particular, Sr. Bertrande Meyers' *The Education of Sisters* (1941), and Sr. Madeleva Wolff's *The Education of Sr. Lucy* (1949). Margaret Thompson has re-

searched the development of United States religious sisters in the preparation of a forthcoming book, *The Yoke of Grace: American Nuns and Social Change.* Her paper "Pressures By and On a Marginal Group," given at the American Political Science Association meeting in August 1986, traces the development of the sister formation movement and other influences that have shaped the experience of religious life among American women.

2. Religious communities were encouraged by various pastoral instructions from the Vatican and from canonical advisers to renew their way of life with emphasis on three principles in particular: (a) fidelity to their founding charism, (b) collegiality and subsidiarity in internal structures, and (c) the option for the poor. I have discussed the impact of this emphasis on ministry in the introduction to my book *Between God and Caesar* (New York: Paulist, 1985), 1–17.

3. "Report to the Vatican: Religious Orders Today," a joint report of the Leadership Conference of Women Religious and the Conference of Major Superiors of Men of the United States (April 1978).

4. "Religious Life and Human Promotion," pastoral instruction of the Vatican Congregation for Religious and for Secular Institutes (1980).

5. The Smith article appeared in the *National Catholic Register* (25 November 1979). The tubal ligation controversy was documented in a private memo by Sr. Emily George, RSM, August 1984.

6. This information appeared in an article in the *Baltimore Sun* in late 1982.

7. Madonna Kolbenschlag, *Authority, Community and Conflict* (Kansas City, MO: Sheed & Ward, 1986), includes the pertinent information, documents, letters, and commentaries on this case.

8. John Paul II, letter to the United States bishops' conference, 4 November 1986.

9. "Nuns: Battered Women of the Church?" *National Catholic Reporter* (21 December 1984), 25.

10. My observations were developed on the basis of the information I gathered from a survey in preparation for the book *Between God and Caesar* and another survey related to a project on "Religious Women and the Mission of the Church," a forthcoming publication.

In the preparation of this commentary, I wish also to acknowledge many conversations and interviews with women in religious communities who, in the spirit of the times, wish to remain anonymous.

III. THE CHURCH AMERICAN
The Negative Impact of a Repressive Regime

The American Scene
A Would-be Wasteland

The intensified campaign of repression began in Europe in the first half of 1979 with the silencing of the French Dominican theologian Jacques Pohier. Quickly then the scene of repression moved to the United States, where an admonitory letter was received by Father Anthony Kosnik, the chairman of the committee of the Catholic Theological Society of America that had published—with the approval of the society—its report *Human Sexuality*. Kosnik was removed from his teaching position at the seminary in Michigan.

In September of 1979 John Paul II visited the United States. Plans for his *pièce de résistance*, the celebration of the Eucharist on the Mall in Washington, D.C., included forbidding women to serve as ministers of the Eucharist at the celebration. Naturally there was an outburst of protest, part of which was organized by the Jesuit William Callahan; subsequently he was forcibly removed from his post in Washington. Because of this action and the many restrictive statements of the pope in his journey around the United States, John Paul II quickly lost popularity and his Washington visit shifted from being a *pièce de résistance* to a *place de résistance:* the crowd at the Eucharist was only a fraction of what was expected.

Again the main theater of Vatican repression shifted back to Europe, first with the inquisition of Schillebeeckx, followed by the attack on Küng's Catholicity. Then in the wake of the fierce reaction of the progressive elements in the Catholic church throughout the world there followed a period of relative quiet— but only relative. With Cardinal Joseph Ratzinger as the point man in the Vatican attack against progressive Catholics after 1983 (when Ratzinger was appointed Prefect of the Congregation of the Doctrine of the Faith), the repressive atmosphere began to intensify. Women religious in America came under increasing fire from the Vatican on a number of fronts. Renewed pressure was applied to Schillebeeckx concerning his writings, now not on Christology but on ministry in the church. And Latin American liberation theology was persistently pilloried and one of its leaders, Leonardo Boff, was dramatically silenced.

In 1986 Father Terry Sweeney, a Jesuit sociologist, developed a questionnaire on controversial questions in the church. Interestingly, almost all of the topics dealt in one way or another with sex: contraception, married clergy, women priests, divorce, abortion, and homosexuality. With all the appropriate ecclesiastical approvals, Sweeney sent his questionnaire to all the United States Catholic bishops. The results were telling: large numbers of bishops, sometimes majorities, took positions (anonymously) in dissent from the established Vatican positions! The Vatican, through Sweeney's Jesuit superior, told Sweeney he had to destroy his material. He demurred—and was dismissed from the Jesuits.

About the same time, Archbishop Hunthausen of Seattle was suddenly thrust into the limelight when he was largely stripped by the Vatican of his episcopal responsibilities, which were handed over to Auxiliary Bishop Wuerl. It came out that a number of ultraconservative Catholics had been complaining to Rome about the archbishop's position on a variety of matters, political, sexual, liturgical, and pastoral, and Rome rushed in where fools did not fear to tread. As a result, the American bishops in general were extremely angry at Rome—but did essentially nothing. Fortunately—and as a result of who knows what pressures and forces—in early summer of 1987, Archbishop Hunthausen had his powers restored, and Bishop Wuerl was transferred.

Matching this peak of repression was the Vatican attack on Father Charles E. Curran, professor of moral theology at the Catholic University of America in Washington, D.C. Father Curran, although a theological moderate, was seen by the Vatican and conservative clerics as a leading symbol of theological dissent since the failed attempt to dismiss him in 1967 and his leading the dissent to "Humanae vitae" in 1968. The loss of those battles still rankled the conservatives, and they finally succeeded in removing him from the faculty in 1986. As of this writing, Father Curran is still struggling to regain his teaching post, although he states that the effort will probably be fruitless. But for the sake of rights in the church and academic freedom, he intends to use every legal means to defend himself.

It is into this would-be Catholic American wasteland that Pope John Paul II is coming in September 1987, and it is within this context that the following reflections by American Catholic theological and other scholars have been written.

L. S.

19. On Hope as a Theological Virtue in American Catholic Theology

DAVID TRACY

Baron von Hügel once argued that a religion is as strong as the individual strengths and interrelationships of its three principal elements: the mystical, the intellectual, and the institutional. By such standards, American Catholicism can be judged a remarkable success. The mystical heart of the religion remains vibrant: its sacramental envisionment of all existence concentrated in a strong eucharistic life; the biblical movement's rediscovery of Word itself as sacrament; the retrieval of the many classic traditions of spirituality in new and ancient forms; the powerful sense of social justice as at the heart of the Christian prophetic tradition; the expressions of individual and group piety among the people. As European commentators from de Tocqueville to the present have observed, Americans are a surprisingly religious people. In our period, de Tocqueville would have a second surprise: American Catholics have become not only a religious but a decidedly theological people as well. The intellectual element of the religion now matches the mystical element in strength.

Part of this latter development is no doubt a result of the great interest in the creative possibilities of theology set loose by that explosion of hope, the Second Vatican Council. Another part is undoubtedly the strength of Catholic education in this country from our grammar schools through the great American Catholic colleges and universities. Yet another part is the emergence of a high proportion of an educated laity after the period of a once largely immigrant church. But the greater part, by far, of this remarkable birth of American Catholic theology is directly related to the diversity, strength, and openness of American Catholic religious life in all its variety. Americans always puzzled Europeans by managing to be a genuinely religious people in a highly developed modern culture. The emergence of peculiarly American theologies, however, is a new and more recent step forward. Here, too, in fidelity to the diversity of American Catholicism itself, the spectrum ranges widely. American Catholic feminist theologians have led the way for all American Christian theology as well as for worldwide Catholicism in fashioning a new critique of the tradition as well as a retrieval of forgotten, often repressed, feminist aspects of that tradition. The eruption of new "people's theologies" (once named by John Shea "street theologies") have fashioned new ways of theologizing in and for particular groups in highly particular circumstances: from the new American liberation theologies of the "base communities" of the South Bronx, through the forging of new narratives and new theologies from Chicago to San Antonio to Monterey. Theologians in more traditionally academic settings have worked on new methodologies for theology. There a characteristically American experiential approach has proved its fruitfulness for all theological methods both here and, increasingly, in Europe and Asia. Neoconservative theologians have aided the wider pluralism by their epiphanic retrievals of classic resources of spirituality and thought in the ancient, two-thousand-year-old tradition.

To read the proceedings of the Catholic Theological Society of America, *Theological Studies,* the *Catholic Biblical Quarterly,* and *Horizons,* the journal of the College Theology Society, as well as the many excellent journals of opinion in American Catholic life should be sufficient warrant for my belief that both American Catholic religious life (von Hügel's mystical element) and American Catholic theological life (the intellectual element) are, without exaggeration, strong at present and entirely promising for the future. American Catholic theology is alive, intense, ecumenical, pluralistic, and honest in its willingness to face the ambiguities in both our American cultural heritage and our Catholic religious tradition.

The mystical and intellectual elements of American Catholic life are, in a word, flourishing. A fair-minded observer can also judge our institutional life positively. The American bishops have filled an invaluable role for the country and the church universal through their collaborative efforts on the pastorals on nuclear war and the economy. Moreover, the very way the bishops performed this service was as admirable as the substantive results: a listening to different views; a way of speaking to both the entire Christian community on inner-Christian warrants and to the wider public on grounds acceptable, in principle, to that public. In sum, the bishops have here attempted to persuade, not coerce. I have the impression that, if left to themselves, the American bishops could and would also take the same road of collaborative inquiry and persuasive discourse on the burning inner-church issues of our day. It is improbable, after all, that the bishops initiated the crises of the last few years. All those disturbing actions: the hounding of the women religious who signed the *New York Times'* statement, the Hunthausen and Curran cases, the attacks on the Dignity groups, the damage to Catholic-Jewish relationships through new Vatican instructions to Cardinal O'Connor, the debilitating effects of new decrees on Catholic higher education— all these actions, after all, were initiated not here but in Rome.

The bishops, indeed, have a difficult road to travel at the moment. In their honest attempt to be faithful to their ecclesial responsibilities to both Rome and thereby the church universal and to the pluralistic American church, they must find a new path: one that is both just and charitable, Catholic and catholic, open and responsible. One can only hope that the bishops will communicate to officials in Rome and to Pope John Paul II on his visit here the true ecclesial American situation (as distinct from the situation fantasized by periodicals like *The Wanderer*) as well and as courageously as they have communicated to officials in Washington on nuclear war, the economy, and Central America. The pragmatic and pastoral performance of most of the present members of the American episcopate and most of the heads of women and men religious, the leaders of various church services, and Catholic academic leaders gives one solid grounds to hope that the present series of crises in the American church need not lead to interminable conflict.

It is well for all of us to remember that optimism and pessimism alike are natural virtues or vices. Indeed whether we construe them as vices or virtues depends largely on our assessment of their intellectual accuracy and usually on our own temperamental proclivities. Hope, however, is another matter. Hope is a strictly theological virtue—and the courage it elicits is the virtue most needed today as the struggle in the American church intensifies. Catholic theology in the United States is too strong, too pluralistic and, in the true sense, too Catholic to concede the field to any purveyors of pessimism and confrontation. History alone should remind us of certain salient facts: the tragic experience of the modernist and Americanist crises earlier in the century are there for all to see. What should have been an intellectual argument became an institutional coercion—and with a price to intellectual integrity that we are all still paying. The twentieth-century Protestant theological experience is illuminating by comparison: Protestant neoorthodox theology (Bultmann, Barth, Tillich, the Niebuhrs) was a self-critical moment within the paradigm established by their liberal predecessors. Neoorthodoxy, however critical of the great liberals, was not a return to a pre-liberal paradigm. The controversy between Protestant liberals and neoorthodox was intense; but like all properly theological controversies, it was also free, open, argumentative. It was a theological argument—an exercise in persuasion, not coercion.

The Catholic controversies surrounding modernism and Americanism were equally intense. But when institutional leaders yielded to the temptation of coercion, not theological persuasion, the tragedy unfolded: honest scholars dishonored, academic institutions raided, intellectual inquiry silenced. The modernist and Americanist crises should be acknowledged as Catholicism's Vietnam experience. To think of repeating them is a folly that should not be camouflaged. Even by neoconservative theological standards there is no necessity for such shameful conduct to be repeated. Neoconservative theologians, like all other theologians, live by the persuasive power of their own theological arguments, not by the power of their institutional roles. Theology—which is, after all, a major part of any vibrant religious tradition—can best perform its services when the mystical and institutional elements are also strong. But theology, as intellectual inquiry, must also be free and open—open even to make those mistakes which are the inevitable price of all intellectual advance and whose correction one can trust to the larger theological community of inquiry. All theologians, to be sure, need to be open to true persuasion from any quarter. But theologians, like all inquirers, would betray their vocation and indeed their own way of being religious, if they simply yielded to coercion. There is, after all, the reality of intellectual integrity. When that integrity is gone, all true inquiry ceases. When persuasion is abandoned, the vacuum is soon filled by the furies let loose by coercion. Along that way lies presumption for the few and despair for the many. But presumption and despair are theological vices whose only service is to clarify anew the need for hope as the central theological virtue of our period—a hope grounded in faith, intellectual integrity, and courage; a hope functioning as the love empowering all true persuasion in the community of hope.

20. Destructive Tensions in Moral Theology

CHARLES E. CURRAN

Tension between theology and Catholic practice on the one hand and official church teaching authority on the other hand has been very evident in the United States in the area of moral theology, especially sexual morality.

My own case well illustrates this tension but is far from the only example. In August of 1986, seven years after I was first informed that I was under investigation by the Congregation for the Doctrine of the Faith, Cardinal Ratzinger, the prefect of that congregation, informed me that I was "neither suitable nor eligible to exercise the function of a professor of Catholic theology."

In the beginning, the issues at stake between the congregation and myself centered on the specific areas of sexual and medical morality as well as on the methodological aspects of moral theology. In the end the congregation expressed disagreement with my dissent (which in my judgment was always quite nuanced) on the questions of the indissolubility of consummated sacramental marriage, abortion, euthanasia, masturbation, artificial contraception, premarital intercourse, and homosexual acts. Many other theologians in the United States and abroad (e.g., the board of directors of the Catholic Theological Society of America) have pointed out that my positions in these areas are moderate and nuanced and must be described as being in the mainstream of Catholic moral theology.

This action by the congregation against me is quite ironic in light of the fact that I have written very little in the area of sexual ethics in the last decade. I made a decision in the early seventies to concentrate my work in the area of social and political ethics. It seemed to me that this was the area in which the teaching of the church needed to be probed at a greater depth and put into practice on a daily basis.

Church authority has frequently taken action about sexual morality in the last few years. Imprimaturs have been removed from a number of books dealing with sexuality, such as Philip Keane's *Sexual Morality.* Both the Vatican and the United States bishops strongly criticized the book *Human Sexuality: New Directions in American Catholic Thought,* which was the work of a committee commissioned by the Catholic Theological Society of America. Anthony Kosnik, the chair of the committee, is no longer teaching in his former seminary position and is not able to teach sexual ethics. John McNeill, who wrote *The Church and the Homosexual,* has recently left the Society of Jesus after facing an ultimatum to keep silent on the question of the morality of homosexuality or face dismissal from the society. The threatened disciplinary action against the religious women who signed a statement on abortion which appeared in the *New York Times* has created widespread resentment on the part of many Catholics in the United States. However, the emphasis on sexual morality has not been limited only to the United States. Recall the action taken by church authorities against Ambrogio Valsechi in Italy and Stephen Pfürtner in Switzerland. All would have to agree that the area of sexual morality is one of the primary areas of tension in the church today between theologians and members of the church on the one hand and the teaching authority of the church on the other hand.

REASONS FOR THIS TENSION

The factual situation raises the interesting question of why. Why is sexual morality such a significant area of tension in the church today? A number of reasons help to explain this reality.

First, the tension between theologians and the hierarchical magisterium is bound to be more acute in practical matters such as church organization or morality. In these areas the practical daily life of people is at stake. The possibility of dissent from non-infallible teaching in sexual and medical morality has many practical ramifications. The relationship between the hierarchical magisterium and theology would be quite smooth if one could make the facile distinction that theology deals with speculation and the hierarchical magisterium deals with the teaching which is to be put into practice. It is not necessary to say that theologians constitute another magisterium in order to justify the possibility of dissent even in practice, but one must be willing to admit the inherent limits of the noninfallible teaching office of the church.

Second, there is no doubt that sexuality often raises great fears and anxieties on the part of many. When the two areas of authority and sexuality come together, one has all the ingredients of a very explosive situation.

Third, the tension between authority and moral theology and moral practice in general in the Catholic church is more pronounced than in many other areas precisely because the Roman Catholic tradition has claimed that its moral teachings in the sexual area are based primarily on natural law and human reason. The Catholic church has never claimed that its sexual ethics are based exclusively or uniquely on Catholic faith. By definition, in this area the conflict between authority and reason must always be decided in favor of right reason. It is true that reason might be wrong, but nonetheless the Catholic church has claimed its teaching in the area of sexuality is based on human reason.

The best of the Catholic moral tradition as exemplified in Thomas Aquinas has always insisted on an intrinsic morality. Morality is based on what is good for the person living in community. Something is obligatory and commanded because it is good and not the other way around. Moral obligation is ultimately grounded in the human reality itself and not in the extrinsic will of any type of legislator. Thus the authority in this matter must always conform itself to the true and the good.

Fourth, there is a great difference between the moral methodologies employed by many contemporary Catholic moral theologians and the methodology followed by the official teaching office and by the Congregation for the Doctrine of the Faith. There is no doubt that a manualistic neo-scholasticism still reigns supreme in official Roman documents, especially in the area of sexuality. In the judgment of the majority of Catholic moral theologians writing today, this methodology is centered too much on the sexual faculty and the sexual act and fails to give enough importance to the total person and the personal relationships within which one exists. Rome refuses to recognize at the present time the legitimacy of any moral methodology in sexuality other than this manualistic neo-scholasticism. However, the vast majority of Catholic theologians writing in this area have already abandoned such a methodology.

Perhaps the most significant methodological differences between the Roman, manualistic neo-scholasticism and the approach of many contemporary moral theologians concerns the latter's use of a more inductive methodology. Such a methodology gives importance to the experience of Christian people that thus becomes a *fons* or *locus theologicus.* One cannot uncritically accept the experience of Christian people or merely reduce morality to an opinion poll. However, the experience of people of goodwill is an important aspect that must enter into theological method. Precisely on the basis of this experience, it is necessary at times to question and perhaps even change those teachings which were rooted in a different historical and cultural experience. The fact that such experience today is often in contradiction with the official teaching of the hierarchical magisterium makes the contemporary problem even more acute.

Fifth, some people in the Roman Catholic church today would find it very hard to admit the possibility of dissent or to change the teaching of the hierarchical magisterium on these issues of sexual morality. The church has invested much of its life and energy in proposing and defending these norms. The hierarchical magisterium would have to admit that to some extent it has been wrong in its teaching. Could the Holy Spirit ever allow the magisterium to be wrong in such important practical matters? There is no doubt that this is a primary reason why many oppose the legitimacy of dissent in the church. However, the ultimate problem seems to come from the fact that the hierarchical magisterium has claimed a greater certitude for this teaching than should have actually been claimed. Noninfallible teaching by definition is reformable. All must recognize that the primary teacher and the primary forgiver in the Christian community is the Holy Spirit.

THE PRESENT STATUS

What has been the effect of this growing divergence between theologians and Catholic practice and the hierarchical teaching office in the area of human sexuality? From the viewpoint of the discipline of moral theology, moral theologians will continue to be even more reluctant to write in the area of sexuality. Many theologians today prefer not to write in this area precisely because of the difficulties entailed in taking positions contrary to the official church teaching.

From the viewpoint of the Catholic faithful, there are a number of different reactions that have occurred. Some Roman Catholics have become disillusioned with the church primarily because of its teaching in sexual matters. Andrew M. Greeley and his associates have concluded that the issuance of the encyclical "Humanae vitae" in 1968 with its condemnation of artificial contraception seems to have been the occasion for massive apostasy and for a notable decline in religious devotion and belief. Greeley attributes the great decline in Catholic practice in the United States in the decade 1963–1973 to this encyclical with its condemnation of artificial contraception. On the other hand, many Roman Catholics continue to consider themselves good Catholics but disagree in theory and in practice with the official hierarchical church teaching on some matters. The vast majority of Roman Catholics today approve the use of artificial contraception in marriage. Many Roman Catholics who are divorced and remarried now feel in conscience that they can and should fully participate in the liturgical, sacramental, and community life of the Roman Catholic church. Homosexuals do not think that they should be banned from the Eucharist and many who live in permanent relationships are participating in the church's life.

It is important to point out that in these cases people can make the decision to disagree in theory and in practice with church teaching and still consider themselves good, loyal Roman Catholics. These decisions are made in conscience and the individual then acts in accord with that conscience. Dissent in practice can and undoubtedly will continue even though Rome might try to clamp down on any kind of theoretical dissent. In a sense, then, there is no great problem created by the present teaching of the hierarchical magisterium for such people.

However, this growing difference between official hierarchical teaching and the practice of many and the positions of the majority of Catholic theologians cannot continue to exist without grave harm to the church. The credibility of the church and especially its teaching office are challenged. Even though there are ways in the present situation to solve the individual dilemma of conscience despite the official church teaching, the present situation cannot continue for a long time without grave damage to the life of the church itself.

21. John Paul II and the Growing Alienation of Women from the Church

ROSEMARY RADFORD RUETHER

The Roman Catholic Church has long assumed that it could count on women to be the majority of churchgoers and the primary carriers of "the faith" to their children. Thus it comes as a surprise to many churchmen to realize that women today are becoming increasingly disaffected from the Catholic church. This is not a question of "secularism" finally catching up with women, as the culturally more conservative sector of society. Rather, Catholic women are becoming disaffected from the Catholic church because they perceive it to be an agent of discrimination against women. As they become sensitized to questions of sexism, women perceive the Catholic church not only as an institution that has been shaped by patriarchal society, but one which continues to play a major role in legitimating sexism both in the church itself and in society.

This new sensitivity to sexism among Catholic women has paralleled the generally expanding critical consciousness after Vatican II. For many Catholics there was an optimism between 1965–76 that the Catholic church was ready to respond to new challenges positively. But the last ten years, and particularly the pontificate of John Paul II, have seen increasing evidence of reactionary backlash on all areas of renewal in the church, but particularly in matters having to do with sexuality and the status of women in the church. This increasingly reenforces women's perception that patriarchal domination and sexual repression are a deepseated pathology in Catholic Christianity that is all but incurable. The present pope seems to sum up this pathology in his personal attitudes. This personal misogyny of the pontiff makes a vivid impression on women, who increasingly see Catholicism as an agent of evil rather than good. Thus the pope has contributed markedly to the loss of the ethical credibility of the church for women, as well as feminist men.

This alienation from the church is also painful for Catholic women. The church has played a cultural role as parent, combining imagery of mother-church with the fatherhood of God, represented by priests. The church has claimed to mediate one's relationship to God as father and to the true nature of reality created by God. Alienation from the church, as an institution hostile to women's human well-being and development, creates deep conflicts. The entire moral universe in which a woman has been raised is perceived as thwarting rather than upholding her fulfillment. Such a woman is made to feel that she must rebel against all that has hitherto claimed to nurture her in order to seek her authentic human potential. The result can be a profound and destructive sense of disorientation. Some women feel that they have to reject God because they cannot differentiate God from the church and from the patriarchal cultural imagery for God. All the language for God and God-world relationships is perceived as having been shaped to exalt the male as the normative human person and to subordinate women.

This patriarchal enculturation of theology affects not simply abstract theorizing about God by professional theologians. Rather it comes home daily in the language of prayer and worship. Thus Catholic women find themselves increasingly blocked from the worship life of the church, and are doubly offended when their suggestions for modest cultural adaptation in language are rebuffed. Hostile reception of suggestions for inclusive language enforce the suspicion that patriarchy is essential, not simply superficial, to Catholic Christianity.

This experience leaves Catholics deeply scarred, starved for positive spiritual nurture. Women feel themselves suffering from linguistic deprivation and eucharistic famine. They find they can no longer nurture their souls in alienating words and symbols that systematically ignore or deny their existence. This increasingly forces some Catholic women to seek autonomous gatherings for theological reflection and worship on the margins of the institutional church where they can meet that need for spiritual nurture denied them in most parishes.

Is this perception that Catholic Christianity particularly suffers from a deeply ingrained misogynist pathology fair? Certainly Christianity did not invent patriarchy, but it did inherit and absorb traditions from both Judaism and Greco-Roman culture that justify male domination over women. Throughout its history, beginning at least with New Testament texts, such as 1 Tim 2:9–14, Catholic Christianity has upheld the idea that women are secondary in the order of creation, more responsible for sin, and are to be silent in church and subordinate in society. This continues to have social, as well as ecclesial, expressions. The Vatican, as well as American bishops, opposed women's suffrage in the early decades of the twentieth century. Although some recent statements of the popes and the bishops have suggested a more positive view of women's rights in society, nevertheless concrete legislation, such as the Equal Rights Amendment, was not endorsed by the hierarchy.

Although Catholic theology has never gone so far as to exclude women completely from the image of God and from salvation (to do so would have been to lose women altogether as members of the church!), the idea that women have a humanity inferior to men and relate to God only under men "as their head" is deeply engrained in the Catholic theological tradition. Saint Augustine, in his treatise on the Trinity, denied that women possessed the image of God in their own right, the male representing the collective image of God in humanity. Aquinas used the patriarchal biology of Aristotle to define women as "misbegotten males" who possess a defective humanity—mentally, morally, and physically. This patriarchal anthropology was used to deduce fundamental theological propositions that made maleness essential to the nature of Christ and denied ordination to women on the grounds that they could not represent Christ. Such a Christology makes it questionable whether women are actually represented or redeemed by Christ at all. Christ is presented to women as the reenforcer of their oppression, not as their redeemer.

These ideas of women's inferiority and proneness to sin in Catholic theology and culture appear contradicted by other traditions which idealize the feminine and link it with superior moral purity and spirituality. The Virgin Mary has been the primary representative of the idea of the feminine as faithful receptivity to God and moral perfection. But this image of Mary as ideal femininity has generally been used by Catholic spirituality to heighten the disparity between this exceptional woman, born without original sin, and all real women who are daughters of Eve. In the light of this perfect woman, real women are simultaneously disparaged and called to an impossible ethic of sexual repression and total submission to male authority. Thus Mary does not become a model of woman as autonomous person, but rather appears as a fantasy by which celibate males sublimate their sexuality into an ideal relationship with a virgin mother, while projecting the hostility caused by this sexual repression into misogynist feelings toward real women. The present pope seems to be a particular example of this combination of Marian piety and misogyny.

Female disaffection with the Catholic church focuses particularly on three areas: (1) reproductive rights, (2) ordination of women, and (3) inclusive language and symbols. Recently some bishops have tried to put the opposition to abortion into the context of a comprehensive "life" ethic. But this view loses its credibility as long as the Catholic church also continues to oppose birth control or to make untenable distinctions between methods of birth control. De facto what is really promoted by this ethic is involuntary motherhood and the denial to women of reproductive self-determination. Needless to say, such a policy promotes, rather than helps eliminate, abortion, since abortion is never a free choice for women but a desperate response to involuntary pregnancy in inhospitable circumstances. Thus the Catholic church's opposition to reproductive self-determination both ties women to a life-style of unchosen pregnancy that makes it very difficult to combine marriage and motherhood with enlarged work and development opportunities, and carries with it a suggestion of the need of the celibate male to punish women for their sexuality.

The second area of discrimination, namely, the denial of ordination to women, still rests on the fundamental structure of a patriarchal theology. The 1976 Vatican declaration against women's ordination expressed in crude and graphic terms women's inability to "represent Christ." As long as the theology of this document stands as normative, women's second-class status in redemption remains basic to Catholic views of women, whether or not a woman might actually aspire to the priesthood. Such a view of the essential maleness of Christ and women's inability to represent Christ is incompatible with the doctrine that the incarnation of God into human nature is an inclusive representation of female as well as male humanity. The logical response to such a document is to conclude that if women can't represent Christ, then Christ does not represent women. Women are not included in salvation in Christ at all.

Finally the question of inclusive language must be seen, not simply as a tinkering with grammar, but as a fundamental challenge to the androcentric bias of all theological words and symbols. Feminist theology not only calls on the church to acknowledge in its verbal declarations that its human members include women as well as men, sisters as well as brothers, daughters as well as sons of God, but also that God is the ground of personhood for women and men. As long as one continues to use exclusively male language for God, one implicitly asserts that women do not possess the image of God. A God who is truly the ground of the being and the new being of women must be imaged as both beyond gender and nameable in language drawn from both genders.

Thus feminist theology calls on the Catholic church to repent of its long history of androcentrism, misogyny, and anti-creational dualism. It calls on the Catholic church to become a credible representative, in both its words and its actions, of divine love and redemptive hope for all humans, female as well as male. The words and actions of the present papacy have raised real questions about whether "Catholic" Christianity is capable of being that sacrament of universal love and hope.

22. The Lay Reaction
ANDREW M. GREELEY

Sociology cannot dictate either theological conclusions or magisterial decisions. It is limited to describing how men and women act, not how they should act. While it may provide raw material on which theologians and teachers can reflect—assuming, as Catholicism always has, that the voice of the Spirit may be heard among the people as well as their leaders—it cannot constrain the direction of such reflection.

It may also speculate on the models which seem to be the basis for certain policy decisions and examine those models in the light of the available empirical data. It is this activity to which I will devote myself in the present paper. I shall ask what model of the Catholic laity seems to underlie the repression which is currently taking place in the church and whether there is support in the data on American Catholics for such a model.

One often hears from ecclesiastical leadership that the laity are confused and that the problem of such confusion can be solved by eliminating those scholars who have created the confusion and by preaching authentic Catholic doctrine with all possible clarity. Thus Cardinal Bernard Law observed that the Catholic people welcome the repeated insistence of their church on the birth control doctrine. Similarly Cardinal Law has insisted on the need of a universal catechism which will state clearly and unequivocally the essence of Catholic teaching.

Let us leave aside the patronization of the laity involved in such a model and inquire whether (1) the laity's response to the crisis in the church of the last two decades indicates confusion and (2) whether repeated and forceful insistence on certain doctrinal (usually ethical) norms eliminates this confusion.

In response to the first question, the following points must be made:

1. There has been no appreciable increase in defection of American Catholics from the church. Moreover, after the

sharp decline in weekly church attendance following the birth control encyclical, attendance stabilized in 1975 and has remained stable ever since.

2. The overwhelming majority of American Catholics reject some, but by no means all, of the church's sexual teachings.

3. American Catholics have registered their protest against the way authority is exercised, particularly authority in sexual matters, by a sharp, not to say catastrophic, lowering of their financial contributions to the church.

They stay in the church, reject some sexual teachings, and protest with diminished financial support, a combination of responses which suggests a sophisticated (if not orthodox) response, hardly what one would expect from men and women who have been confused by false teachers.

In 1963, some 12 percent of those who were raised Catholics no longer described themselves as Catholics. In 1975, this percentage had increased to 15 percent. In 1985, it had risen to 17 percent. However, if one takes into account the different age distribution of the population, the figure that can properly be compared with the 1963 number is 13 percent.

Moreover, while church attendance fell from 65 percent every week in 1963 to 50 percent in the years from 1975 to the present, the proportion never going to church has not increased more than a couple of percentage points and almost two-thirds of American Catholics are inside a church for Sunday (or Saturday evening) Mass once a month. Finally, projections based on life cycle curves indicate that those who were born as recently as the early sixties will attend church through their life cycle at about the same rates as their parents.

American Catholics, in other words, have survived the turbulence of the years since the Second Vatican Council with their basic affiliation to the church relatively unchanged.

However, in overwhelming numbers they no longer accept the church's teaching on birth control, divorce, and premarital sex and are willing to permit abortion if the mother's life is in danger or if the child is expected to be handicapped. On these issues approximately nine out of ten American Catholics are in dissent—with the exception of the matter of premarital sex being always wrong, a subject in which four out of five dissent.

The premarital sex issue seems to be linked with the birth control issue. Acceptance of the official teaching on premarital sex began to fall several years after the decline in acceptance of the birth control teaching and has fallen since then just as precipitously. Having lost credibility on birth control, church leadership also lost, as a delayed chain reaction, its credibility on premarital sex. If sex need not be limited to procreation, the laity seemed to argue, then it need not be limited to publicly committed married partners.

However, the chain reaction has *not* affected Catholic attitudes on abortion on demand, homosexuality, and extramarital sex. Some two-thirds of American Catholics continue to accept the Church's teaching on these subjects, the same proportions as twenty years ago.

While Church leadership can hardly be expected to be pleased by this picture, it would seem that the laity are not so confused that they are unable to make distinctions. Rejection of the birth control teaching has had no effect at all on attitudes towards some other, not unimportant, sexual matters.

How can Catholics justify continued reception of the sacraments while at the same time rejecting certain doctrines which the teaching authority presently deems of paramount importance? My research suggests that they do so by an appeal from church leaders, who they think do not understand, to God, who they think does understand. I do not, be it noted, endorse such reasoning. I only report it. And I note that such an appeal is not likely to be deflected by a catechism that church leaders produce, since the latter are already dismissed as not understanding.

In 1960, Protestants and Catholics both contributed 2.2 percent of their incomes to their churches. In 1985, Protestants still contributed 2.2 percent. But Catholic contributions had fallen to 1.1 percent. The cost of this decline in 1985 was $6 billion. Over the quarter century the cost in contemporary dollars is $65 billion. The difference between Catholics and Protestants in church contributions is especially great among the better educated, those with small families, regular churchgoers, and the politically and socially liberal. In other charities, Catholics are as generous as Protestants.

About 15 percent of the decline can be accounted for by lower rates of church attendance, the same proportion by a younger age

distribution in the population (younger people give smaller proportions of their income than do older people), and about 20 percent of the decline cannot be accounted for by the available
mathematical models. The rest of the change can be explained by
parallel and correlated declines in the acceptance of sexual teaching and ecclesiastical authority. The Catholic laity seem to be voting, negatively, with their checkbooks. Thus those who think they
are dealing with a simple, docile, and confused laity can find little
support for such imagery in the data.

Moreover, there is no reason to think that clear, forceful, and
insistent repetition of teaching will change the mind of the
American laity. In the eight years since his election, Pope John
Paul II has left little doubt about his opposition to the ordination
of women. Surely every American Catholic who can read knows
about this opposition. Yet between 1975 and 1986, Catholic lay
support for the ordination of women has almost doubled, from 29
percent to 56 percent. Indeed, support for women priests seems
to increase every time there is a statement from church leadership saying that such a change is impossible.

Finally, on the issues of sexual ethics about which the pope has
been so clear and so forceful in the last half-dozen years, especially since his visit to the United States, there has been little change
in Catholic attitudes. Between 1980 and 1986, Catholic opposition to abortion on demand declined from 70 percent to 68 percent; disapproval of homosexuality diminished from 71 percent
to 69 percent; and disapproval of premarital sex fell from 23 percent to 21 percent. In 1980, 16 percent of American Catholics
thought that abortion ought not be permitted when a mother's
life was in danger. In 1986, the percentage had gone down to 13
percent. None of these differences are statistically significant. But
the point is that the continued, persistent, and vehement procla-
mations of the Vatican had no effect at all on the attitudes of
American Catholics.

The purpose of this paper, to repeat, is to portray not what reality should be, but what it is. But what if one is asked how one
thinks church leadership should react to such a portrait?

First of all, they should stop deceiving themselves that reality is
different.

Second, they should, to quote Archbishop John R. Quinn at the synod on the family a number of years ago, engage in dialogue with the laity on the issues involved.

Since the word dialogue has been corrupted by its recent usage in the church, one should perhaps note that it means not only *speaking at* the laity, but *listening to* them—which church leaders find difficult indeed.

23. Women and the Seminaries
ARLENE ANDERSON SWIDLER

Catholic women continue on their journey. They theologize.
They restudy the Scriptures. They restate the problems the
church should be facing and reevaluate their own tasks. They develop new styles of liturgy. They pray in new ways. But until all
their achievements can be integrated into general Catholic
church life the overall effect will be slight, and the distance between feminists and the rest of the church will widen dangerously.
How do we keep together? Or, to borrow a term from the academic world, how can women's discoveries and insights be "main-
streamed" into ordinary parish life? In large part through a
priesthood that has been made aware of and sensitive to the
issues.

It is in the seminaries that our Catholic clergy can learn to study
and work with women as peers and to integrate the thought and
experience of the other half of the church into their own theology, preaching, and prayer life. Once these men are safely en-
sconced in their rectories, feminist influence will be minimal.
Women in seminaries—as divinity students, as professors, as spiritual directors—are clearly essential. Much is riding on their continued presence.

When in June of 1981 John Paul II mandated a study of United
States seminary education, many of us in the Women's Ordination Conference (WOC) were immediately apprehensive. The
WOC staff, therefore, sent out a questionnaire to fifty-five seminaries in the United States and Canada to discover the extent of
women's participation. The responses from twenty-seven seminaries, almost exactly one-half, can give us some sense of trends at
that crucial time.

The Vatican study, or "apostolic visitation," was coordinated
by Bishop John Marshall of Burlington, with Bishop Donald

Wuerl, since of Seattle, as his executive secretary for the first four years. Under Bishop Marshall's direction, teams of examiners visited each seminary and prepared in-depth reports on each of the thirty-eight "free-standing" seminaries in the country. (The WOC study had included seminaries involved in collaborative models as well.) The results are presented in a letter from Cardinal William W. Baum, prefect of the Vatican Congregation for Catholic Education, to the United States Catholic bishops, released 5 October 1986 and titled "The State of U.S. of Free-Standing Seminaries" (published in *Origins*, 16 October 1986).

According to Cardinal Baum, the Holy Father "initiated the visitation" to " 'take the pulse' on priestly formation and to see how Vatican Council II is being implemented" in American seminaries. Because "the Holy Father has taken a great interest in the work of the visitation and having been kept thoroughly informed of its findings has expressed his satisfaction with its progress," the letter and visitation are meant to be taken as representing papal policy.

Whether women were from the beginning intended as a target is not, of course, known. Along with its questionnaire, WOC sent out its own "pulse tester," asking for seminary opinions. Reactions varied. One rector wrote, "In the context of Church operating procedures it is not as alarming as it may seem." Another responded, "The women's issue is undoubtedly on the agenda."As it turned out, women's fears were quite justified.

Three areas are of interest: women as faculty members, as spiritual directors, and as students (put last here because the discussion is most complicated).

WOMEN AS FACULTY MEMBERS

Cardinal Baum's letter reiterates the principle that "as a general rule professors for the sacred subjects ought to be priests," adding that nonclerical professors may be appointed, provided they at least conform to secular standards. The WOC study, which had not distinguished between teachers of sacred and profane matters, discovered that from 1976 to 1981 the number of full-time women faculty in the responding seminaries had grown from thirty-seven to seventy-two and part-time women faculty had increased from thirty-one to seventy.

Women professors of theology are necessary if we are to straighten out our skewed theology. To deal with just one area: our male bias in imaging and speaking of and to God in masculine terms only, and all the linguistic, liturgical, and homiletic questions that flow from that theology, must be treated in courses in fundamental theology and Scripture. Priests who have really studied and reflected on the questions—and how few these are even today—can explicate the issues, but only a feminist theologian can communicate all the pain and the degradation heaped upon women by misogynist theology.

Suggestions that matters like these be treated in other courses are unrealistic. To take them out of their proper context and relegate them to the peripheral category of women's concerns would already veil their significance. But even such attention is unlikely. The section on "social justice" within Cardinal Baum's letter, for example, completely ignores women. "A sound spirituality . . . based on the example and teaching of the Lord himself" will assure, it says, "that the future priest will forgo the natural attractions of functioning only among those of his own class and his own culture"—and there it stops.

WOMEN AS SPIRITUAL DIRECTORS

Women have also become more involved in spiritual direction in seminaries. Although responses to our WOC survey noted that the term is defined in more than one way and that some seminaries either did not include spiritual direction as an "official function" or had no such category, the numbers we did receive showed that ten seminaries had a total of fifty women spiritual directors in 1981 and that six of these ten had had no women in that position five years before.

The Baum letter is quite explicit in excluding women—and members of the Great Unordained in general—from directing seminarians. "In a number of cases prior to the apostolic visitation of the theologates spiritual direction was being entrusted to people who were not themselves ordained to the priesthood. We have asked for a realignment of spiritual direction in these seminaries." Just what constitutes spiritual direction being somewhat fluid, seminarians, like other people, will probably continue seeking counsel as they see fit.

Nevertheless the theology behind the decision is disturbingly patriarchal. An emphasis on the priest-director as "role model," as one "vocationally oriented" in the same direction, assumes that life experience of the priesthood is essential for guiding seminarians. Yet these same men will be sent out to direct, guide, and judge married laity with no inner experience of that life. There is no sense of dialogue between the various lived spiritualities.

Feminist spirituality has much to offer, beginning with the insight that pride—overestimating oneself—is not, after all, the besetting sin for everyone. Many people, including men, are far more likely to be guilty of underestimating themselves and fearing to shoulder their share of the world's decision making and creative work. Certainly, integrating such reflections on women's experiences needs to be a part of seminarians' development.

WOMEN AS STUDENTS

The lay students in seminaries (those not on the ordination track are never referred to as seminarians) fall into three categories. First there are those who come in for adult education or for formation for some specific apostolate. As the letter notes, such classes are often scheduled during times when the facilities are unused and thus cause few problems. Undoubtedly many Catholics find a real value in studying at what they consider the heart of the diocese.

Two other groups of laity, primarily women, attend the seminary, and the letter does not distinguish between them. In the first group are people working for a graduate degree—often an M.A.—in theology or religious education. The other group consists of people who actually take the same courses as the seminarians and, when they graduate, get the same M.Div. degree. The former group, in our responses, had grown from 375 to 634 in five years; the latter had increased from 69 to 120.

Cardinal Baum's letter sees several difficulties in the presence of these students, indicating problems which seem to be laid at the feet of an unreasonable and overdemanding laity. First, a good deal is made of the weak preparation of nonseminarian students, their lack of philosophical and scriptural background, which results in "a lowering of theological standards." It is difficult to take such a problem seriously. In such cases where it does in fact exist, it is surely easily dealt with by a brief reprimand to the admissions officer.

Secondly, there is a concern with the overloading of faculty and fragmentation of the seminary's work by what are actually graduate schools of religion being run in some seminaries. As the letter says, "It is unwise and unfair to expect a seminary to serve all a local church's needs of theological learning and formation for ecclesial service." This warning, too, seems misdirected. Often the seminaries themselves, feeling the financial crunch, aggressively recruit nonseminarian students, sometimes to the detriment of well-established local Catholic theological graduate programs.

A third objection deals with the distinction between priests and laity. "The specialized nature of priestly formation" is emphasized, as is the distinction between priestly and lay ministries. The letter fails to confront the fact that women in divinity programs, for the most part, see their vocation in much the same light as the male seminarians—in fact, it is quite possible for a careful reader to peruse the whole document without realizing that women are studying in the divinity programs. These women, too, look forward to counseling and healing, to teaching and preaching, to preparing liturgies and preparing people for the reception of the sacraments, to ministering in parishes, college campuses, hospitals, and prisons. The presence of such women will in no way dilute "the vocational orientation of the group."

THE NEED FOR WOMEN IN SEMINARIES

There are several reasons why women are needed in the divinity program. The first—not, of course, acceptable to Vatican visitators—is simply that we need a pool of women who are willing and able to move into ecclesial roles as they open. As Cardinal Baum remarks in another context, "There are some people who are determined to be priests by hook or by crook."

Secondly, we need the ministry of these women now.

Thirdly, it is only in a situation in which seminarians and women work as peers—testing, correcting, building upon, adopting one another's ideas—that we can train priests who will treat women as equals.

Although the general report of this Vatican-mandated study has been made public, specific observations were sent directly to the individual bishops. How they will affect the presence of women, we do not as yet know. There is much disagreement with the Vatican position.

One of the respondents to the 1981 WOC survey wrote that the bishop sees "the presence of women on both faculty and student body as wonderful, bringing great wealth, variety, and richness." A second said, "I would strenuously argue against any move to eliminate women from any of the seminary's programs." Another rector told us, "Seminaries will have rather serious deficiencies in their overall priestly formation programs if women are not part of the administration, faculty and spiritual formation teams. This is a point of view shared by most people I meet who are engaged in the ministry of priestly formation."

24. Theology in Catholic Higher Education

RICHARD P. MCBRIEN

Catholic theology enjoyed something of a renaissance during and immediately following the Second Vatican Council. The names of Congar, Rahner, Schillebeeckx, and Küng were as celebrated at Vatican II as were those of Montini, Suenens, Frings, and Alfrink. Cooperation between the hierarchical magisterium and theologians had rarely been closer or more productive.

Two events substantially altered this situation: the 1968 birth control encyclical of Pope Paul VI, "Humanae vitae," and the election ten years later of Cardinal Karol Wojtyla to the papacy.

The first event provoked a storm of dissent, signaling that theologians were prepared to use their newly acquired influence to challenge official teachings. Father Charles Curran of the Catholic University of America began his slide toward eventual Vatican censure when he organized a public protest against the encyclical in that fateful summer of 1968.

The suspicions and animosities which many conservative Catholics have always harbored toward theologians resurfaced with uncommon force. They insisted, especially in private communications, that "something be done."

But there was an obstacle. The incumbent pope, Paul VI, had no stomach for censorship and suppression. It would have been contrary to his whole background (including ministry to university students and Catholic intellectuals) and to the leading role he assumed at Vatican II. So, however conservative the aging pontiff had become in the latter years of his papacy, he would not proceed even against Hans Küng, the urgings of his more militantly conservative advisers notwithstanding.

The situation changed when, in August 1978, the pope died. The remarkable events of that year are still vivid in our memories. Venice's patriarch, Cardinal Albino Luciani, was elected to succeed Paul VI, but he himself died suddenly after serving only thirty-three days. The cardinals, summoned hastily back to Rome, were not about to select another mild-mannered, physically delicate colleague. They broke a centuries-old precedent and elected a relatively young and unmistakably vigorous Pole, Krakow's Cardinal Karol Wojtyla.

Cardinal Wojtyla had known only two kinds of political regimes in his entire adult life: nazism and communism. In the absence of a free press, an independent labor movement, and a flourishing system of higher education, the Catholic church for him and for all Poles became, almost by default, the one countervailing institutional force against a hostile government.

In a situation of this sort, dissent within the church was simply out of the question. Public conflict of any kind between clergy and bishops, or among the bishops, would have been politically suicidal. On the other hand, the wearing of clerical dress and of nuns' veils became political statements. They gave enduring visibility to the loyal opposition: "loyal" to Poland, "opposition" to its government.

It has become something of a cliché in recent years to attribute to this Polish background Pope John Paul II's theological conservatism, his impatience with dissent, and his strong-willed exercise of papal authority. But the cliché, in this instance, is very probably correct.

To say, as many have, that the present bishop of Rome does not understand the church in the United States or in other parts of the free world is not to condemn him. If a different sort of man had been elected during the most recent conclave—England's Cardinal Basil Hume, for example—one could have said of him that he doesn't understand what it means to live under communist oppression. As our hypothetical pope, Cardinal Hume would have been severely ill-advised to act as if his experiences as an English Benedictine could be applied, without modification, to every other portion of the church.

This, it appears to many, is Pope John Paul II's problem. He seems to assume that the only effective way to combat our common enemies—in today's world, they are atheism and materialism—is through a completely united front. No dissent, no public quarrelling, no breaking from the ranks.

Thus, he prefers organizations like Opus Dei and Communione e Liberazione to the Jesuits and the Franciscans. The former act *en bloc;* the latter tolerate, and even encourage, pluralism and diversity. The former follow the pope's lead without question or delay; the latter proceed on the basis of consensus and always in freedom. The pope's preferential option for a united front may also explain his hard-line course against independent-minded theologians and his support for the proposed Vatican schema on higher education.

Like many Catholics of his generation who have been trained as philosophers rather than as theologians, he seems to work out of a theological framework that shaped the seminary textbooks of the pre–Vatican II period. Within this framework, it is often difficult to distinguish, not only between theology and philosophy, but also between theology and catechesis.[1]

How well, therefore, does Pope John Paul II understand the *academic* character of theology and the place of theology in higher education? Speaking to a plenary meeting of the Congregation for Catholic Education in November 1986, he acknowledged the criticisms that had been made of the proposed schema on Catholic higher education, but he endorsed it nonetheless. "Every Catholic university in fact must show itself to all not only as a scientific workshop [*sic*]," he said, "but also as a solid rock of Christian principles, to which scientific activity can be anchored."[2]

Few Catholic educators or theologians would quarrel with that ideal. But the pope's assertion begs an important question: Who determines the Catholic character of such institutions? The Vatican schema assigns this responsibility to the hierarchy in general and to the local bishop in particular (and, given the schema's ecclesiology, ultimately to the pope). At least 110 United States Catholic college and university presidents find this to be the "real crux" of the document, namely, "the assertion of a power on the part of the bishop to control theologians (Norms, Chapter IV, Article 31) and to assure 'orthodoxy' in their teaching. . . . What is proposed here," the presidents insists, "is contrary to the American values of both academic freedom and due process, both of which are written into most university statutes and protected by civil and constitutional law."[3]

The Vatican schema seems to assume that these institutions were founded by the hierarchy and so should remain subject to the hierarchy. In almost no instance, however, were they founded, chartered, or funded by the hierarchy. Indeed, it is the state and not the church that charters United States Catholic colleges and universities. Significantly, the state leaves these academic institutions free to carry out their educational mission and even assists them with funds as long as academic standards are met and academic freedom respected. This is not the case in Poland, to be sure, or in most of the rest of the world.

Does this mean that the safeguarding of the Catholic character of a United States Catholic college or university is somehow left to chance? Not at all. It is the responsibility of their duly elected boards of trustees. To assign this responsibility to any other agency outside the college or university is to change the nature of the institution and the character of the academic enterprise that is conducted therein.

"Obviously, if church or state or any power outside the university can dictate who can teach and who can learn," argues Father Theodore M. Hesburgh, C.S.C., president of the University of Notre Dame from 1952 to 1987, "the university is not free and, in fact, is not a true university where the truth is sought and taught. It is rather a place of political or religious indoctrination. The latter is perfectly fitting for a catechetical center, but not for a university."[4]

The bishop of Rome's view of the Vatican schema on higher education, therefore, is at odds with those who know Catholic colleges and universities best (keeping in mind that almost all of them are, in fact, in the United States). If his view were to prevail, Father Hesburgh warns, the best Catholic institutions would be faced with a "terrible and basic dilemma." They would have "to choose between being real universities and being really Catholic when, in fact, they are already both."[5]

The Vatican's inability to see that is rooted in its abiding tendency to collapse theology into catechesis and universities into catechetical centers. And that tendency is, in turn, rooted in an ecclesiological perspective which continues to define the church primarily, if not exclusively, in hierarchical terms.

NOTES

1. I have addressed this issue more directly in "Theologians Under Fire," *The Tablet* 240 (28 June 1986): 675–77.
2. NC News Service, "Pope-Universities," 13 November 1986, p. 18.
3. See "Catholic College and University Presidents Respond to Proposed Vatican Schema," *Origins* 15 (10 April 1986), 703. The schema itself is published in the same issue, "Proposed Schema for a Pontifical Document on Catholic Universities," 706–11.
4. Theodore M. Hesburgh, C.S.C., "The Vatican and American Catholic Higher Education," *America* 155 (1 November 1986), 250.
5. Ibid., 250, 263.

25. The Problem That Has No Name

EUGENE C. KENNEDY

Great cultural transformations are, like mysterious changes within our bodies, difficult to name accurately. Until we find the correct diagnosis we are uncertain about the choice of effective remedies or reactions. Indeed, the word *diagnosis* contains, within its own linguistic history, revelations and hints about the central problem of contemporary life in general and Catholic life in particular.

The root *gno*, as in *gignoskein*, means to know, think, or judge. It is found in *gnomon*, a judge or interpreter, and as the sturdy foundation of *gnaro*, knowing or expert, as well as of *gnarrare* (L. *narrare*), to tell or to relate. Diagnosis, defined as *discernment*, is in itself a family reunion of popular contemporary Catholic themes and longings. We want to know, to discern our own gifts, to tell our own story, to judge ourselves. We are suspicious, if not disdainful, of those who profess to be able to do any of these things in our regard. In short, the problem of our time is that of authority. Whether it is rough beast or terrible beauty we are unsure, for it stands still unnamed on the ark of our experience. We still do not know how to live with it.

Most discussions of authority are really condemnations or reassertions of *authoritarianism*, a controlling phenomenon well versed in techniques of shaming and debasement that is very different from the mature generative character of healthy authority. The revolt against the former, however, has made the recognition or recovery of the latter very difficult. In psychology alone there are, for example, dozens of books and hundreds of articles and research projects on authoritarianism and its evils. There is hardly any interest, much less research or writing, about authority as a sound and indispensable element in human growth. Any institution, including the family and the church, charged with responsibility for fostering healthy development must be knowing about the nature of authentic authority. Being pro-life, in a real sense, means being in favor of constructive authority.

This difficulty in identifying sound authority is compounded by our enchantment with media shorthand in any discussion of the American Catholic church. Television and the newspapers, revealing their own intrinsic need for conflict, almost always style stories about the Catholic church in the negative language of repression and rebellion. In fact, however, very few Catholics want to rebel against church authority. Hardly any want to overthrow the pope, or, for that matter, be arbitrary in their judgments about curial decisions. Something psychologically far different is occurring, and it is urgent for participants and observers to discern its proper nature. Without that kind of knowing, there can be no accurate telling of the story of what is happening in the contemporary American Catholic church. Within the limits of this essay, I would like to propose a different interpretation of our engagement with the problem of authority in the relationship of American Catholics to their church.

First of all, segments of American Catholicism that seem to be in violent disagreement about authority are actually troubled by the same problems and are seeking, by different routes and from differing viewpoints, a resolution of this same difficulty. Whether they be called liberals or traditionalists, these groups, each obviously profoundly attached to the Catholic church, are searching, not to destroy or falsely exalt authority, but to discover a *credible authority* in which to invest their trust, and to identify *effective healthy leaders* whom they can willingly follow.

The medieval model of authority based on a pre-Copernican notion of the universe—a hierarchical map divided with the heavens above and the earth below—does not function well in a space age because such charts no longer reflect our experience of ourselves or of the cosmos. That manner of interpreting reality according to supposed divisions descending from the highest, purest, and most privileged pinnacle of creation to the lowest, basest, and least trustworthy material aspects of being, supported a hundred commonplace Catholic notions about everything from the quasi-divine right of religious superiors to states of life labeled from most to least perfect and body parts that ranked from more noble to less noble. Even "offering things *up*" depended on a geographically divided universe for its validity.

The daily drama of grace's loss or gain was acted out in the tense and protean environment of nature pitted against super-nature, spirit against flesh. An authoritarian church, crippled, as all authoritarianism is, by an inability to observe itself, prided itself on a hierarchical form derived from these supposedly God-authored divisions of the universe. We have come literally to the end of the world, the end of that imagined hierarchically ordered authoritarian world that has, like an ancient star, collapsed from within not because of assault from without. It no longer provides a credible reflection of historical, physical, or spiritual experience.

The church's present conflicts over embracing the collegiality taught by Vatican II reflect this continuing uncertainty about the nature of authority. Collegiality, however, is a vehicle that, properly implemented, can allow the development and enhancement of healthy authority in the next century. The present seemingly enormous reluctance to adopt collegiality is the product of rear guard actions being desperately fought against the inevitable changes that the space age is forcing upon us in every form of governance. Authority and its exercise are the problem almost everywhere in the world, including Soviet Russia, which has stagnated under ultra-authoritarianism. It has also discovered, as church authorities soon must, that it cannot successfully control the flow of information in the age of communication. The nuclear accident at Chernobyl could not be hidden precisely because of space age satellites. The church must come to terms with the same truth about its own inability to censor, disallow, or render itself insensitive to the real meaning of human experience or the impact of new knowledge in realms as different as human sexuality, freedom of inquiry, and the evolving understandings of theology.

The authoritarian defense of religious metaphors as literal truth kills their inner spiritual meaning. Authoritarian leaders are, however, comfortable with unambiguous concrete faith, and ill at ease with mystery, the central identifying component of all true religion and all true human experience. That is why such leaders possess so little true spiritual authority, that is, authority that naturally attracts the attention of searching believers. Even America's bishops seem distinctly ill at ease with reflections on the spiritual aspects of our contemporary experience. It may explain why they do not hesitate to speak as nuclear experts or economists, while they do not spontaneously or easily explore the spiritual dimensions of these staggering issues. Perhaps nothing illustrates this better than their distinct awkwardness, the "yes but" quality of their dealings with women. As ecclesiastical leaders move uneasily around the issue of women's equality in the church, they reveal not only something about themselves but something about the deepest historical authoritarian instincts of the bureaucratic church.

The obvious intense struggle between these authoritarian elements of the male hierarchy and the rising voice of women aware of their dignity, equality, and their abilities, constitutes what psychology terms an unobtrusive measure of the larger problem of the search for healthy modes of authority within the church. One can read it, as Professor Rudolph Bell has suggested in his brilliant study *Holy Anorexia* (University of Chicago Press, 1985), in the varying historical styles of female sanctity throughout the history of the church. He identifies the constantly developing modes of heroic holiness as the dynamic female response to an ever vigilant and steadily responsive male hierarchy's efforts to maintain control over women.

Extreme fasting, akin to today's anorexia, was employed by Saint Catherine of Siena and Saint Clare of Assisi, among hundreds of others, as their only way of escaping male clerical control and establishing some autonomy of their own. Dominated by the male church in every other way, they could defy and frustrate confessors and ecclesiastical authority through controlling their own eating habits, their own bodies, in a reflection of a familiar contemporary claim. Beneath the surface accidents, the struggle for individuality, for breaking the male ordering of their existences, was the true story of their lives. As Bell observes, "It . . . became evident that woman's holiness was the consequence of sacrifice and willpower; no longer could the female saint be viewed simply as the receptacle of divine grace, always in need of

304 / EUGENE C. KENNEDY

male guidance. Woman as object, possessed of no interior spirituality, gave way to woman as subject, creator of her own destiny" (p. 150).

The Reformation, according to Bell, included an enormous reaction against this feminine claim to spiritual territory outside the control of what he calls a "hierarchical male prelacy." As he notes, "this meant a counterattack on the lay piety, with its emphasis on individual responsibility, that for three centuries since Bernard of Clairvaux and Francis of Assisi had flourished within mother church's bosom and that had now become its mortal enemy" (p. 151). The subsequent massive efforts to control female spirituality by placing it once more firmly under the control of men led to a decline of fasting and, through the centuries, to the rise of female struggles to free themselves again. The succeeding style of piety, which included apparently bizarre forms of illness, for example, exemplified by saints who spent most of their time in bed (and therefore outside control of their communities or church authority) are the crooked lines writing straight about the same struggle with male authority. A further shift in which female holiness became expressed in zeal for charitable works extended into this century. Women effectively expressed their extraordinary capacity for independent achievement in running hospitals, schools, and carrying out other good works. Mother Cabrini has been succeeded by Mother Teresa, who stands, ironically, not as a symbol of old authority, but of women's ability to overcome it and to achieve spiritual and personal autonomy. Just as popes and bishops admired but feared holy women a thousand years ago, so they respect but are rendered powerless in the presence of Mother Teresa today. She seems to support church authority but stands independent of it; it would be difficult to imagine any pope, bishop, or monsignor telling her how, where, or when she should work.

The present conflicted relationship between the church and women is but the latest episode in a long and difficult story. And today, as never before, women can and do operate independently of the asserted authority of the church. This mirrors the deep feelings of many Catholics, even quite traditional ones, who stand spiritually independent of the authority of ecclesiastics. The religious life is ending because it can no longer function as a male dominated culture, not because human beings lack profound spiritual aspirations. The male bonded culture of clerical life is in ruins because it is a vestige of the great days of privilege, not because people lack interest in ministry.

This turning away represents a search for authority rather than a rejection of it. Church leaders must read the signs of these times accurately, for it is they, not their members, who have failed to understand and express the healthy spiritual authority that, like the voice of the true shepherd, cannot be mistaken by the flock. The more church leaders, still wearing its symbols in their medieval court regalia, seek to reestablish authority as authoritarianism, the more surely they destroy their possibility of having any but remembered authority in the future.

26. Democracy, Dissent, and Dialogue
A Catholic Vocation
LEONARD SWIDLER

How does a person or a community know it has a vocation, a call-ing? Probably the most important way, as pointed out by Pope John XXIII and Vatican II, is through the "signs of the times." It seems clear to me, then, that the "signs of the times" in both secu-lar and church history point very clearly to the need to move away from the authoritarian, patriarchical style in the Catholic church which has carried over from the time of the Roman empire to one of mature adults schooled in democracy: responsible freedom and dialogue. In this contemporary vocation, moreover, American Catholics bear a special responsibility since it is in America that both responsible freedom, with its necessary concomitant, possi-ble dissent, and dialogue have been most highly developed both individually and communally: a church providing a model of de-mocracy, that is, deliberation, dissent, dialogue, and decision would be their special contribution to the church universal. Let us look at the arguments for this view.

"The Christian faithful . . . have the right and even at times *a duty* to manifest to the sacred pastors their opinion on matters which pertain to the good of the Church." "Those who are en-gaged in the sacred disciplines enjoy a lawful freedom of inquiry and of prudently expressing their opinions on matters in which they have expertise." These are not the wild words of some radi-cal group of non-Catholics, or even the words of a group of liberal Catholics. They are Canon 212,3 and Canon 218 of the new Code of Canon Law of the Roman Catholic Church. This might seem to some to seal the argument in favor of freedom, possible dissent, and dialogue, but there is more.

"Christ summons the Church, as she goes her pilgrim way, to

that continual reformation of which she always has need. . . . Let everyone in the church . . . preserve a proper freedom . . . even in the theological elaborations of revealed truth. . . . *All* are led . . . wherever necessary, to undertake with vigor the task of renewal and reform. . . . Catholics' . . . primary *duty* is to make a careful and honest appraisal of whatever needs to be renewed and done in the Catholic household itself." Who this time are the radical advocates of freedom and reformation "even in the theological elaborations of revealed truth"?—all the bishops of the world gathered together in ecumenical Council Vatican II.[1]

The Council also firmly declared that "the human person has a right to religious freedom. This freedom means that all human beings are to be immune from coercion from individuals, social groups and every human power. . . . *Nobody is forced to act against his convictions in religious matters in private or in public.* . . . Truth can impose itself on the mind of humans only in virtue of its own truth.[2] The Council further stated: "search for truth" should be carried out "by free enquiry . . . and dialogue. . . . Human beings are bound to follow their consciences faithfully in all their activity . . . they must not be forced to act against their conscience, *especially in religious matters.*"[3]

DEMOCRACY

How was this freedom and responsibility, this democracy, put into action in the history of the church? Judging from the earliest documentary evidence we have, the Christian church operated with wide participation in decision making from the beginning. This was true not only of the more freewheeling, charismatic churches related to Paul, but also the more "ordered" ones. Thus we find in the Acts of the Apostles that, for example, "the whole multitude elected Stephen" (Acts 6:5). Again, when a large number of people in Antioch was converted to Christianity, it was not just the Apostles or the elders, but rather the *whole* church at Jerusalem which sent Barnabas to Antioch (Acts 11:22). Still later in the Acts of the Apostles there is the statement: "Then it seemed good to the Apostles and Elders, with the whole Church, to choose men from among them and send them to Antioch with Paul and Barnabas" (Acts 15:22).

In Eusebius's *History of the Church,* one of the major sources of the postbiblical history of the church, we find Peter not referred to as the leader or bishop of the church at Rome, either the first or subsequent. Rather, Linus was said to be the first bishop of Rome.[4] Moreover, Peter *is* indirectly referred to by Eusebius as the first bishop of Antioch![5] However, it should be noted that Ignatius of Antioch (d. 107), said to be Peter's second successor as bishop of Antioch by Eusebius—and who provides the earliest evidence of monepiscopacy (a single bishop being in charge of the church in a district) in some areas of the Christian world at the beginning of the second century—does *not* refer to a bishop at Rome; the *Shepherd of Hermas,* probably written during the second quarter of the second century, describes the leadership of the church at Rome as a committee of presbyters. All other early documents—the New Testament pastoral epistles, First Clement, the Didache, the Kerygma of Peter, the Apocalypse of Peter, the Epistle of Barnabas, and the Epistle of Polycarp—give no evidence of monepiscopacy at Rome or anywhere else. Only Ignatius points to monepiscopacy, and then only in Syria and Asia Minor.[6] It is only around the middle of the second century that we have clear evidence of monepiscopacy at Rome.[7]

In sum, it is clear that from the earliest period of Christianity there were various forms of community structure, from the very charismatic Pauline community at Corinth to the more presbyterially ordered community at Jerusalem. Then later, through a long period of development, the monepiscopal structure gradually arose and slowly spread, until by the end of the second century it was generally accepted and practiced. However, even the monepiscopacy of that time and the following centuries was by no means the nearly absolutist authoritarian power center it later became. It operated more like a limited monarchy, or just as accurately said, a limited democracy.

ELECTION OF LEADERS

The fundamental act of choice on the part of the Christian people from the initial period of monepiscopacy and for many centuries thereafter was that of electing their own leaders, their own bishops—and priests and deacons. In this, of course, they were simply continuing the same primordial custom reflected in the

New Testament documents. We find corroboration in two other first-century documents, the Didache and Clement of Rome's first letter: "You must, then, elect for yourselves bishops and deacons. . . ."[8] Bishops should be chosen "with the consent of the whole church. . . ."[9]

Early in the third century, Hippolytus made it clear that it was an "apostolic tradition," which was still practiced, for the entire local community along with its leaders to choose its own deacons, presbyters, and bishop.[10] His testimony is closely followed by that of Saint Cyprian of Carthage (d. 258), who often referred to the election of bishops by the presbyters and people. He himself was so elected and consequently made it his rule never to administer ordination without first having consulted both the clergy and the laity about the candidates: "From Cyprian to the presbyterium, deacons, and all the people, greetings! In the ordaining of clerics, most beloved brethren, it is our custom to take your advice beforehand and with common deliberations weigh the character and qualifications of each individual."[11] Cyprian also reported a similar democratic custom in the church of Rome: "Cornelius was made bishop by the . . . testimony of almost all the people, who were then present, and by the assembly of ancient priests and good men."[12]

Cyprian likewise bore witness to the custom of the people having the right, not only to elect, but also to reject and even recall bishops: "The people themselves most especially have the power to choose worthy bishops or to reject unworthy ones."[13] Saint Optatus, a sucessor to Cyprian as bishop of Carthage, attests to the continuance of the practice of electing bishops into the fourth century when he reports: "Then Caecilianus was elected by the suffrage of all the people."[14] And over in Asia Minor, the Council of Ancyra (314) confirmed the right of election and rejection of bishops by the people.[15] Every Catholic schoolgirl and -boy knows the stories of the election of Saint Ambrose as Bishop of Milan and Saint Augustine as bishop of Hippo (fourth and fifth centuries) by the acclamation of the people: "Nos elegimus eum!" A little later Pope Saint Celestine said: "No one is given the episcopate involuntarily. The consent and desire of the clerics, the people and leadership are required."[16] That redoubtable Pope Saint Leo the Great, who faced down Attila the Hun and saved Rome from the sack, wrote: "Let him who will stand before all be elected by all."[17] These principles from the early centuries of Christian practice were reiterated in various synods until at least as late as the Council of Paris in 829.[18]

Basically the election of bishops by the clergy and people remained in effect until the twelfth century—over half the present span of Christianity. Even at the beginning of the United States of America, our first bishop, John Carroll, was elected, with the full approval of Rome, at least by all of the priests of the United States, and he then proposed a similar election of all subsequent bishops in America—only to be blocked by Rome.[19] In fact, as late as the start of the twentieth century less than half the world's bishops were directly named by the pope. Thus it is only in our lifetime that the right of choosing our own bishops has been almost completely taken away from the priests and people—against almost the whole history of Catholic tradition.

PARTICIPATORY DECISION MAKING

It was not only in the election, and recall, of their deacons, priests, and bishops that the laity of the ancient church were involved in church decision making. Eusebius reports that already in the second century the "*faithful* . . . examined the new doctrines and condemned the heresy."[20] Cyprian noted that he often convoked councils: *Concilio frequenter acto.*[21] On the burning church issues of the day, he wrote to the laity: "This business should be examined in all its parts in your presence and with your counsel."[22] And again: "It is a subject which must be considered . . . with the whole body of the laity."[23] And yet again: "From the beginning of my episcopate I have been determined to undertake nothing . . . without gaining the assent of the people."[24] Furthermore, this custom of participatory decision making was also prevalent in the Roman church then, for the Roman clergy wrote: "Thus by the collaborative counsels of bishops, presbyters, deacons, confessors and likewise a large number of the laity . . . for no decree can be established which does not appear to be ratified by the consent of the plurality."[25]

It was not only on the local and regional levels that the laity were actively involved in ecclesiastical decision making; from the beginning that was also true on the church universal level as well.

In the fourth century the great worldwide ecumenical councils began, the first, of course, being held in 325 at Nicaea—and note, called and presided over by a layman, the emperor Constantine. In fact, all the ecumenical councils from the beginning until well into the Middle Ages were always, with one exception, called by the emperors. That one exception was Nicaea II in the eighth century, which was called by the empress Irene! Moreover, the emperors and empress called the councils on their own authority, not with prior consultation and approval of the papacy—not even, necessarily, for that matter, with the subsequent approval of the papacy. That is, the decrees of the ecumenical councils were promulgated and published by the emperor without necessarily waiting for the approbation of the papacy. Laity were also present at the ecumenical councils, as well as the large regional councils, such as the ones at Cyprian's Carthage in the third century, the Council of Elvira in the fourth century, and again the (fourth) Council of Toledo in the sixth century, and on down through the centuries, reaching a high point in some ways at the ecumenical councils of Constance and Basel in the first half of the fifteenth century. Even in the sixteenth-century Council of Trent, laity were present and active. Only with Vatican Council I in 1870 did lay participation in ecumenical councils shrivel to almost nothing.

Thus, in summary, one can say that, of course, in the beginning the church was the people, who naturally chose their leaders out of their midst, and on occasion recalled them. They also took an active role in deciding about a whole range of things, including doctrinal matters. It is only in the late Middle Ages and the modern period of history that the rights of the laity to choose their own church leaders and actively to participate in church decision making were eroded to the miserable remnant which we experienced growing up—and we were told that that is the way it always was!—reaching its low point in the middle of this century just before Vatican II (1962–65). That council, of course, started the process of restoring our ancient tradition of shared responsibility, and in fact was followed up in this regard by the 1971 Synod of Bishops when it stated: "The members of the Church should have some share in the drawing up of decisions, in accordance with the rules given by the Second Vatican Ecumenical Council and the Holy See, for instance, with regard to the setting up of councils at

all levels"[26]—would that that latter were implemented! Unfortunately we appear to be returning to a preconciliar mode at the
present time. Nevertheless, we must conclude that the Catholic
church not only could, and therefore should, be a democracy; it in
fact *was* a limited democracy—which has been dismantled. It
needs to be reestablished.

DISSENT

What then of our very contemporary issue of whether there
can be any legitimate dissent in the Catholic church today? Let us
look at some of the pertinent current documents. In 1973, the
Congregation of the Doctrine of the Faith stated that the "conceptions" by which church teaching is expressed are changeable:
"The truths which the Church intends to teach through her dogmatic formulas are distinct from the changeable conceptions of a
given epoch and can be expressed without them."[27] But how can
these "conceptions" be changed unless someone points out that
they might be improved, even be defective, that is, unless there is
deliberation, possibly dissent, and then dialogue leading to a new
decision on how to express the matter?

There is more: "Doctrinal discussion requires perceptiveness,
both in honestly setting out one's own opinion and in recognizing
the truth everywhere, even if the truth demolishes one so that one
is forced to reconsider one's own position, in theory and in
practice."[28]

Even John Paul II encouraged responsible dissent and supported theologians in their invaluable service done in freedom. In
1969, then archbishop of Krakow, he said: "Conformity means
death for any community. A loyal opposition is a necessity in any
community."[29] A decade later, as pope, he declared: "The
Church needs her theologians, particularly in this time and age.
. . . We desire to listen to you and we are eager to receive the val-
ued assistance of your responsible scholarship. . . . We will never
tire of insisting on the eminent role of the university . . . a place of
scientific research, constantly updating its methods . . . *in freedom
of investigation.*"[30] Later he even went so far as to remark: "Truth
is the power of peace. . . . What should one say of the practice of
combatting or silencing those who do not share the same

views?"[31] (Ironically, that statement was issued on 18 December 1979, just after the interrogation of Edward Schillebeeckx in Rome and on the very day of the quasi-silencing of Hans Küng.)

But this support for, indeed, advocacy of responsible dissent by the highest Catholic officials really should not at all be surprising. It is part of the proper pattern found in the whole history of humankind. The human being is by nature a historical being, and therefore subject to constant change. It is to be expected that established positions, whether in theory or practice, will upon occasion cause problems. The way this conflict is responded to is, first, deliberation and then, if judged proper, dissent, then dialogue, and finally decision—which decision may in the future again become the cause of further deliberation, dissent, dialogue, and decision, etc. For humankind this is the natural law.

We see this already in our religious history in the Hebrew Bible with its prophetic tradition. The prophets dissented from the establishment very loudly and clearly. True, they were sometimes resisted, and even put to death, by the establishment. Still, the prophetic tradition was accepted by Israel, God's chosen people, as a whole. Jesus, who was a good, observant Jew, also stood in this prophetic tradition—indeed, he was called a prophet by his followers. He challenged the religious establishment. He was a dissenter. And are not Christians said to be his followers?

His immediate followers, the disciples and Apostles, did in fact follow him in this. They too were religious dissenters, and consequently they likewise fell afoul of the religious establishment, sometimes even suffering the same fate as their leader and many of the prophets before him. The point here is that from earliest Christianity, just as in Judaism, there has been deliberation, dissent, dialogue, and decision. The first "pope," Peter, experienced this when Paul "withstood him to his face"—and Peter changed.

This practice of decision making in the church by dialogue and consensus, this *deliberatio, dissensus, dialogus, consensus,* continued through the early centuries and ran strong for well over a millennium of Catholic history. Indeed, even at the high point of the centralizing power of the medieval papacy, the ultimate autocrat, Pope Boniface VIII, had incorporated into his *Decretals* the old Roman principle: "Whatever affects everyone must be approved by everyone."[32] But of course such dialogue and ultimate arrival at a consensus, by its very nature, included the possibility of dissent. There can be no *con*sensus without the possibility of *dis*sensus.

It will probably also come as somewhat of a shock for many to learn that not always in the history of the Roman Catholic Church were the pope and bishops the supreme teachers of what was true Catholic doctrine. For almost six centuries it was the teachers, the theologians, who were the supreme arbiters in deciding what was correct Catholic teaching. This occurred in the first three centuries of the Christian era and again from the thirteenth through the fifteenth centuries.

Let me give only one example from the fourteenth century, that of the French theologian Godefroid de Fontaines. He poses the following question—and note how he poses it—"Whether the theologian *must* contradict the statement of the bishop if he believes it to be opposed to the truth?"[33] He answers by saying that if the matter is not concerned with faith or morals, then he should dissent only in private. But if it is a matter of faith or morals, "the teacher must take a stand, regardless of the episcopal decree . . . even though some will be scandalized by this action. It is better to preserve the truth, even at the cost of a scandal, than to let it be suppressed through fear of a scandal." And, Godfroid pointed out, this would be true even if the bishop in question were the pope, "for in this situation the pope can be doubted."

Even in the twentieth century, under the pall of the modernist heresy hunt, we find the traditional theological manuals, which every bishop over fifty today studied in his seminary days, putting forth the doctrine that "the consensus of the faithful is a certain criterion of the Tradition and faith of the Church" (*Consensus fidelium est certum Traditionis et fidei Ecclesiae criterium. Sententia communis*).[34] But, of course, as noted, without the possibility of *dis*sensus there can be no such thing as *con*sensus. We would not be consenting if we were not able to dissent—we would simply be like Pavlov's dog, automatically responding to stimuli.

Equally if not more interesting is the fact that all these over half-a-century-old bishops and priests also learned in their moral theology the ethical system known as "probabilism." Simply stated, probabilism means that in a disputed moral issue a Catholic may in good conscience follow a position even though it is espoused only by a minority of reputable moral theologians.

For example, before 1960 no Catholic moral theologian openly espoused the position that artificial birth control could under some conditions be in good conscience used by Catholics. Hence, no Catholic could legitimately do so at that time. Then, in the late fifties, a Belgian, Father Louis Jansens, published an article that argued that there were some circumstances under which it would be morally proper for Catholics to use some forms of artificial birth control, and shortly thereafter came Vatican II with its historicizing and liberating influences, and the questions of birth control and responsible parenthood were widely discussed. More and more Catholic theologians began to espouse the legitimacy of artificial birth control. Hence, it was then possible for Catholics to use birth control with a good conscience, since at least a minority of reputable Catholic theologians espoused that position. By 1968 the vast majority supported it. It was then that Pope Paul VI sided with the 5 percent of his international commission which argued against it and wrote his encyclical "Humanae vitae" against artificial birth control. Now as the probabilism—which Paul VI and all the other priests of that time had learned—posited, since Paul VI and a small number of other theologians espoused the negative position, Catholics could in good conscience follow the pope's position on birth control (for he specifically did not claim to be speaking infallibly on the matter). Many Catholics, of course, found that there was still greater reason for them to follow the massive majority of Catholic theologians who favored possible moral use of artificial birth control.

Lest anyone think that only radicals, in fact, publicly dissent from an officially stated teaching of a pope, it should be recalled that in 1968 in response to "Humanae vitae" the bishops' conferences of at least Belgium, Germany, Canada, and the United States issued public statements which essentially said that in the end individual Catholic couples may—indeed, must—follow their own consciences on the matter of artificial birth control, even if that led them to oppose Pope Paul VI's position (according to present polls, over two-thirds of American Catholics approve of artificial birth control). The United States bishops even explicitly stated that "the expression of theological dissent is in order. . . . If the reasons are serious and well-founded, if the manner of dissent does not question or impugn the teaching authority of the Church, and is such as not to give scandal."[35]

In responding to the objection that public dissent supposedly might give scandal to the faithful, the Association for the Rights of Catholics in the Church stated: "If giving scandal means harming the faithful by leading them astray, scandal is given not when dissent is expressed publicly, but when harmful teachings are not corrected as a result of the public dialogue arising out of dissent."[36]

Despite the great accumulation of documentation and precedent over the centuries in favor of responsible dissent in the church, in August 1986, Archibishop Hickey of Washington, D.C., publicly tried to retract that right, with the claimed support of the Vatican. Referring to those 1968 United States bishops' norms for theological dissent mentioned above, he commented, "I think we've seen these norms, as applied to public dissent, are simply unworkable." What was even more remarkable was his claim that the Holy See had said that "there is no right to public dissent" (all this concerned the Vatican's move to dismiss Charles Curran from Catholic University of America in August 1986). It is of course apparent that some in Rome wish to forbid responsible dissent, as if Vatican II and its freedom fallout had never occurred. This, however, is clearly in contradiction to the majority of the long history of the Catholic tradition.

In 1864, Pope Pius IX in his "Syllabus of Errors" condemned "that erroneous opinion most pernicious to the Catholic Church . . . called by our predecessor Gregory XVI 'madness' [*deliramentum*], namely, that liberty of conscience and of worship is the right of every human being."[37] A century later, Vatican II's "Declaration on Religious Liberty" taught that, "Religious freedom in society is in complete harmony with the act of Christian faith" (no. 9). How then did the church move from the condemnation to the commendation of religious freedom? Obviously many Catholics dissented substantially and publicly over a long period of time— and sometimes at great cost (as late as the middle fifties the American Father John Courtney Murray was silenced by Cardinal Ratzinger's predecessor, Cardinal Ottaviani, for publicly advocating freedom of conscience. Father Murray later was the major author of Vatican II's "Declaration on Religious Liberty").

In 1917, the Code of Canon Law forbade "Catholics from participating in disputations or discussions with non-Catholics without the permission of the Holy See" (Canon 1325,3). And in 1919, 1927, 1948, 1949, and 1954 the Vatican explicitly repeated its rejection of Catholic involvement in the ecumenical movement. But in 1965, Vatican Council II "exhorted all the Catholic faithful to . . . take an active and intelligent part in the work of ecumenism. . . . The concern for restoring unity involves the whole Church, faithful and clergy alike. It extends to everyone."[38] How was the move made from the excoriation to the exhortation of Catholic ecumenism? Again, only a great deal of public deliberation, dissent, and dialogue led to this radical reversal. And that is precisely why the Association for the Rights of Catholics in the Church (ARCC) has stated in number 8 of its *Charter of the Rights of Catholics in the Church:* "All Catholics have the right to express publicly their dissent in regard to decisions made by Church authorities."

RIGHTS

Discouraging to some as the present situation is, it is important to recall some of those sustaining quotations from contemporary church leaders cited above. Indeed, even our new 1983 Code of Canon Law, for all of its deep disappointments, offers us a foundation on which to build our claim to Catholic rights. The highly respected canonist Father James Coriden, in the introductory article to the forthcoming book on ARCC's *Charter of the Rights of Catholics in the Church,* makes the persuasive argument that the heart of the Catholic "bill of rights," the Vatican vetted *Lex Fundamentalis,* which was so worked over during the 1970s, in fact is to be found in the new code, largely in Canons 208 to 223. To those who would argue that those canons should not be interpreted in such a fundamental, broadbased way, but in the narrowest, most restricted manner possible, in keeping with the mind of the lawgiver, it must be said that the officially expressed mind of the lawgiver is in fact on the side of the "bill of rights" interpretation. In his address to the Roman Rota just one month after the promulgation of the new code, Pope John Paul II called specific attention to the "bill of rights" in the code:

The church has always affirmed and protected the rights of the faithful. In the new code, indeed, it has promulgated them as a *"carta fondamentale"* (See Canons 208-223). It offers opportune judicial guarantees for protecting and safeguarding adequately the desired reciprocity between the rights and duties inscribed in the dignity of the person of the "faithful Christian."[39]

This "bill of rights" in the 1983 Code of Canon Law includes:

1. Equality of all Christians in dignity and activity in which "all cooperate in the building up of the Body of Christ" (Canon 208).
2. The right of all Christians to follow their informed consciences, that is, "in matters concerning God and God's Church . . . they have the right to embrace and to observe that truth which they have recognized" (Canon 748,1).
3. The right of all Christians to petition, that is, to make known their needs and desires to church leaders (Canon 212,2).
4. The right of all Christians to recommend, to advise church leaders regarding the good of the church, and to participate in public opinion and informing the faithful (Canon 212,3).
5. The right of all Christians to association, that is, to found and direct associations for religious purposes (Canon 215).
6. The right of all Christians to assemble, that is, to hold meetings for the same purpose as to associate (Canon 215).
7. The right of all Christians to Christian education (Canon 217).
8. The right of all Christians to academic freedom, that is, to inquiry and expression of opinion (Canon 218).
9. The right of all Christians to be free in the choice of their state of life (Canon 219).
10. The right of all Christians to a good reputation (Canon 220).
11. The right of all Christians to privacy (Canon 220).
12. The right of all Christians to due process of law in the church, that is, to "vindicate and defend the rights which they enjoy in the Church before a competent ecclesiastical court in accord with the norm of law" (Canon 221,1), and "be judged in accord with the prescriptions of the law to be

applied with equity" (Canon 221,2), with sanctions imposed "in accord with the norm of the law" (Canon 221,3).

Of these and the other fundamental rights of the "bill of rights" in the 1983 code, Professor Coriden says:

These rights and freedoms are not peripheral or inconsequential. They go to the heart of the reasons for belonging to a church. They are central to participation in a Christian community of faith and love. They are to life within the church what freedom of speech, freedom of religion, due process of law, suffrage and representation are to life as citizens. They are tantamount to what we refer to as constitutional rights.

It is true that a number of important rights are missing from the 1983 code, and consequently they have been incorporated into the ARCC *Charter of the Rights of Catholics in the Church*. Besides the ones already mentioned above, they include:

2. Officers of the church have the right to teach on matters both of private and public morality only after wide consultation prior to the formulation of their teaching. . . .

5. All Catholics have the right to a voice in all decisions that affect them, including the choosing of their leaders. . . .

15. All Catholics, regardles of race, age, nationality, sex, sexual orientation, state-of-life, or social position have the right to receive all the sacraments for which they are adequately prepared. . . .

16. All Catholics, regardless of canonical status (lay or clerical), sex or sexual orientation, have the right to exercise all ministries in the Church for which they are adequately prepared, according to the needs and with the approval of the community. . . .

26. All Catholic women have an equal right with men to the resources and exercise of all the powers of the Church. . . .

28. All married Catholics have the right to determine in conscience the size of their families and the appropriate methods of family planning. . . .

30. All married Catholics have the right to withdraw from a marriage which has irretrievably broken down. All such Catholics retain the radical right to remarry. . . .

31. All Catholics who are divorced and remarried and who are in conscience reconciled to the Church have the right to the same ministries, including all sacraments, as do other Catholics. . . .

32. All Catholics have the right to expect that Church documents and materials will avoid sexist language and that symbols and imagery of God will not be exclusively masculine. . . .

ARCC is convinced that these rights of Catholics, which are not expressed in present canon law, are in fact founded in Scripture and/or reason and therefore ought to be incorporated in Catholic law and practice—and it is to that end, among others, that it is working. With the claim, after responsible and prayerful *deliberation*, that these are Catholic rights, the Catholics who make up ARCC and those many other Catholics all over the world who have been involved in the drawing up of the *Charter of the Rights of Catholics in the Church*, felt called in conscience to move to responsible *dissent*. They are now calling for responsible and open *dialogue* on the issues, so as to come to a new, future responsible *decision*.

Nevertheless, as Father Coriden has pointed out, a substantial "bill of Catholic rights" is present in the new Code of Canon Law. These rights, however, must be made real, must be made actual. That takes study, reflection, imagination, courage, and, above all, concerted effort. Catholics cannot individually make their rights real; rather, they must work in concert, each contributing her or his talents—of which everyone has at least some. That is why organizations such as the Association for the Rights of Catholics in the Church, and others, are indispensable. For, as the bishops in their 1971 synod wrote:

While the Church is bound to give witness to justice, it recognizes that anyone who ventures to speak to people about justice must first be just in their eyes. Hence we must undertake an examination of the modes of acting and of the possessions and life style found within the Church itself. Rights must be preserved in the Church. None should be deprived of ordinary rights because of association with the Church.[40]

DIALOGUE

Catholic Christianity is a living faith, not a dead imitation of a past which no longer exists. Catholic theology is a contemporary reflection in today's thought categories on present questions and problems about what it means to think and live as a Christian in this concrete world. Simply to parrot the past is to pervert it. To be a Christian means to make what Jesus thought, taught, and wrought understandable and applicable in today's language and life. Christian life and theology must be something dynamic, not dead, and therefore at its heart there must be deliberation, dissent, dialogue, decision—which of course leads to further deliberation, dissent . . .

One of the main functions of the magisterium, and especially the Congregation of the Doctrine of the Faith, therefore, ought not be to put a stop to deliberation, dissent, and dialogue, but instead precisely to encourage, promote, and direct it in the most creative possible channels. As a 1979 petition in support of Father Schillebeeckx, signed by hundreds of theologians, urged:

The function of the Congregation of the Doctrine of the Faith should be to *promote dialogue* among theologians of varying methodologies and approaches so that the most enlightening, helpful, and authentic expressions of theology could ultimately find acceptance.

Hence, we call upon the Congregation of the Doctrine of the Faith to eliminate from its procedures "hearings," and the like, substituting for them dialogues that would be either issue-oriented, or if it is deemed important to focus on the work of a particular theologian, would bring together not only the theologian in question and the consultors of the Congregation of the Doctrine of the Faith, but also a worldwide selection of the best pertinent theological scholars of varying methodologies and approaches. These dialogues could well be conducted with the collaboration of the International Theological Commission, the Pontifical Biblical Commission, universities, theological faculties, and theological organizations. Thus, the best experts on the issues concerned would work until acceptable resolutions were arrived at. Such a procedure of course is by no means new; it is precisely the procedure utilized at Vatican II.[41]

Indeed, even the pope and the curia wrote of the absolute necessity of dialogue and sketched out how it should be conducted. Pope Paul VI in his very first encyclical, "Ecclesiam suam" (1964), wrote that dialogue "is *demanded* nowadays. . . . It is *demanded* by the dynamic course of action which is changing the face of modern society. It is *demanded* by the . . . maturity humanity has reached in this day and age." Then in 1968 the Vatican declared that,

the willingness to engage in dialogue is the measure and strength of that general renewal which must be carried out in the Church, which *implies a still greater appreciation of liberty.* . . . Doctrinal dialogue should be initiated with courage and sincerity, *with the greatest freedom* . . . recognizing the truth everywhere, even if the truth demolishes one so that one is forced to reconsider one's own position. . . . Therefore *the liberty of the participants* must be ensured by law and reverenced in practice.[42]

The 1971 Synod of Bishops added its affirmation of freedom of expression and the need for dialogue: "The church recognizes everyone's right to suitable freedom of expression and thought. This includes the right of everyone to be heard in a spirit of dialogue which preserves a legitimate diversity within the Church."[43]

For these reasons the ARCC *Charter of the Rights of Catholics in the Church* contains the following right: "20. Catholic teachers of theology have a right to responsible academic freedom. The acceptability of their teaching is to be judged in dialogue with their peers, keeping in mind the legitimacy of responsible dissent and pluralism of belief."

CONCLUSION

What must we Catholics then do today when, largely in contradiction to our tradition, the return of a centralizing authoritarianism appears so much to be the order of the day? First, we must not leave the church but love it, and that means live it, live from it, live in it, and live with it, that it might help us lead more fully human lives—which is what Jesus is all about (our "salvation," *salus,* "full healthy lives"—loving ourselves, our neighbor, the world around us, and thereby the Source). But that loving, that living the church means growing in "salvation," *salus,* maturity, and for that we need deliberation; and then where appropriate, dissent (even if painful to us); a reaching out to dialogue (even when rebuffed); so that ultimately a new, ever more mature decision can be made. . . . That is our Catholic vocation.

NOTES

1. Decree on Ecumenism, no. 4.
2. Declaration on Religious Liberty, nos. 1, 2.
3. Ibid., no. 3.
4. Eusebius, *History of the Church,* 3,2.
5. Ibid., 3, 36.
6. See T. Patrick, Burke, "The Monarchical Episcopate at the End of the First Century," *Journal of Ecumenical Studies* 11 (1970), 499–518.
7. Eusebius's account of the Easter controversy describes Anicetus in a monepiscopal role in Rome shortly before the death of Polycarp in 155—*History of the Church,* 4.22.1–3. See James F. McCue, "The Roman Primacy in the Patristic

DEMOCRACY, DISSENT, AND DIALOGUE / 323

Era. The Beginnings through Nicea," in *Papal Primacy and the Universal Church. Lutherans and Catholics in Dialogue V*, ed. Paul Empie and T. Austin Murphy (Minneapolis: Augsburg, 1974), 44–72.

8. *Didache*, 15:1–2.
9. *1 Clement*, 44,5.
10. Hippolytus, *Traditio Apostolica*, 2,7,8.
11. Migne, *Patrologia Latina*, 4, 317–18. "Cyprianus presbyterio et diaconibus et plebi universae salutem. In ordinationibus clericis, fratres charissimi, solemus vos ante consulere, et mores ac merita singulorum communi consilia ponderare."
12. Ibid., 3, 796–97.
13. Cyprian, Epistle, 67, 3. *Corpus scriptorum ecclesiasticorum Latinorum (CSEL)*, 3.2.737. "Plebs . . . ipsa maxime habeat potestatem uel eligendi dignos sacerdotes uel indignos recusandi."
14. Optatus, *CSEL*, 34.2.407. "Tunc suffragio totius populi Caecilianus elegitur et manum imponente Felice Autumnitano episcopus ordinatur."
15. Canon 18. See C. J. von Hefele, *Conciliengeschichte*, I (Freiburg, 1873), 237.
16. Celestine, Epistle, iv, 5; *PL*, 50, 431. "Nullus invitis detur episcopus. Cleri, plebis, et ordinis, consensus ac desiderium requiratur."
17. Leo, Epistle, x, 4; *PL*, 54, 634. "Qui praefuturus est omnibus ab omnibus eligatur."
18. Jean Harduin, *Acta Conciliorum et Epistolae Decretales ac Constitutiones Summorum Pontificum*, IV, 1289ff.
19. See Leonard Swidler, "People, Priests, and Bishops in U.S. Catholic History," in *Bishops and People*, ed. Leonard Swidler and Arlene Swidler (Philadelphia: Westminster, 1970), 113–35.
20. Eusebius, *History of the Church*, *Patrologia Graeca*, 20, 468.
21. Cyprian, Epistle, xxvi.
22. Cyprian, *PL*, 4, 256–57. "Cyprianus fratribus in plebe consistentibus salutem . . . examinabuntur singula praesentibus et judicantibus vobis."
23. Cyprian, Epistle, liv. Quoted in Johann Baptist Hirscher, *Sympathies of the Continent*, trans. of *Die kirchlichen Zustände der Gegenwart*, 1849, by Arthur C. Coxe (Oxford, 1852), 123. "Singulorum tractanda ratio, non tantum cum collegis meis, sed cum plebe ipsa universa."
24. Cyprian, *PL*, 4, 234. "Quando a primordio episcopatus mei statuerim, nihil sine consilio vestro, et sine consensu plebis, mea privatim, sententia gerere."
25. Cyprian, *PL*, 4, 312. "Sic collatione consiliorum cum episcopis, presbyteris, diaconis, confessoribus pariter ac stantibus laicis facta, lapsorum tractare rationem. . . . Quoniam nec firmum decretum potest esse quod non plurimorum videbitur habuisse consensu."
26. Reprinted in part in the *Charter of the Rights of Catholics in the Church*, 2d ed. (Association for the Rights of Catholics in the Church, January 1985), 17. Available from ARCC, Box 912, Delran, NJ 08075.
27. "Mysterium ecclesiae," 24 June 1973.
28. Secretariat for Unbelievers, "Humanae personae dignitatem," 28 August 1968 in *Acta Apostolicae Sedis* 60 (1968), 692–704; English in *Vatican Council II*, ed. Austin Flannery (Collegeville, MN: Liturgical Press, 1975), 1010.
29. Cited in Hans Küng, "Kardinal Ratzinger, Papst Wojtyla und die Angst vor der Freiheit," *Die Zeit* (4 October 1985).
30. John Paul II, "Address to Catholic Theologians and Scholars at the Catholic University of America," 7 October 1979. Emphasis added.
31. Reported in the *Washington Post*, 19 December 1979.

32. Regula 29: "Quod omnes tangit, debet ab omnibus approbari."
33. This citation and the rest in this paragraph, as well as a more extensive discussion, are found in Roger Gryson, "The Authority of the Teacher in the Ancient and Medieval Church," in *Authority in the Church*, ed. Leonard Swidler and Piet Fransen (New York: Crossroad, 1982), 176–87.
34. Adolf Tanquerey, *Synopsis Theologiae Dogmaticae Fundamentalis*, 24th ed. (New York: Benziger, 1937), 752.
35. Reprinted in *National Catholic Reporter*, 5 September 1986.
36. ARCC statement "Dissent and Dialogue in the Church," September 1986.
37. "Quanta cura" (1864), cited in Leonard Swidler, *Freedom in the Church* (Dayton: Pflaum, 1969), 89.
38. "Decree on Ecumenism," nos. 4, 5.
39. *Acta Apostolicae Sedis* 75 (1983), 556; *Origins* 12 (1983), 631.
40. Cited in *Charter of the Rights of Catholics in the Church*, 17.
41. Reprinted in Leonard Swidler, *Küng in Conflict* (New York: Doubleday, 1981), 516f.
42. "Humanae personae dignitatem," in Flannery, *Vatican Council II*, 1010. Emphasis added.
43. Cited in *Charter of the Rights of Catholics in the Church*, 17.